A Great New Beginning

The 1981 Inaugural Story

A Chronicle of the Inauguration of the 40th President of the United States
and an Historic Picture of Past Celebrations from 1789 to the Present

Created by the 1981 Inaugural Book Committee

Copyright © 1981 by the 1981 Presidential Inaugural Committee. All rights reserved.
Library of Congress Catalog Number: 80-600198.

Contents

Introduction	7
Message From the Co-Chairmen	9
Starting From The Beginning	11
The Privilege And The Power	19
A Vision For The Nation	27
A Need to Contribute	35
The First Lady	41
The Reagan Family	45
A Portrait of Barbara Pierce Bush	49
The Bush Family	53
The President and His Cabinet	57
The Inaugural Heritage	61
The Joint Congressional Committee	73
The 1981 Presidential Inaugural Committee	75
Notes On Inaugurals	81
The Inaugural Prelude	89
Taste Of America	*90*
A Spine-Tingling Opening Ceremony	*92*
Co-Chairmen's Reception	*99*
Americana Potpourri	*100*
A Rousing Round of Receptions	*105*
Concerts and Candlelight	*111*
Distinguished Ladies' And Vice-President's Reception	*120*
All Star Inaugural Gala	*124*
Inaugural Day—1981	132
I Do Solemnly Swear	*137*
The Inaugural Address	*144*
Begin the Celebrations!	*146*
Festivities And Fireworks	*154*
White Ties And Tales	*156*
A Spirit Renewed	*165*
A Great New Beginning	166
Acknowledgments and Credits	174

Introduction

*T*he Inauguration of a President is an occasion with many meanings.

It is, quite literally, an oath of office—a promise to the American people to uphold the laws of the Constitution and to faithfully execute the duties of office.

But the Inauguration is much more. To governments and peoples beyond our shores, the orderly ascendency of a U.S. President to office represents stability and certainty in a world sometimes troubled by disorder and confusion. This solemn occasion, albeit brief, is a shining testament to a system of government that recognizes that its greatness lies in the hearts and the spirit of its people.

It is more.

The Inauguration is, quite appropriately, a time of respect and honor. A time to reflect on past glories and to hold true to the traditions and customs we share as a people united.

And, as it should be, the Inauguration is a festive event, a joyful celebration of the ideals and aspirations that have maintained and sustained the nation through more than 200 years.

The Inauguration of Ronald Wilson Reagan as the 40th President of the United States and of George Walker Bush as Vice President, represents a new birth, a redirection of national energies and priorities to build an even greater America. A time to rekindle not only the ethereal flame of hope and promise, but to assure the reality of accomplishment and deeds realized and to come.

It is appropriate the two should take this pledge standing for the first time on the West Front of the Capitol from which they could face a proud nation to offer their commitment and dedication to the American people, in the hope that together we can accomplish the great goals we set out to achieve.

Through the pages of this book are depicted the moods, scenes, events and activities of the 1981 Inaugural; in remembering them, we ask you to project them against the backdrop of Inaugurations past, and to carry forward that same spirit of optimism and vision our founding fathers bore as they took their first steps toward liberty and democracy.

If the past is, indeed, prologue, it is hoped this chronicle of the 1981 Inaugural events will add to the memory of the occasion and serve as a testament and tribute to . . . A Great New Beginning.

Starting At The Beginning

Who could have known, back in those hectic Spring days of 1966 when I worked as a precinct captain in the Montclair neighborhood of Oakland for Ronald Reagan in the California gubernatorial primary race that my candidate would someday become the President of the United States.

Not that I doubted his ability to be President. Just that my attention was riveted firmly on helping him win the Governorship of California. After all, well-known and admired as he was, Ronald Reagan had never held elective public office.

It was what he said, what he believed, what he stood for that attracted me to Ronald Reagan. It was the chance to help him put his principles into practice, and the leader-

By Ursula (Mrs. Edwin) Meese
Honorary Book Chairman

11

ship qualities he demonstrated, which encouraged me to join the grass roots volunteer effort on his behalf.

The primary and general election victories which followed, especially the landslide he won in November, 1966, sent a message throughout the country that Ronald Reagan—and what he believed in—deserved to be taken very seriously.

My husband Ed, and I, were among those who attended Ronald Reagan's 12:01 AM swearing-in ceremony in the State Capitol Rotunda on January 1, 1967—full of admiration and hope for California's future.

Ed was Deputy District Attorney in Alameda County. Soon he would be leaving that job to become a member of Governor Reagan's staff as Legal Affairs Secretary. For the next eight years, the opportunity to work for this man—later as Governor Reagan's Executive Assistant and member of the Cabinet—served to widen our horizons of public service.

Public service had been a tradition in our families. My father was a 1915 graduate of West Point and spent his life, first as an Army officer and later as Manager of the Veterans Administration Hospital in Oakland and then as Postmaster there. In June, our oldest son will graduate from West Point, continuing the tradition established by his grandfather.

Ed's father served for three decades as Tax Collector and Treasurer of Alameda County.

During the two terms Ed served on Governor Reagan's staff, we came to know, in a firsthand way, the great qualities and the extraordinary strengths of the man who now takes his place as the 40th President of the United States.

Watching Ronald Reagan during his years as Chief Executive of America's most populous state—the closest thing to a "nation state" given its great economic and geographical diversity—was, in a sense, like experiencing a man and philosophy ahead of their time. His influence as Governor of California transcended the boundaries of our state, but it would take time for the wisdom of his ideas to become fully understood and appreciated in other parts of the country.

Ronald Reagan, from the beginning, rejected the notion that be-

cause things had always been done in a conventional way in state government they should be perpetuated for their own sake.

He sought out leaders in the private sector for new ideas. He recognized the danger to the fiscal and social soundness and stability of a people whose state government had grown too big, too expensive and too unresponsive to the wishes of those whose work and taxes made it all possible.

He was not afraid to make the hard decisions necessary to put California government back in the black. He did not shy away from innovating new approaches to solving management and fiscal problems.

At the end of his two terms, he left his successor with a healthy budget surplus and a management structure which still endure.

He listened to the people. He showed he cared about the taxpayer and the disadvantaged in the state.

The leadership he brought to the state, his exposure to a wide variety of public policy issues and the experience he gained in successfully dealing with them were the basis on which Ronald Reagan was able to

effectively communicate a proven philosophy of government beyond the boundaries of California which gradually, in recent years, captured the imagination of millions of Americans.

The "mashed potato" circuit of speeches across the country, the syndicated newspaper columns, the radio commentaries and the recent presidential campaign all combined to convey a message of a leader concerned about the direction in which the nation was moving and the offer of renewed hope for strong leadership to make America great again.

If Ronald Reagan's ideas were ahead of their time as Governor, the American public now has come to recognize them as providing new and practical hope for the future of the nation.

The road ahead—the challenge to put America back on track, to restore the nation's economic and defensive strength, to give priority to upholding traditional family values and to regain control of the government—will not be easy. But, through the years, I have watched

15

16

this man, Ronald Reagan, put his shoulder to the wheel, in the face of adversity, and get the job done.

He cares deeply about his country. He is a great patriot, at a time when we need many great patriots. He is a man of vision, at a time when we need many men and women of vision. He is a leader who views America's past as the prologue to an even greater future for all of us—and especially our children and their children's children.

Being the President of the United States has to be the most difficult job in the world. The enormity of the responsibility is staggering. But, I have watched Ronald Reagan. He is a man who, with our prayers and continuing support, is equal to the task he has been given.

Etched across the face of a State Building across the street from California's Capitol are these words: "Give me men to match my mountains." Ronald Reagan is such a man.

Thinking back to that Inaugural swearing-in when he became Governor of California, and all that has happened since, I am happy and proud to have shared with so many others the faith in Ronald Reagan's wisdom and greatness as he assumes the formidable challenges which lie ahead.

The Privilege And The Power

By Hugh Sidey

For all of its recent troubles and the doubts generated by a season of political inaction and frustration, the American Presidency remains the most powerful, sensitive, encompassing and adaptable position awarded to a single person in this world. That person can make a difference.

There is no system on earth that is at once so huge and forceful and yet so flexible, wherein an individual can on a great range of issues make decisions and order them implemented. Wherever one looks right now the forces of communism seem to be locked in internal committee struggles or taught with anticipation as old men get older. The Kremlin political maneuvers which Premier Leonid Brezhnev must sustain to hold his job and bring about unified action within that cumbersome system would make the persuasive duties of an American President appear simple. Democracy, having held its political contest in the open under great scrutiny, then rewards the winner with unmatched authority.

Even such a power lover as Lyndon Johnson sometimes marveled. When he walked out of the Glassboro (N.J.) summit meeting with Alexei Kosygin back in 1967 Johnson seemed unusually philosophical. Not until he gathered the reporters around him on Air Force One while speeding to his ranch in Texas was the reason apparent. At 37,000 feet over the hills of Pennsylvania, L.B.J. allowed as how he never ever would fully appreciate the job of President. "There I was," he explained, "the leader of the greatest democracy on earth and I could make almost any decision I wanted. And there was Kosygin, representing the greatest dictatorship on earth, and he had to call Moscow every time he wanted to go to the men's room." As always, Johnson had a point; though, as always, quaintly homespun.

A rare moment in history. Two future Presidents, Lyndon B. Johnson and Richard M. Nixon congratulate President John F. Kennedy at his inauguration in January, 1961.

With privilege and power, as with almost everything else in this life, comes responsibility. Presidents do not just press buttons. They must know themselves and where they want to go. They must know their people and their country. They must educate and cajole, sometimes threaten and sometimes ignore. But, always, they must be in the spirit of the United States. That is the energy source. A President who is wise and bold knows those moments when he can move from where they are to where they have not been. That is leadership. A President who is sensitive and intelligent can hear the discordant strains in his nation and help clarify them, then lift the banner and move on.

What was it that John Kennedy heard on an April evening in 1961 when he sent the word out of the Oval Office that America would send a man to the moon? He was only 43 years old and he was no scientist and there was no great clamor for the U.S. to invest billions

in a race with the Soviets into space that ultimately might be lost. Something stirred within the man and his decisions set in motion the grandest, peaceful, creative human endeavor that the modern world has seen.

Or Richard Nixon? Something sounded in far-off China and he heard it when others did not. He launched his secret probes that produced the opening to China and then one day in 1972 Nixon stood on the Great Wall while an American satellite hovering over the Pacific beamed the television pictures back to the U.S.

Franklin Roosevelt led the battles against want and tyranny and his main weapons were confidence and hope. Harry Truman one gray night decided that the United States must send aid to Greece and Turkey and the Truman Doctrine was born, later expanded and enriched with the Marshall Plan which saved Western Europe.

And Dwight Eisenhower, with a wisdom that just now we are begin-

Dwight D. Eisenhower, paused for a moment during a particularly tense meeting to reflect on the decisions and responsibilities demanded of him during the Presidency.

President Eisenhower conferring on the White House lawn during the Cold War conflict in his first term with Secretary of State John Foster Dulles, British Prime Minister Winston Churchill and Foreign Secretary Anthony Eden.

Franklin D. Roosevelt thrived on his relationship with the nation's press. Here he elaborates and answers questions following one of the famous fireside chats.

Herbert Hoover took great pleasure in throwing the ceremonial first ball at the opening of each baseball season. Pictured here he opens the 1929 season of the Washington Senators in old Griffith Stadium in Washington.

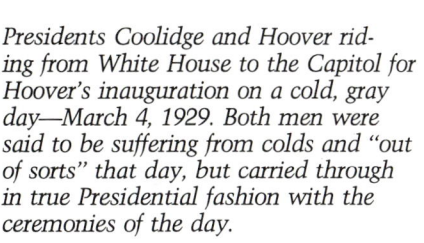

Presidents Coolidge and Hoover riding from White House to the Capitol for Hoover's inauguration on a cold, gray day—March 4, 1929. Both men were said to be suffering from colds and "out of sorts" that day, but carried through in true Presidential fashion with the ceremonies of the day.

ning to fully appreciate, mixed restraint with strength. He established the commanding margin of American nuclear power that assured peace but kept American forces out of Indochina when the French were beseiged. Jerry Ford was thrust into a job he never dreamed he would have. Without hesitation he took the steps he thought necessary. He vetoed more than 70 bills sent down by Congress and that action helped to drive inflation down from 10 percent to 5 percent. Ford began to rebuild U.S. arsenals to meet the relentless march of Soviet weaponry.

Of course being President of the United States is impossible. No President can do everything he wants to or do what his people would like him to do. But if he is courageous and has a vision and is determined he can do something—*something*. That is often enough for this nation which for all of its ailments, real and imagined, remains the wealthiest, most imaginative and creative force in the world. F.D.R.'s nostrums for curing the great depression did not work but he sustained the country with his jaunty defiance of disaster. It is true that Ike got a bit bored with politics and the job of being President and maybe went out to putt on the South Lawn more than he should have, but in his marvelous Kansas fashion he put his trust in the American people and that was enough to help nurture the greatest productive boom that mankind has seen.

Being President is a burden. Presidents over the years have said a lot of nasty things about the job, such as it was not fit for a gentleman (Buchanan) and it was a crown of thorns (J.Q. Adams) and a splendid misery (Jefferson). Kennedy once exclaimed: "I'm going to give this damned job to Nixon." He never did. And none of the others of recent vintage have walked willingly away from it. The burden is bearable. You like being President, don't you, Johnson was asked one night right in the middle of Vietnam. He looked startled. He looked guilty. He shuffled a bit, pawed the floor, then said, "Yes." You enjoy the job, don't you, Jimmy Carter was asked not long ago. His eyes bright and with no hesitation he answered: "Yes."

Certainly the challenge is larger. Surely the complexities have grown. Danger has increased with interdependence, the demand for energy and the spread of nuclear weapons. Modern arms have created great wounds on the thin skin of civilization. The massing of people in our urban centers has produced social tension and conflict. Our very system of constitutional government sometimes appears clumsy and hesitant. But men and women still covet the Presidency and once there relish its vantage point because it remains an office where one person can make a difference. The belief is father to the fact.

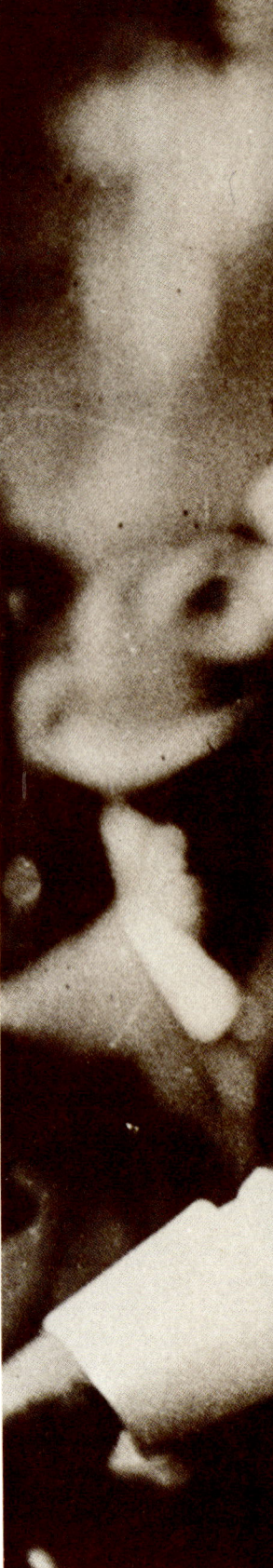

"I will confess to you confidentially, that I like the job," Teddy Roosevelt said to a friend at the end of his long White House stay.

A Vision For The Nation

Perhaps it is the special openness of the horizon in the Middle West, an openness that reveals no obstacle to travel in any direction. Perhaps it is the remarkable flatness of the prairie, which suggests that God had good times in mind—perfectly smooth infields for countless baseball diamonds—when he created central Illinois. In any case, those of us who sensibly chose to be born and raised in central Illinois like to think we acquired there a distinctive cheerfulness.

It has been said that a talent for happiness is like a talent for a good French accent! It is acquired in childhood. If so, Ronald Wilson Reagan's temperament is a testimonial to Tampico and Dixon, Illinois. He seems to have acquired early, and permanently, the fundamental optimism that has moved generations of Americans, for nearly four centuries, to head west.

To Americans, "the West" is not just a geographical expression. It also is an idea, with several meanings. The American West always has been a beckoning place, a place for fresh starts and fresh ideas, a place of open spaces and open minds. Its most precious resource is renewable: an extravagant sense of possibility. But since 1945 the phrase "the West" has had another meaning for Americans. It denotes a community of shared values that unite the free nations of the world. Ronald Reagan is a man of the West, in both senses.

By George F. Will

Ronald Reagan has succeeded at several careers—sometimes at several simultaneously. But all his careers—in acting, in the labor movement, in politics—have depended on, and developed, different facets of a particular skill, the ability to communicate. In a democracy, politics is primarily a task of communicating. In a democracy, politics is not a business for people who are impatient. It is, above all, the craft of building coalitions. That means compromise, which requires persuasion. Under some other forms of government, those who govern can deal with the people by issuing commands. Our way is harder, and better. Persuasion is the vocation of all public officials, but especially of Presidents. That is why there is such fascination with Ronald Reagan's gifts as a communicator.

It is impossible to pinpoint the moment when his political career began. He first ran for office in 1966. But two years earlier he acquired, quite suddenly, a national following, because of a singularly effective speech on behalf of the Republican presidential nominee, Barry Goldwater. And long before that, Ronald Reagan held the highest office in his trade union. Suffice it to say, he has been actively involved with public issues for more than three decades. And the long trail has led to a Presidential Inauguration.

Such Inaugurations are the greatest ceremonies of our civic life. They are at once solemn and festive. They express seriousness about the power conferred upon Presidents, and they express pride in the splendidly civilized way in which a free people can confer power. But after the ceremonies, after the parade passes and the dancing is done, every President finds that, great though his power is, there is precious little a President can do alone.

27

John and Nelle Reagan pose in an early photograph with their sons Neil (left) and Ron (right).

Ronald Reagan's grade school class in Dixon, Illinois. Ron is the serious looking one, second row, far left.

Little, that is, except be persuasive, and by moving the nation, move the rest of the government.

The fact that there is "the rest of the government" is, for any President, tiresome. The constitutional system of separation of powers, of checks and balances, is, inevitably, frustrating for the man in the Oval Office. But the Founding Fathers knew what they were doing when they divided powers in a way that is symbolized by our Inauguration ceremonies. These ceremonies link two great buildings, the White House and the Capitol, that are 16 blocks apart. Certainly the nation's new Chief Executive seems to have an executive's disposition. Ronald Reagan likes to decide and to delegate.

What he cannot delegate is the task of articulating a vision for the nation—a vision of the past that is inspiring, and a vision of the future that is energizing. Churchill said that "to govern is to choose," and in American government the crucial question always is: What does the President choose to communicate? The political message Ronald Reagan has communicated with notable consistency can be put in a word: confidence.

His confidence about his fellow citizens is similar to the confidence expressed by another Californian, Eric Hoffer, the blue-collar author and philosopher who worked for years as a stevedore on the San Francisco docks. The American nation, Hoffer said, is "lumpy with talent." It is a wonderful phrase, and accurate. A paradox of our age is that Ronald Reagan has made politics his vocation because he believes that political decisions have become too intrusive in American life, and that they are becoming impediments to the flowering of American talents.

Internationally, the nations of the free world have much more to rejoice about than to regret in their

While still in high school, young Ron worked as a lifeguard in Dixon, Illinois.

"Dutch" Reagan as the sports broadcaster for WHO-Radio in Des Moines, Iowa. His first announcing job was for a station in Davenport, Iowa, where he was hired to cover the Chicago Cubs.

Captain Ronald Reagan when he first entered the Army Air Corps in 1945.

Nancy and Ronald Reagan cut the cake following their wedding on March 4, 1952, in the home of his best man, William Holden.

31

Ronald Reagan is sworn in as the Governor of California in January, 1967.

experiences, individually and collectively, since 1945. But these have not been easy years, and there seems to be a readiness for a fresh affirmation of the determination to let freedom ring. In recent years, Americans have been belabored by various voices purporting to explain why the United States must lower its expectations for itself and must pull back from the leadership of the free world. Ronald Reagan's campaign for the presidency rested on a stubborn refusal ever to consider the possibility that the trajectory of American history has passed its apogee. His stubbornness seems to have found a sympathetic audience.

When the 1980 presidential season is recollected in tranquility by the participants, or studied by historians, two aspects will seem striking. One is that the winner survived a political steeplechase race more grueling than any previous race. The second is that Ronald Reagan, perhaps more than any candidate of modern times, assembled a "constituency of issues" rather than a "constituency of interests." His was a campaign of ideas, ideas about the proper relationship of the American people to their government, and about the proper relationship of the United States to its friends and adversaries.

I suspect that if you distilled to a single sentence Ronald Reagan's political credo, it would be this sentence I once saw at a political rally: "America isn't perfect—but we're not through working on it yet." That sense of endless renewal is what unites the United States on Inauguration Day.

33

A Need To Contribute

"*Our father's philosophy about the need to contribute came through quite early. When George talks about that in his speeches, he means it.*"

Prescott Bush, Jr., on his younger brother.

Here, now, comes George Bush: his hair, though newly combed only ten minutes before, is not quite in place; his tie, though neatly knotted and of appropriate hue, is nevertheless slightly off-center; his coat and pants, though freshly pressed just this morning, are in sore need of a hot iron. What we see, obviously, is a busy man at the ragged end of a long workday. But wait: the smile is as undaunted, the handshake as earnest, the wit as keen, the enthusiasm as contagious, as when he began fourteen—or was it sixteen?—hours before.

It is said of George Herbert Walker Bush (by panting aides, trying to keep pace with his schedule) that the man has been engineered to move in only two gears:

By Vic Gold

third and overdrive. Overdrive is when he is up-and-moving in what, seen in others, would pass as a jogger's pace. Third gear is reserved for his moments of workday repose, when he has either been trapped behind a desk or placed under the constraint of an airplane seatbelt.

Ah, yes, George Bush, in workday repose: he will be found either rattling off countless letters and memos; talking into a dictaphone; scribbling thank-you notes (personal and hand-written) to friends, acquaintances, anyone who might have done him or Barbara or some member of their family a service or kindness; reviewing briefing papers and otherwise cutting into the backlog of books, magazines and journals that clutter his battered briefcase; or merely peppering those around him with questions about news breaking along the international front, on the national scene, or in the race for the National League pennant. (*How did the Astros do last night? Did Ryan go the distance?*)

The need to contribute: it is an inner compulsion to give of himself,

35

George Bush was the youngest commissioned pilot in the Navy during World War II. This picture was taken when he received his wings at age 18 in 1942.

As the captain of the Yale baseball team—George Bush is seated center, first row, following Yale's capture of the NCAA eastern regional championship.

his energies, his total commitment, reflected by the resume . . . *president of his senior class and captain of the baseball team at Yale; Phi Beta Kappa, after taking his economics degree in only two-and-a-half years; youngest commissioned pilot in the U.S. Navy during World War Two; awarded the Distinguished Flying Cross after being shot down and rescued in combat; successful businessman, after moving West to help build his own company; elected to the U.S. House of Representatives as the first Republican Congressman to represent Houston; U.S. Ambassador to the United Nations; Chairman of the Republican National Committee; America's second envoy to the People's Republic of China; Director of the Central Intelligence Agency. . . .*

What the resume tells us of the man, beyond his "need to contrib-

An early family picture of the Bushes with their first son, George Jr., who was born in 1946.

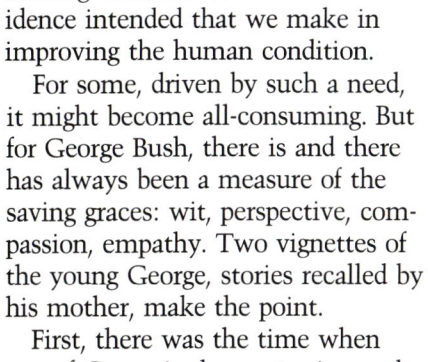

ute," is the compulsion he draws from the roots of his native New England, his adopted Texas. It is, to be sure, the consummate American need: the passion to excel, to extend oneself, one's community, one's nation, to the limit of possibility in making whatever contribution Providence intended that we make in improving the human condition.

For some, driven by such a need, it might become all-consuming. But for George Bush, there is and there has always been a measure of the saving graces: wit, perspective, compassion, empathy. Two vignettes of the young George, stories recalled by his mother, make the point.

First, there was the time when one of George's classmates in an obstacle race . . . "was so fat that when

37

Congressman George Bush pauses a few moments during his first days as a Congressman from Houston, Texas, in 1967.

he had to crawl through a barrel, he got stuck," Dorothy Bush remembers. "Everybody broke out laughing, but George didn't think it was funny, and with tears streaming down his face, he ran out on the field and pushed the boy through the barrel." Then there was Dorothy Bush's nickname for her son—"Have Half"—because whenever young George was given something, "he would turn to the person next to him and say, 'Here, have half.'"

Thus, for young George Bush, as for the man who came to hold his country's second highest elective office, the "need to contribute" has always held larger meaning than simply the achievement of honors and distinctions to be captured in a

During a particularly tense moment at the United Nations in 1972, Ambassador Bush waits to make a point.

George and Barbara Bush with Deng Xiao Ping in Peiping, China, in 1975.

career resume. Asked by a reporter what, of all his accomplishments, he takes most pride in, he answers: "That my children still come home."

"I am a realist," our new Vice-President is fond of saying. "I see the world as it is, not as I wish it were."

He kids himself. Like his countrymen, he is a dreamer with double-vision, and the world he sees is not simply that of the present but one of the future, enriched by the contributions we leave behind.

Ambassador and Mrs. Bush get a chance to explore the Forbidden City in China during his assignment as the country's second envoy to the People's Republic of China.

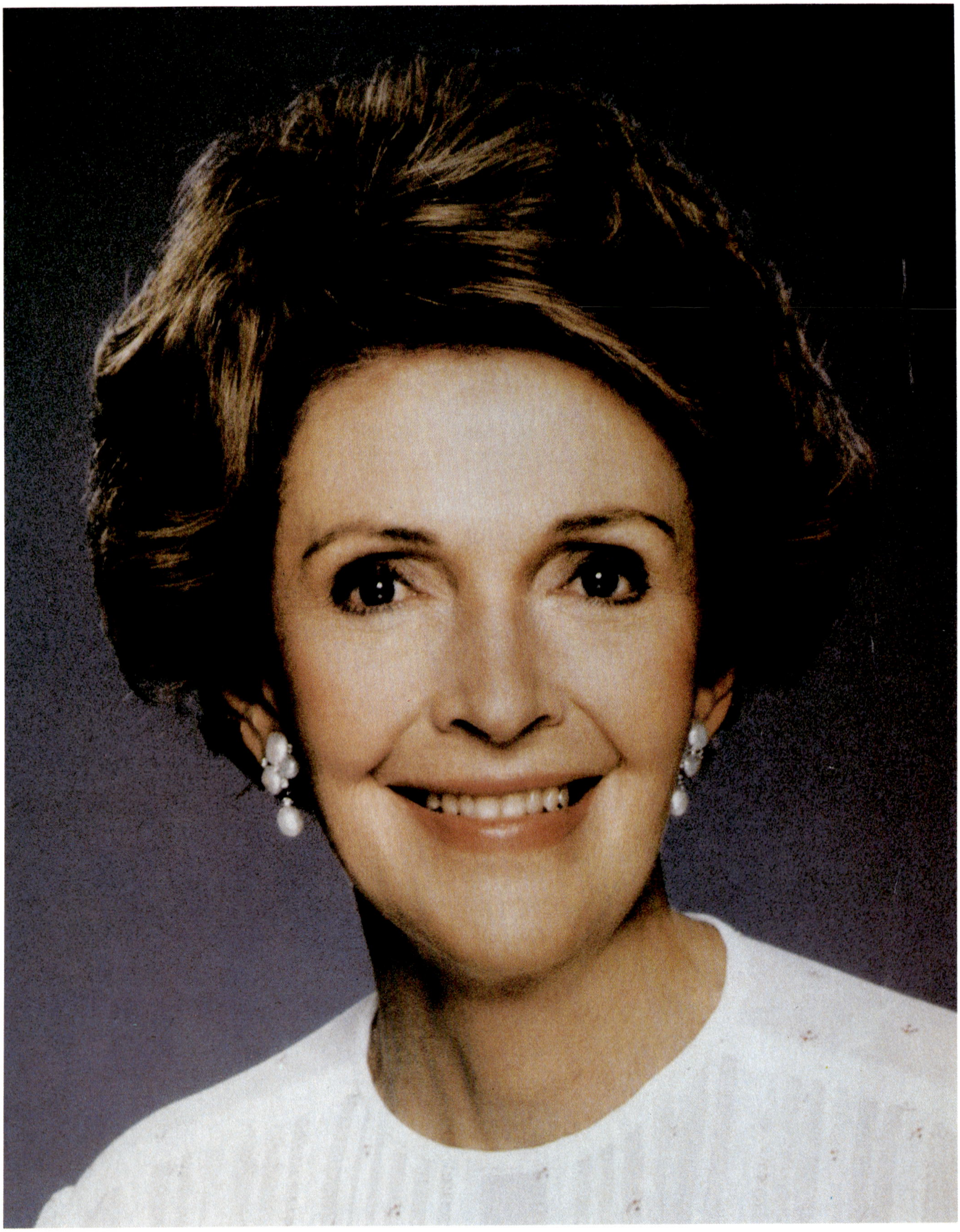

The First Lady

★
★
★

She might have been born in New York on the Fourth of July, but her mother, so the story goes, was an avid baseball fan who couldn't pass up an Independence Day doubleheader. Thus Anne Frances Robbins came on stage July 6th. The "Frances" quickly yielded to "Nancy," and with her mother's remarriage to Dr. Loyal Davis, she grew up as Nancy Davis—schoolgirl in Chicago, Smith graduate in Massachusetts, professional actress, wife, homemaker, mother, for eight years the First Lady of California, and now First Lady of our land.

Nancy Reagan is quintessentially feminine. Looks are deceptive, they say, and hers are. She doesn't look her age. She isn't tall, but she stands tall. She can seem fragile, with the kind of delicacy that asks for a protective cloak around her shoulders, but reporters who have followed her on the campaign trail know better. She has the stamina of a marathon runner. Her brown eyes, set wide apart, mirror the woman within. We of the press have seen those eyes flashing with anger and glinting with mischief; we have seen them full of tears, and full of laughter. We have seen Nancy tired and Nancy impatient, but I cannot recall a Nancy bored or a Nancy disheveled. What other words come to mind? Poised. Fastidious. Composed. This is a lady with class.

After graduation from Smith, she spent nearly eight years in the sophisticated world of Broadway and Hollywood. It is a world, by its very nature, of artificial emotions, of masks and make-believe. None of the permissiveness rubbed off. In her 1980 autobiography, she set that firm chin of hers—it is indeed a very firm chin—and sounded off:

"I cannot accept as admirable a modern morality that makes permissible almost any act. The truly important ingredients of life are still the same as they always have been—true love and real friendship, honesty and faithfulness, sincerity, unselfishness and selflessness, the concept that it is better to give than to receive, to do unto others as you would have them do unto you. These principles are still around, they haven't gone away, but it's not considered chic to discuss them or

By James J. Kilpatrick

write about them. I believe these ideals and precepts have endured because they are right and no less right today than yesterday."

That is the essential Nancy Reagan speaking. Again and again in her book, she returned to these themes.

"Human beings need moral standards to guide them. Society needs them to keep it from flying apart. Moral standards evolve, of course. They're not fixed in the stars. We need such standards because they encourage the most important asset of civilized people—self-restraint. Self-restraint marks the difference between adult and childish behavior.

A grown person who lives without self-control can have no central purpose in his or her life."

Nancy tends to divide her life into two almost equal segments—the 28 years before she met her husband and all the years that have passed since then. The watershed came in 1951. She was Nancy Davis, 28, budding actress. He was Ronald Reagan, 40, president of the Screen Actors Guild. The future President of the United States arrived for their first date on crutches: He had broken a leg in a charity baseball game. They both fibbed. It would have to be an early dinner, he said, wary that things might go wrong, because he had an early call in the morning.

"So do I," she lied. After all, as she would later recall, a girl has to have some pride.

"I don't know if it was love at first sight," Nancy has written, "but it was something close to it." In her old-fashioned phrase, "we were taken with one another." The following year, March 4, 1952, they were married. They went on an old-fashioned honeymoon, complete with a bouquet of roses in the bridal suite.

Her husband, she says, "is a very sentimental man." Twenty-two years later, Ronald Reagan had an engagement on the east coast that compelled him to miss a community dinner in Los Angeles. He wrote a note to his host, expressing his regrets; and please, he added, "tell your guest of honor that I will be calling on her when I get back to California.

"I have long admired her," Mr. Reagan continued, "and upon my return to California intend not only to tell her that . . . but also that I love her more than anyone in the whole wide world."

That sense of closeness abides. I remember one night on the campaign trail in 1976, when we were flying from Somewhere to Somewhere, and I went forward to speak with a staffer. It had been an exhausting day. In the half-light of the darkened cabin, the Governor still was reading in his window seat, turning the pages carefully with his right hand so as not to disturb Nancy. She was wrapped head to toe in an airline blanket, sound asleep, snuggled contentedly against his shoulder. She is his love. And he is hers.

43

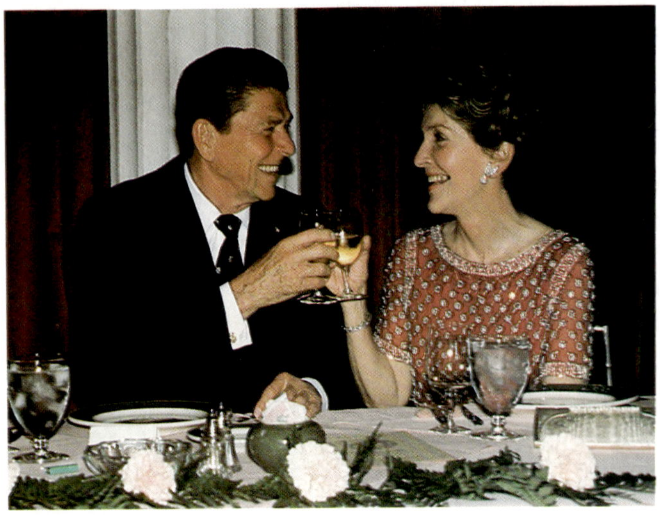

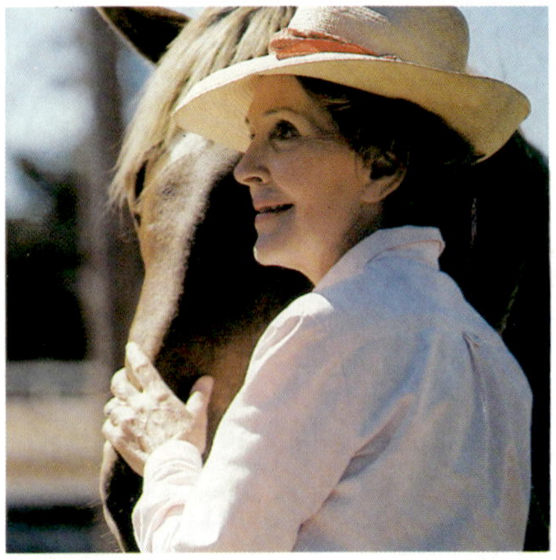

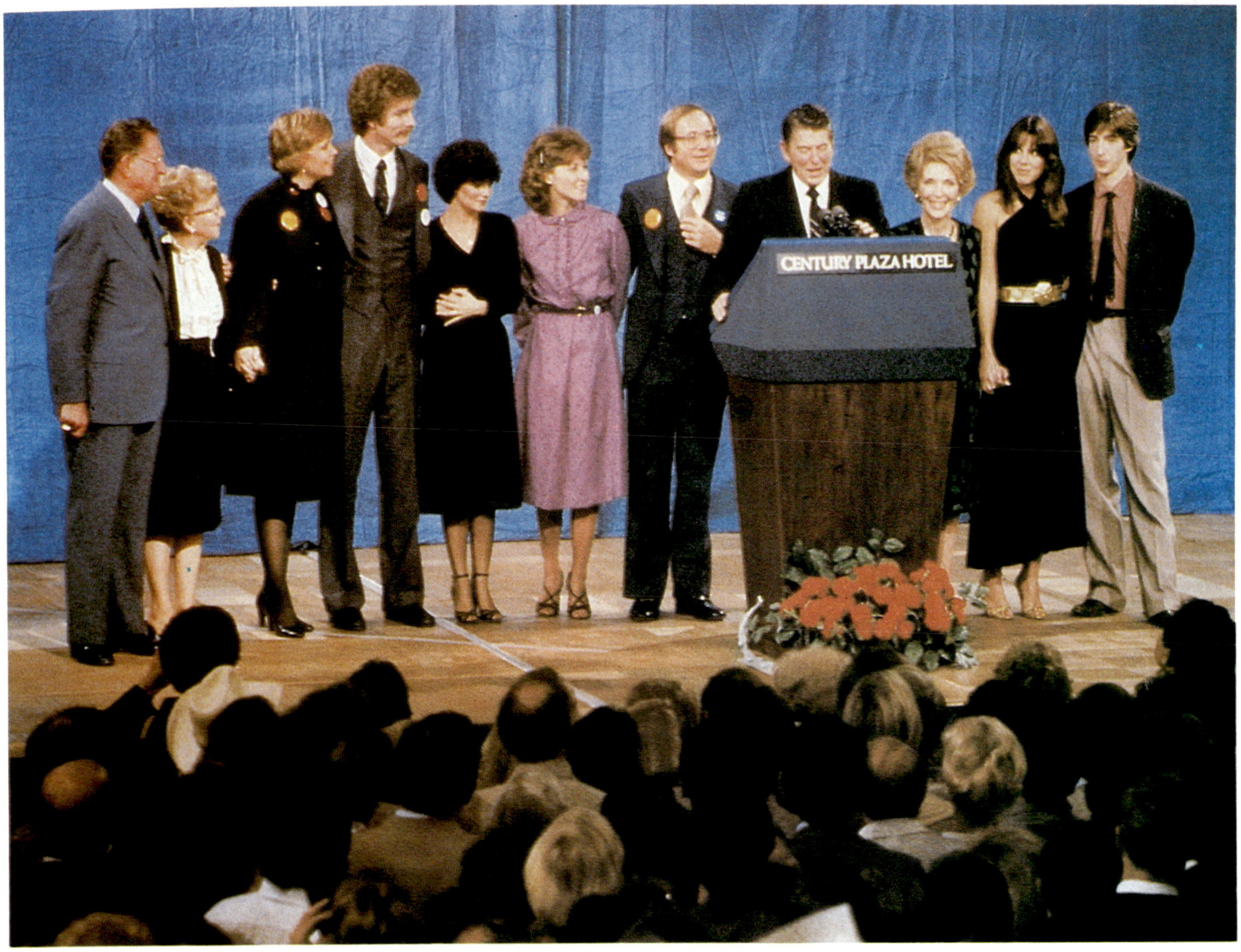
CENTURY PLAZA HOTEL

The Reagan Family

★

★

★

The Reagan family is a microcosm of what America is all about—at least its best parts. Through grace, tensions, love and adjustments in personal relationships, we find cohesion and apartness—love and rivalry—religious commitment and free thinking—firm principles and flexible application—love of country and differences in approach.

The cohesion of the Reagans is evidenced by the closeness of each to the other, although the family unit is parted geographically by independent careers.

When their children were going to school, Nancy and Ronald Reagan unselfishly devoted their time to parent-teacher-student activities. The Reagans' dedication to doing what was right and good for their children and the school was evidenced in the yearly school May festivals. During the entire festival day, one would find Ronnie in the back of the hot dog booth dishing up hot dogs, mustard, relish, together with assorted clean-up duties. In the front of the booth, Nancy would be passing back orders, making change, and benevolently dishing up the chili made by the mothers.

Nancy and Ronald Reagan are committed church-goers, an example of peace with oneself and one's God. The children evidence boldly an inner dedication to personal ideals, not necessarily represented by ceremonial evidence.

By Mary Jane & Charles Z. Wick

46

A strong mother and a strong father sometimes produce mild and meek progeny. In the Reagan family all the children and their parents are strong willed in adhering to principles as they see them. There is an unspoken rivalry among the children to achieve in his or her own way the fulfillment of personal commitments.

"God Bless America," the Irving Berlin song, in its simple eloquence summarizes the Reagan philosophy. The Reagans all have different ways of expressing this same feeling.

Yes, the Reagan family is a microcosm of what America is all about—a thought to make patriots proud.

It has been the great privilege of our family to have had the pleasure of sharing a succession of personal, family and public events through the years where that special quality of this family, touched by destiny, has enriched all of our lives.

47

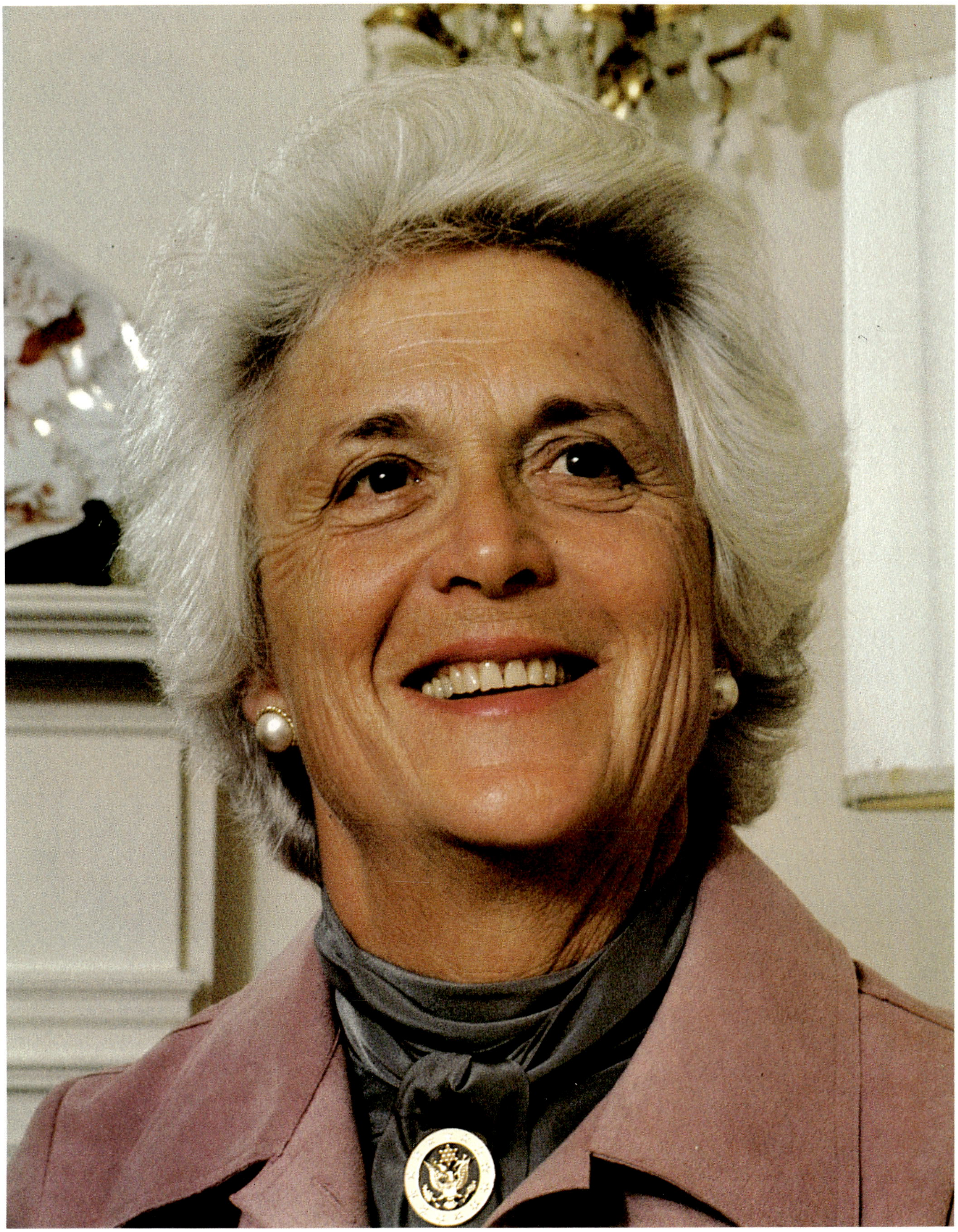

A Portrait Of Barbara Pierce Bush

★
★
★

"She comes into the room like a fresh breeze and everybody feels a little better," says a friend of Barbara Bush. After fifteen years of a warm bipartisan friendship, I can't think of a better way of saying it— Barbara Pierce Bush is a person who affirms life by her presence. She is attractive, friendly, equable, kind, and, on occasion, very very funny. She can be reserved or brisk, but never distant. An amazing number of people of all ages call her friend.

Like millions of other American women, Barbara Bush has lived a life defined by others—as the wife of a man in business and public life, as the devoted mother of six children, as a woman called on to play supportive official roles. She has emerged a strong and vibrant person, handsome and youthful of manner, in no way diminished or limited by the life she has chosen. She has accepted every responsibility as a means of learning, enjoyment and growth, and, as one intimate puts it, "with discipline, incredible balance, and a core of common sense that must have been there from the beginning."

In many ways, as Barbara Bush would be the first to admit, hers has been almost a storybook life. She was born into a large well-to-do family in the pleasant Westchester community of Rye, New York, attended private schools and Smith College. She met her husband, George Bush, at a dance when she was sixteen and he, seventeen. They fell in love, and a few years later, were married when he, then a World War II Navy flyer, was on rotation home from overseas.—"I became a sophomore dropout from Smith to go away with George." One can truthfully say, as the old tales go, they have lived happily ever after. Her own reflection on her life is characteristically positive. "I count myself extraordinarily fortunate to have shared this life with George. What else could I have done that would have been more interesting or filled with such great experiences?"

It has not been, however, a life untouched by difficulty. Again like many another American wife in the post World War II era she has had to be extremely flexible. The war years left her young husband unwilling to take up a life of investment banking as had his New Englander father and grandfather. "He wanted to deal with things he could feel and see. He wanted to act and to do...." So, after graduating from Yale after an accelerated college course of only two and one-half years (during which their first child was born) George Bush accepted a job with Dresser Industries and the young Bushes were off to Odessa, Texas. They lived in five different places in California while he was in management training and finally came back to Midland, Texas, where they lived for eleven years.

By Abagail McCarthy

49

The demands of change attendant on George Bush's subsequent varied career—his running for office, his service in Congress, his acceptance of leadership positions at precarious times for party, agency or mission—has called for great adaptability on the part of his wife. She has lived, for example, in 28 different homes in 17 cities while managing to make a close family life possible for her husband and children. "One of the strongest influences in my life," she says, "was that of George's mother who also lived a public life. By her example she showed me the importance of close family ties in the midst of pressures."

Any triumph or gain in the Bushes' life has been tempered by the loss of their second child, a beautiful four-year-old daughter who died of leukemia. "But," says Barbara Bush simply, "we do not forget that we were more fortunate than many others who have suffered such a loss without the helps we had—a sharing, loving extended family and the means to do everything possible. We believed in God. And we learned what to value."

Today she lists her ever-growing family of children and grandchildren with something like wonder. "As of this June we will have five daughters and four sons! There is George, our oldest, married to Laura, Jeb to Columba, Neil to Sharon and Marvin, just graduated from the University of Virginia, who will be married to Margaret Molster. Then there is our own Dorothy at Boston College. And there are our two grandchildren."

Barbara Bush feels that her intense interest in reading as a tool for children's development stems from her experience with her own children and grandchildren. "It seems to me so clear that reading is basic in opening up the world for a child.

The ability to read is the first step in achieving the American dream." Not only has she accepted a position on the board of Reading Is Fundamental, an organization of volunteers which makes books and reading itself accessible to underprivileged children—partly in tribute to one of its founders, her friend, Mrs. Robert McNamara—but her hope and her plan is to extend her assistance to, and to promote, in every way she can, the many existing professional programs and the experts who are promoting reading and working to alleviate reading disabilities. "I met such people all across the country; I hear from them; and I have a file this thick,"—she demonstrates, holding her hands wide apart—"I want to help them, to put them in touch with each other, and with others who need the help." She sees her role as second lady of the land as in every way a supportive one.

Her faith and the philosophy that being blessed by fortune obligates one to give—of goods, love and work—are part of Barbara Bush. Many know of the thousands she raised for various charities by lectures sharing her China experience, but only those close to her know Barbara Bush, the volunteer who rejects honorary titles to do the real work wherever she goes. "She works in cancer wards, tending and feeding patients in a hospital for the chronically ill."

It is that Barbara who chose to open the Bible to the Sermon on the Mount for her husband's oath-taking. " 'Pray in secret . . . do not your alms before men to be seen of them . . . judge not . . . build your house upon a rock'—I like those words," she says.

51

52

The Bush Family

★

★

★

Meet the Bushes, gathered for a family picture on a very special occasion: Election Night, November 4, 1980. A conscientious photographer has arranged them in proper symmetrical order, with George and Barbara Bush second row-center, alongside George's mother who, under ordinary circumstances, would be considered the family elder—save for the fact that there are no ordinary circumstances whenever the Bushes get together and, in any case, Dorothy Bush is a rather extraordinary version of a family "elder."

Consider, for example, her recent bicycle accident, which occurred during her daily two-and-a-half mile, three-speed, ride into Kennebunkport. Earlier in the evening, before the photographer arrived, George Bush was once again marveling at the story of how his mother, having taken a spill and broken her collarbone, had asked a neighborhood youth to go to his house and ask his parents to call a doctor.

"I'll go, but it won't do any good," the boy had answered. "They're playing tennis and I don't think they'll want to break away from the game."

By Vic Gold

Telling the story, George Bush looked at his mother, shook his head, and laughed. "Now to some people, that might have sounded callous," he said, "but as a tennis fanatic, mother understood perfectly."

But that had happened several weeks before and now Dorothy Bush, looking none the worse for the incident, is standing patiently amid bedlam while the photographer, trying to capture this historic moment, works frantically to put things and people in place. His problem is that the younger Bushes, while aware of the significance of this night, simply won't settle into a proper frame of mind. The occasion calls for a certain degree of solemnity, but no sooner than one of the younger Bushes settles down, another begins cracking one-liners, mugging for the camera or otherwise upsetting the harmony of the camera's eye. Meanwhile, the future Vice President, far from doing anything to discourage this disarray, is actually part of the problem, cracking one-liners and mugging with the rest.

What most impressed her about her future husband when they first met, says Barbara Bush, wasn't his academic credentials or status as captain of the Yale baseball team. It was his sense of humor. He was a young man on-the-move, ambitious and hard-driving—but one who seemed to take his work, not himself, seriously.

That attribute, along with Barbara Bush's own wit and perspective (and a good measure of their grandmother Dorothy's resilience), has clearly been passed along to the five Bush children, from the oldest, George, 34, to the youngest, Dorothy, 21.

George, who holds a master's degree in business administration from Harvard and a degree in history from his father's alma mater, Yale, is president of his own oil and gas exploration company, and with his

53

wife, the former Laura Welch, makes his home in Midland, Texas.

Jeb, 29, a Phi Beta Kappa graduate of the University of Texas with a degree in Latin American studies, is married to the former Columba Gallo, and left his job as Assistant Vice President of the Texas Commerce Bank in Caracas, Venezuela, in 1979, to join the rest of the Bush family in his father's campaign. Jeb, Columba and their two children, George, 4, and Noelle, 3, moved to Miami, Florida on January 1, 1981, where the second of the Bush sons is now engaged in a real estate business.

Neil, 25, holds both an undergraduate and master's degree in business administration from Tulane University. It was during the primary season in the winter of 1979–80, that Neil met Sharon Hart. They were married in Kennebunkport, Maine the following summer, and are now living in Denver, Colorado, where Neil is employed in a training program with Amoco.

Marvin, 24, is a graduate of the University of Virginia, where he studied history and English. The fourth of the Bush sons is engaged to Margaret Molster of Richmond, with wedding plans set for the couple in mid-June, 1981.

Finally, there is Dorothy—"Doro" to members of her family and friends—the youngest of the George and Barbara Bush children, who completed studies at the Katherine Gibbs School in Boston and is now working toward her bachelor's degree at Boston College.

Individualists all, yet they come together as a close-knit family, each sharing not only the wit and perspective of their extraordinary "elders," but also the keen sense of personal and social responsibility that also has passed down through the generations.

"It was George's idea that our children should know responsibility at a young age," Barbara Bush once told a friend. "He was right, and we've never regretted it."

Wit, perspective, a sense of responsibility—George and Barbara Bush's family share all these attributes, and one more thing that their grandmother Dorothy understands perfectly: As reported in the official biography of the 1980 campaign, they are all "avid tennis players."

55

56

The President And His Cabinet

*S*ome of the most important issues in the world have been thrashed out and decided in the 23 × 28 foot portion of the West Wing of the White House known as the Cabinet Room. Here assembles the President's Cabinet, that top group of executive appointments whose collective status has no constitutional or legislative basis.

Although the functions of the Cabinet officers and their departments are prescribed by law, the functions of the Cabinet itself are not. The Cabinet's activities have evolved through custom and the specific needs of individual presidents.

American presidents have not always utilized their Cabinets as fully as they might. George Washington made little use of his Cabinet in the early experimental days of the new democracy. Before leaving the capital on one occasion, Washington gave Vice President John Adams permission to bring his associates together if a crisis developed during his absence. Within twenty-four hours after the Chief Executive had left the city, Adams called the first meeting of a United States Cabinet.

In administrations from George Washington's on, Cabinets have experienced varying degrees of importance. President Jackson's Cabinet was one of musical chairs. Jackson went through four Secretaries of State, five Secretaries of the Treasury, three Secretaries of War, three Secretaries of the Navy, three Attorneys General and two Postmasters General, in his quest for a complementary group. President Polk frankly stated he preferred to conduct the affairs of government without the Cabinet's aid. Yet he still set an all-time record of four hundred meetings in four years. And a member of Franklin Roosevelt's Cabinet, who was under no illusion as to his essentiality, said, "The cold fact is that on important matters we are seldom called upon for advice. . . ."

All too often Cabinet gatherings have been haphazard and carelessly planned conclaves, meeting in an atmosphere of indecision, aimless discussion, and even recrimination with members hashing over trivia.

President Eisenhower, on the other hand, used his Cabinet as a non-voting board of directors before which looming executive problems and future opportunities and plans were presented. Eisenhower knew the requirements for an effective Cabinet system: "The teams and staffs through which the modern commander absorbs information and exercises his authority must be a beautifully interlocked, smooth-working mechanism. Ideally, the whole should be practically a single mind."

By Robert Keith Gray

Counsellor to the President Edwin Meese III

Secretary of Agriculture John R. Block

Secretary of Education Terrel H. Bell

Secretary of Transportation Andrew L. Lewis Jr.

Secretary of Health and Human Services Richard S. Schweiker

Attorney General William French Smith

Director of Central Intelligence William J. Casey

Secretary of Housing and Urban Development Samuel R. Pierce Jr.

Secretary of State Alexander M. Haig Jr.

Although a Cabinet can administer, implement and advise, it is the president alone who must make the final decisions and bear the ultimate responsibility. The completeness of the president's power and responsibility as a majority of one was well illustrated at a meeting of Abraham Lincoln's Cabinet. The discussion was a heated one and tempers flared, for Lincoln found he alone was in favor of the proposal. Every other man at the table was opposed to it. Lincoln argued for, the others against. Finally, the President whammed the table with his fist and said, "Gentlemen, the 'ayes' have it. Next item!"

Presidential attempts to form a collegial "Cabinet government" often have fallen victim to the dissension that arises between members of the White House staff and the Cabinet officers or among the Cabinet officers themselves. Everyone wants to speak to the president in private. The words of one former Cabinet member are instructive, "Putting a pet project on the Cabinet agenda is a good way to get it nibbled to death by ducks."

A true cabinet process is not easy to maintain. Yet President Reagan, when he was Governor of California, instituted a state cabinet system which worked well. It succeeded because of his continuing attentions and efforts. He was committed to its smooth and effective functioning and insistent upon its productivity. A Cabinet, whether on the state or national level, is purposeful only when the Chief Executive is unswervingly determined that it be so. Ronald Reagan, as Governor of California, exhibited a dedication that will continue in Washington.

Ronald Wilson Reagan's Cabinet is destined to be one of the most cohesive, instrumental and accomplished in our nation's history. Its officers are devoted to the goals and ideals of the man who leads them. And the leader is long devoted to the practicalities and possibilities of a strong Cabinet structure. In short, each believes in the other.

To staff his Cabinet, President Reagan has chosen men and women of sterling ability who hold shared values, those values so often stated during the course of the campaign— family, work, neighborhood, peace and freedom. The Cabinet jointly and inseparably believes in the need to rebuild a disintegrating economy, renew a weakened defense, and return the government to the people.

In the final analysis, this community of aspirations is the heart, the soul, the strength of the Reagan Cabinet.

Robert Keith Gray, Co-chairman of the Presidential Inaugural Committee, was Secretary of the Cabinet in the Eisenhower Administration and is the author of "18 Acres Under Glass," published by Doubleday.

Secretary of Energy James B. Edwards

Secretary of Commerce Malcolm Baldridge

Secretary of Labor Raymond J. Donovan

Secretary of the Interior James G. Watt

Secretary of Defense Caspar W. Weinberger

Secretary of the Treasury Donald T. Regan

Director of the Office of Management and Budget David A. Stockman

United States Trade Representative William E. Brock

United States Ambassador to the United Nations Jeane J. Kirkpatrick

PRICE 25 CENTS.
OFFICIAL
PROGRAMME
INAUGURAL
CEREMONIES
Washington D.C.
MARCH 4TH
1897
COPYRIGHT 1897

The Inaugural Heritage

★

★

★

The inauguration of a new President is the one event which unifies people of political differences. Every four years the people of the United States join together in the nation's capital to witness the ceremony and to enjoy the day of pageantry which surrounds this event. Abraham Lincoln best summed the mood of the people on the eve of his own Inauguration in his speech of February 18, 1861 with these remarks:

"Almost all men in this country and in any country where freedom of thought is tolerated, citizens attach themselves to political parties. It is but ordinary charity to attribute the fact that in so attaching himself to the party which his judgment prefers, the citizen believes he thereby promotes the best interests of the whole country; and when an election is passed, it is altogether befitting a free people that, until the next election, they should be as one people."

The Inaugural Day activities center around a simple oath of 37 words. Unchanged since it was first spoken in 1789 by George Washington, it symbolizes the orderly transfer of authority within our government. With each transfer of such authority comes a new hope—a new beginning for all America. As expressed in the words of Harry S. Truman in 1949:

"In the simple ceremony in which the President and Vice President are invested with the duties of their offices, the citizens of the United States symbolically invest themselves with the duties of citizenship—the responsibility of keeping themselves informed on the activities of their Government, of living in friendly understanding with one another, and helping to keep the United States a nation which increasingly provides a better life for its people."

Individuals of differing backgrounds: religious and ethnic groups—from generals to farmers, from ministers to lawyers, from storekeepers to professors, from mining engineers to architects, from the urban to the rural—all repeating the same oath. Regardless of the weather, be it rain, bright sunlight, overcast skies, snow blizzards, or sub-zero weather, the ceremony goes on with little or no interruption. Regardless of circumstances—in war or in peace, in times of prosperity, or in periods of financial crisis—still the transfer of the Government takes the same orderly form.

The Inaugural address, which follows the oath, is the first public expression of the *new* President's own personality, aspirations and goals. In it the President sets the tone for the new administration. Inaugural addresses have been memorized by some and read by others. They have varied in length from the 8,445 word speech of William Henry Harrison to the 135 word address by George Washington.

Following the oath taking ceremonies, the dignitaries leave the Capitol and lead the nation in an Inaugural parade down Pennsylvania Avenue past the White House. This is the one activity that all of the nation can either participate in or watch. Generations of custom have laid down the content and form of the parade with its many military and civilian bands and floats.

The day's activities conclude with the ball, the most lavish celebration the people afford their new President. It is one of our country's old-

Introduction by Herbert R. Collins, Curator, Division of Political History, The Smithsonian Institution.

This beautifully color illustrated Inaugural Program was issued upon the occasion of William McKinley's inauguration in 1897.

est recurring festivals which has played a significant role in most every Inauguration since George Washington's.

Following the day's events, the President retires to his new home and the home of the nation—the White House. The most historic building in Washington, D.C., it has been occupied by every American President since John Adams, whose blessing is engraved on one of its mantels: "I Pray Heaven Bestow on THIS HOUSE and on ALL that shall hereafter inhabit it. May none but Honest and Wise Men ever rule under this roof!" (Nov. 2, 1800)

Inaugurals Past

Snow, wind, rain, traffic jams, lost invitations, crowded hotels, streets and restaurants, and general mass confusion have largely characterized most festivities of past Presidential Inaugural days.

As well-planned as an event may be, circumstances oftentimes beyond anyone's control have redirected schedules and redefined precedents. Inaugurations have been symbolic events heralding in new eras and bright hopes. For some, it has been a prized day, the trophy of a political victor. For others, it is a realization of defeat. Always, the change occurs and the man of the day has every opportunity to achieve historic immortality. Some Presidents have seen Inauguration Day as a somber and serious commencement of the hardest job in the world, while others have reveled and gloried in the pomp and circumstance of the festivity.

Inaugurals past researched and written by Carl Sferrazza with the assistance of the Inaugural staff.

On April 24, 1789 George Washington arrived in New York bedecked in a flotilla of color, docking in lower Manhattan at Murphy's Wharf. Six days later he took the oath of office as the first President of the United States.

This creamware mug from England bears the picture of the new President in 1801, Thomas Jefferson of Virginia.

The ever popular Dolley Madison was described by Washington Irving as "a fine portly buxom dame, who has a kind word for everyone." She hosted the first Inaugural Ball in 1809.

62

This creamware pitcher was made in commemoration of James Madison's Inaugural in 1809.

George Washington gracefully minueted with the ladies of New York society at the private and belated ball held in honor of his 1789 Inaugural.

At his last public reception in 1833, Andrew Jackson invited mobs into the White House to partake of a gift of a giant cheese. The guests threw it around and rubbed it into the rugs, the odor lingering into the Van Buren administration.

This is one in a series of clothing buttons manufactured and worn to commemorate the first Inaugural of George Washington in 1789.

Inauguration Day has been a mirror of Presidential character and taste. As such, past traditions have been broken and established accordingly. The oath, parade and balls have all become folklore of a proud people seeing Inauguration as the winds of change and an opportunity for a new beginning.

April 30, 1789

George Washington, "first in the hearts of his countrymen" became the first President of the United States on April 30, 1789. Many of the Inaugural traditions we revere today, were established on that cool, April morning in New York City.

63

The streets were filled with mobs of people. As Washington's coach moved along the extended parade route, church bells rang and crowds greeted him with cheers and pageantry.

In the city of New York, all work had stopped. Everyone rushed to the waterfront to see Washington's Inaugural barge arrive at Murphy's Wharf. The cannon of the harbor battery fired the welcoming salute and three hearty cheers greeted the entourage. The crowd was so dense that the planned parade was delayed for over two hours.

The next morning, Washington made his way to Federal Hall through the growing crowds. Arriving on the balcony overlooking the harbor, he repeated the oath after Robert Livingston, the chancellor of New York state. According to one source, he was so nervous that he lost his cue. After repeating the oath, he kissed the Bible and added, "So help me God," setting an example for his successors.

The day concluded with a huge fireworks display that was paid for by private citizens. A celebration ball was not held until May 7, at which Washington minueted with the best of New York society ladies.

March 4, 1809

On the glorious morning on which he was to be installed into the most honored position in the land, James Madison commented, "I'd much rather be in bed sleeping." Not so for his wife, Dolley Madison. She enjoyed the day to the fullest and approved the first official Inaugural Ball, held at the Long Hotel in Washington, D.C.

Appearing in a long-trained pale buff-colored velvet gown and a new pearl ensemble, she was the unchallenged star of the evening. Dolley

In 1861 as the Nation was torn apart by Civil War, Abraham Lincoln took his oath of office under an unfinished Capitol Dome. By 1865, however, at his second oath taking, the Dome was complete . . . and the Nation was healing.

Inaugurated in 1877, Rutherford Birchard Hayes had his official state china featuring all sorts of American wildlife scenes.

This paper balloon lantern was used at the Inauguration of Benjamin Harrison and Levi P. Morton in 1881.

danced with outgoing President Jefferson in a matching Parisian turban with two ostrich plumes that came dangerously close to the candle-lit chandeliers. The courtly Virginian, Jefferson, admitted that he was a bit nervous as this was his first ball in over forty years.

As the Marine Band played, setting a precedent for future balls, Dolley strategically situated herself between the Ministers of France and England, whose countries were at war, thereby initiating a new type of social diplomacy.

March 4, 1829

Nothing has ever equalled the Inauguration celebration of Andrew Jackson. From all over the country, people flocked to the Capital to see their hero, "Old Hickory," sworn in. With hordes of admirers and fifteen veterans of the American Revolution

Well-heeled guests in beautiful gowns and tuxedos at Grover Cleveland's 1885 Inaugural Ball looked out onto the crowds and decorated interior of the Pension Building from a spacious balcony high above the dance floor.

This wedgewood pitcher was made in 1881 to commemorate the Inauguration of James A. Garfield.

65

trailing behind him, Jackson walked through the streets of the Capital, refusing the offer of the coach. Following the swearing-in, he delivered his speech unsmilingly.

Just one month before, Jackson had lost his beloved wife, Rachel. So no Inaugural Ball was staged. Instead, the President thought it better to hold an open house at the Executive Mansion.

By the time Jackson arrived at the White House for the reception, crowds of thousands engulfed the White House. The East Room was overrun. Food that had been carefully laid out on tables was thrown on the elegant floors and walls. In the packed house drunken men fought, little children cried for lost parents and ladies fainted. There was such a press to shake Jackson's hand that he found himself trapped, almost suffocating against the wall. A group of supporters formed a cordon around him and helped him escape through a side door. Mounting his horse, Jackson went back to Gadsby's Tavern and spent his first night there.

As the party continued, the crowd became increasingly unruly. China was thrown and smashed, draperies pulled and torn, and muddy boots damaged rugs and silk sofas. A panicked White House staff put the tubs of alcoholic punch out on the South Lawn. The scheme worked and the guests departed.

March 4, 1841

The crowds in Washington were as wild and eager for William Henry Harrison's Inauguration as they had been for Andrew Jackson's. It was the first time an official Inaugural Committee had actually been organized and Harrison, known as the Indian-fighting General, "Old Tippecanoe," was the first President to arrive by railroad for his Inauguration.

The first commercial advertisement at an Inaugural appeared with this rose distributed by a perfume company at Benjamin Harrison's 1889 Inaugural.

This program from Inauguration 1893 was unique in that it commemorated Grover Cleveland's second and non-consecutive term as the 24th President.

After taking the oath of office on the Capitol steps on March 4, 1881, James Abram Garfield immediately turned to kiss his mother.

66

Giving the longest Inaugural Address on record, he stopped in midstream to take the oath and then finished the 8,441 word speech.

Already exhausted from the pre-inaugural activities, Harrison insisted upon dancing with the wives of prominent Whigs at an unprecedented three balls, finally retiring early in the morning. Tired and chilled, the President came down with pneumonia. Exactly one month to the day of his Inauguration, William Henry Harrison died.

March 4, 1865

Abraham Lincoln took his second oath of office under the newly completed dome of the Capitol. The long Civil War was drawing to a close and the Inauguration under the completed dome hopefully symbolized the binding together of the country.

However, on Inaugural Day, not all events went smoothly. The President, who had been at the Capitol earlier in the morning was expected back at the White House by Mrs. Lincoln. When he did not return at the appointed time, Mrs. Lincoln hopped into the carriage and rushed to the Capitol. Recognizing the Presidential carriage, the crowds cheered the first lady, thinking the President was inside. Among precedent setting events, two companies of freed Negroes marched in Lincoln's parade: old man weather did not cooperate, however, and the beautiful paper floats built for the parade were torn and destroyed by the rain. The Inaugural ball was held that Monday and the Lincolns attended. Ominously,

Outgoing President Grover Cleveland graciously escorted President-elect William McKinley to his oath of office March 4, 1897.

one of the guests at the ceremony would see the President again at Ford's Theatre. His name was John Wilkes Booth.

March 4, 1873

On the coldest Inauguration Day in history, with temperatures at −4 degrees and winds up to 40 miles per hour, President Ulysses S. Grant was called on and escorted to the Capitol by a Congressional Committee, establishing a tradition.

Grant's second term Inaugural Ball is probably the most disastrous in history. It took place in a huge

67

This metal badge commemorated William McKinley's Inauguration and was worn that day in 1897.

William McKinley's 1897 Inaugural Ball Program depicts the large and often used Pension Building on its cover.

Theodore Roosevelt's Inaugural was filled with enthusiasm and vigor, remembered here in a song honoring the "bully" TR.

temporary building erected in Judiciary Square. Unfortunately, nobody thought of installing a heating system. Guests danced with their wraps and coats on to keep warm. The mammoth feast prepared for thousands froze solid and musicians, too cold to play their instruments, stood by helplessly. Hundreds of canaries, intended to serenade guests, froze to death on their ceiling perches and fell onto the horrified dancers. It was not a day to remember.

March 3, 1877

Rutherford Birchard Hayes entered Washington under a cloud. He won the Presidency with a hotly disputed single electoral vote. March 4 fell on a Sunday that year. Fearing a reversal of the controversial election, a secret Inauguration was held on Saturday, the third. After dinner in the White House, Rutherford Hayes, accompanied by President Grant and Chief Justice Waite, slipped into the Red Room. Before anyone else was informed, America had a new President. President Hayes then calmly repeated the oath in public that Monday, March 5.

March 4, 1881

By 1881 Washington, D.C. was becoming accustomed to Inauguration Days. Bleachers were built for the crowds. Municipal buildings were decorated with bunting, banners and flags. At intersections along the parade route arches were built and decorated with flowers. For the first time a wooden reviewing stand was built in front of the White House for President James A. Garfield's 80-year-old mother to become the first mother to witness her son's assumption of the Presidency. The night before the Inauguration, she

Teddy Roosevelt's Inaugural parade was a potpourri of variety. Seen here are American Indians who participated in the parade.

Tin plates commemorating William Howard Taft were used both in the 1908 campaign and 1909 Inaugural.

was the personal houseguest of President Hayes. Following the oath taking, President Garfield turned first to kiss his mother.

The Inaugural Ball held at the Smithsonian Arts and Industry Building was warm and well organized, with plenty to eat. Guests danced nonstop to music provided by two groups of 150 musicians. A huge statue of Columbia, symbol of America, was covered with flowers and illuminated by an electric light. Many visitors gasped in wonder at their first sight of electricity.

69

March 4, 1889

Benjamin Harrison's term of office came between two non-consecutive terms of Grover Cleveland. Harrison is the only grandson of a President to become President himself.

Harrison's Inauguration Day was marred by a continuous downpour of torrential rain. Earlier that day a very optimistic outgoing First Lady, Frances Cleveland, told one of her butlers, "Now I want you to leave everything the way it is, as you see it now. For we are coming back in four years from today." She proved correct.

Overscheduling to please the various groups clammering for recognition, the Inaugural Parade was forced to run late into darkness. It broke up quickly though—both marchers and spectators were wet and cold and had no patience left.

March 4, 1905

Six months after the 1901 Inauguration, President McKinley was assassinated and Teddy was rushed to Buffalo to take the oath of office in the presence of the McKinley cabinet.

The 1905 Inaugural reflected President Theodore Roosevelt's universal popularity. Parade participants included an Indian chief in full costume riding in an automobile, rather than on horseback. Teddy's beloved Rough Riders, who had fought with him in Cuba and a Negro Cavalry rode up to the White House portico and leaned forward in their saddles to shake hands with the President who was waiting on the steps.

The evening before the Inaugural ceremonies, Roosevelt received a present he would cherish as long as he lived. Secretary of State John Hay sent him a ring containing hair cut from President Lincoln's head on

William and Helen Taft rode down Pennsylvania Avenue towards the White House on his Inauguration Day, March 4, 1909. It was the first time a President's wife rode back with her husband, and it thereby set a tradition.

This little stuffed doll represents the popular and energetic President Theodore Roosevelt as a Rough Rider.

the night of his assassination. The ring was engraved with Roosevelt's and Lincoln's initials. Hay wrote, "Please wear it tomorrow. You are one of the men who most thoroughly understands and appreciates Lincoln." That tie with Lincoln is said to have encouraged Roosevelt during the difficult periods of the Presidency.

That night at the Inaugural Ball, Teddy Roosevelt's 21-year-old daughter, Alice, thoroughly enjoyed the festivities. Waving to the friends she spied in the audience, Alice had to be restrained lest she fall from the President's box.

Mamie Eisenhower and her penchant for pink influenced everything from roses, wallpaper, and cupcakes to her beautiful Inaugural Ball gown of 1953, now on display in the Smithsonian's Museum of American History.

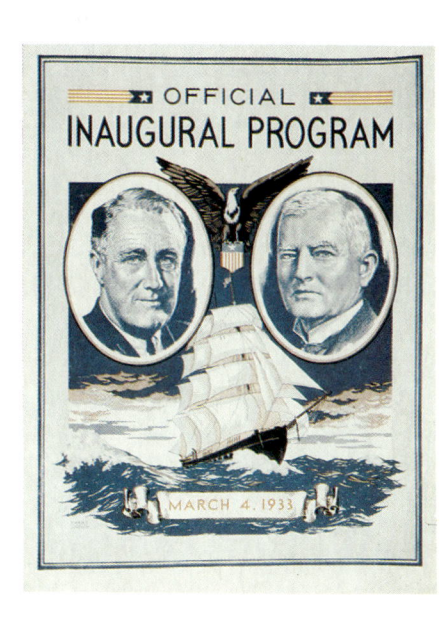

The 1933 Inaugural Program showing F.D.R. and Vice President-elect John Nance Garner.

March 4, 1909

William Howard Taft prophetically commented to a friend early in his career, that "... It would be a cold day before I get to be President." And so it was. One of the winter's worst storms delayed guests and carriages and hampered communications. Because of the storm, Mrs. Taft's ball gown that had been ordered from New York, was delayed in arriving. Despite the blizzard and complications, little Charles Taft remained undaunted, reading the latest copy of *Treasure Island* while his father took the oath of office and delivered his address.

More significantly, in the new era of horseless carriages, President Taft, the traditionalist, rode back to the White House in a carriage accompanied by his wife Helen, who started a tradition continued by all future First Ladies. Even progressive Teddy Roosevelt refused the use of a car in leaving Washington. "I came in by horse and I shall go out by horse." There was, however, a sign of things to come, as a solitary automobile made its way down the Inaugural Parade route.

During their first few weeks in the White House, the Tafts had a hectic social schedule. The strain on Mrs. Taft was serious enough to cause a slight stroke that left her unable to take part in any of the White House activities for over a year.

January 20, 1945

Franklin Roosevelt's fourth inaugural ceremonies took place with little pomp and circumstance on the South Portico of the White House. Because of the President's failing health and the inpropriety of a celebration while the country was still at war, there was no Inaugural Ball. Mrs. Roosevelt and Mrs. Truman greeted thousands of well-wishers in the East Room. Before he took the oath of office the President insisted that all thirteen of his grandchildren be gathered with him for a portrait at the White House. Some people feel he had a premonition that this would be the last time they could all be together, for within three months he was dead.

January 20, 1953

For the first time in almost 70 years, the White House became the home of a former general and his family. Dwight D. Eisenhower and his wife, Mamie, re-instituted the status of the Inaugural Ball which had been temporarily suspended while the country was at war.

Ike wore a homberg hat instead of the traditional formal black topper. He became the first Republican President since William McKinley and was also the first to serve under the new 22nd Amendment that limited the president to two terms.

Television had become very much a part of the American lifestyle. Even though Mamie and Ike delighted in an opportunity to stay home nights and watch television, the President never was very comfortable in front of the camera, especially while he ate his Inaugural luncheon in the Old Supreme Court Room.

The Inauguration is a real catharsis for the American people. In a sense, it is the act of healing after the inevitable division of a political campaign. The Inaugural pageantry reiterates that, although one side did not win, the new leader is going to do everything possible to unite the nation behind him. The Inauguration is our most visible affirmation of the faith the American people have in their institutions.

Seated (left to right): Representative Jim Wright, Senator Mark O. Hatfield—Chairman, Senator Claiborne Pell.

2nd row from left to right: Karleen Durrenberger, Janet Moore, Joe O'Leary, Annette Penney, Hyde Murray, Glee Gomien, Ray Nelson, Don Massey, Bill Cochrane, Linda Melconian, Tom Decker, George White, Architect of the Capitol, and Bill Ensign.

Congress provided in 1905 that a Joint Congressional Committee on Inaugural Ceremonies, made up of both Senators and Representatives, be in charge of planning for the swearing-in at the Capitol. In 1981, the Members of the committee included:

Senator Mark O. Hatfield, of Oregon, Chairman
Representative John J. Rhodes, of Arizona
Senator Claiborne Pell, of Rhode Island
Representative Robert H. Michel, of Illinois
Senator Howard H. Baker, Jr., of Tennessee
The Speaker of the House, Thomas P. O'Neill, of Massachusetts
Senator Robert C. Byrd, of West Virginia
Representative Jim Wright, of Texas

The committee was assisted by: Tom K. Decker, Executive Director; Raymond Nelson, Associate Director; William McWhorter Cochrane, Chief Counsel; Donald F. Massey, Special Counsel; Joe O'Leary, Karleen Durrenberger, Glee Gomien and staff.

The Joint Congressional Committee

January, 1981, was a month of transition for Washington and the Nation. On January 5, the 97th Congress convened with a Republican majority in the Senate for the first time in twenty-six years, and with control of the House and Senate in the hands of separate parties for the first time in fifty years. In the following weeks, the Senate conducted confirmation hearings for Cabinet Secretaries to head each of the executive departments. Then, on January 20, the period of transition was capped with the Inauguration of a new President of the United States of America, a visible sign of the unity of our nation—even during the passage from one administration to the next.

Symbolizing this transition, the Inaugural ceremonies for the first time in history were held on the West Front of the United States Capitol Building. Under this new arrangement, larger crowds could be accommodated and costs were held down. As President Ronald Reagan was sworn in, he looked down the sweeping expanse of the Mall toward the Washington Monument and Lincoln Memorial. Most of his predecessors, at a majority of inaugurations held between 1829 and 1977, had looked across the East Front Plaza, toward the Supreme Court and the Library of Congress.

Our first two Presidents, George Washington and John Adams, were inaugurated in New York City and Philadelphia, when the capital was located in those cities. In 1801, shortly after the federal government had moved to the city of Washington D.C., Thomas Jefferson became the first President inaugurated here, in a ceremony in the Senate Chamber of the Capitol. During the War of 1812 the Capitol Building suffered major damage when British troops set it ablaze, and in the years during its reconstruction, Congress met in a temporary "Brick Capitol" across the street. There, on March 4, 1817, James Monroe took the oath of office on a platform erected outside the hall. Four years later, the inaugural ceremonies had moved back inside the restored Capitol, to the chamber of the House of Representatives. It was Andrew Jackson, the "People's President," who, on March 4, 1829, was the first to be sworn into office on the East Front steps of the Capitol. This was in keeping with Jackson's democratic principles, by which he refused a military escort, parade and carriage, and walked to the Capitol. In 1833 Jackson's ill-health moved the ceremony back indoors to the House chamber, but from that time forward Presidential inaugurations were held out-of-doors on the East Front, before large crowds of cheering onlookers. Only once in the next 140 years was the tradition broken, and then only because a fierce blizzard forced the inauguration of William Howard Taft indoors in March, 1909.

The new location chosen for 1981, the Capitol's West Front, was designed by Frederick Law Olmsted and constructed between 1884 and 1892. Although Olmsted never anticipated the holding of public ceremonies on the West Front terraces, neither did he imagine that the grand entrance of the East Plaza would be so heavily utilized for parking and vehicular traffic. Should the new site prove successful, it may establish a new tradition, as lasting as that set in 1829 when Andrew Jackson stepped forward onto a small platform on the East Front to take his oath as President of the United States.

By Senator Mark O. Hatfield, Chairman, Joint Congressional Committee on Inaugural Ceremonies

The quadrennial Presidential Inauguration has always been our Nation's most significant public ceremony. For this event the entire Federal Government converges, meeting on the steps of the Capitol as the new President takes the oath from the Chief Justice of the Supreme Court, while surrounded by members of Congress and of his Cabinet. Our sense of hope is rekindled. We face our national issues with a new spirit and determination. The orderly transfer of power, both in the legislative and executive branches, stands as a tribute to our constitutional form of government. In 1981, this transition has been exceptionally disciplined, cooperative and harmonious. In this spirit the Joint Committee on the Inauguration has endeavored to provide a dignified ceremony, one worthy of the Nation and its people.

The 1981 Presidential Inaugural Committee

★

★

★

For most Americans the period between the national election and the Inauguration is simply a transition period—a fuzzy, gray time during which the old Administration prepares to leave and the new prepares to arrive. It is interrupted only by the Christmas season—by then most have put the election far behind them and for the most part simply wait for the change to occur.

But, every four years, for a few thousand party workers, Inaugural planners, volunteers and military personnel, Christmas becomes just a fleeting moment in a painfully short two-month period of intensive and hectic planning, promoting and staging. The big moment is January 20.

Home for the 1981 Presidential Inaugural Committee was a temporary compound at Fort McNair in an area of Southwest Washington commonly referred to as Buzzards' Point.

Within days of the election, Inaugural committee co-chairmen had been named. And shortly thereafter, the shabby, rambling cluster of buildings, which had once housed

By F. C. Duke Zeller, Vice Chairman, Inaugural Book Committee

both the War Office and the Government Printing Office, was on its way to being transformed into the nerve center for all inaugural activities.

As construction workers, electricians and telephone technicians converged on the complex, the cold, bleak surroundings took on color and came to life. In came the photos of the two men for whom everything was being done, up went the streamers, in marched the secretarial staff and the schedulers and the event planners and the people to erect the sound systems, along with a cadre of cars and military aides to accomplish all the tasks at hand. Instant Inaugural Committee!

Distinguished party leaders, businessmen and women, entertainers, labor leaders and individuals distinguished in other fields had been asked to chair the various inaugural committees and all donated a great deal of time and services. Although most had never worked on an inauguration before, they brought with them the expertise and wherewithal to get things accomplished. And with a willing army of volunteers behind them, things quickly hit high gear and stayed there.

75

Young and old alike, workers pitched in—doing what each could do best. They drew blueprints, held press conferences, painted posters, checked schedules, stuffed envelopes, addressed invitations and drank gallons of coffee, as they watched time march away from them—and alternately prayed for, dreaded, worried about and welcomed the dawn of Inauguration Day, 1981.

They were reminded of the days remaining, like shopping days to Christmas, by a calendar countdown hanging in the reception room. And throughout it all, they were rewarded from every other wall and door with the grateful smiles and approving eyes of the President- and Vice President-elect.

Sometimes it was too hot, sometimes too cold, too early, too late, too crowded, too hectic or too disorganized, but through it all, this army worked—often right through the long days and into the night—to bring the Inauguration to life and make it, hopefully, the best ever.

Armed with their blueprints and banners and scurrying through the halls performing various and sundry tasks, at times they seemed more like high schoolers planning their big prom. In reality, the committees were fortunate to be staffed with many bright, energetic professionals from all walks of life, all charged with producing the nation's quadrennial celebration of democracy and the orderly exchange of power.

There were many tense moments, short tempers and a few tears, but as

77

Inaugural Executive Directors, Frederick K. Biebel, Robert G. McCune and W. George Kersey.

Mrs. Mary Jane Wick, Inaugural Executive Advisor.

78

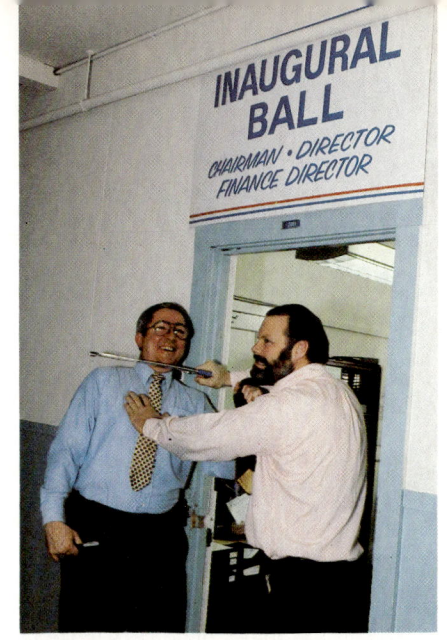

time ticked away, camaraderie carried the day. It was January 20 or Bust!

And when January 20 finally did loom, everyone breathed a collective sigh of relief. The floats had been finished on time, the grandstands stood just where they were supposed to, the ballrooms had been decorated and were ready to greet the happy bipartisan revellers, the official program was finished, the concerts and other events had all been sold out, and the pre-Inaugural glittering, star-studded gala had been a huge success.

With all deadlines successfully met, the group dispersed, leaving with the heady feeling that each had been a part of history and had done his or her part to help lay the foundation for the Inauguration of Ronald Wilson Reagan and the nation's Great New Beginning.

79

The Presidential Inaugural Committee
requests the honor of your presence
to attend and participate in the Inauguration of
Ronald Wilson Reagan
as President of the United States of America
and
George Herbert Walker Bush
as Vice President of the United States of America
on Tuesday the twentieth of January
one thousand nine hundred and eighty one
in the City of Washington

Co-Chairmen
Robert K. Gray
Charles Z. Wick

Notes On Inaugurals

★

★

★

The course of true love never runs smoothly nor does the course of good government. But there is an exception to the latter rule, albeit a fleeting and infrequent one. This is the inauguration of a new President. Government never performs so smoothly and reliably as it does for an inaugural. Not that everything goes perfectly; it does not by any means. Compared to government as usual, however, the manner in which public agencies labor to produce the inaugural ought to serve as a model for administrations to follow.

Nearly everyone in public service with even a slight responsibility for some inaugural event or ceremony takes that responsibility seriously and does level best to fulfill it. This includes the outgoing Administration which will smile through gritted teeth, if necessary, to behave graciously and cooperatively.

For months in advance, public agencies—from the District of Columbia police to the Department of Defense—knock themselves out to insure that every contingency is anticipated and disarmed in advance. Even Acts of God, be it sleet, snow or storm, must be foreseen and rendered harmless. Washington may not have staged an inauguration in the midst of an earthquake or tidal wave, but if it is at all humanly possible to do so, Washington would do it.

The inaugural show is the thing and the show must go on with full dignity and decorum, at least on the surface. Never mind that behind the facade of ruffles and flourishes and unruffled ceremony and celebration, there are many hard-working, heavily stressed people laboring in the wings. By and large, they don't mind either. Inaugurals are history in the making and everyone who has a hand in it, no matter how small, senses the significance of it. Clerks

By Byron Kennard

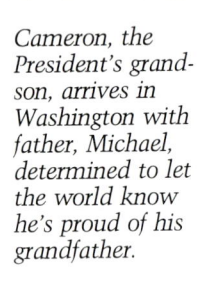

Cameron, the President's grandson, arrives in Washington with father, Michael, determined to let the world know he's proud of his grandfather.

and carpenters, painters and patrolmen, the great and the near- or would-be great all play their part with a special consciousness that this is one time when things must be done right! If somebody steps on your toe or jabs you in the ribs, no sign of pain must crack your demeanor. The face of the nation is on display at inaugural time and it must appear to all beholders, calm and confident, wise and serene.

It is a pity that things do not always function this well in the City of Washington. But, alas, this brief spell of dedicated effort and expansive goodwill fades like the spirit of Christmas on the day after when the mess must be cleaned up and the garbage taken out. Just as every day can't be Christmas, every Tuesday can't be the inaugural. So when

83

the real thing does roll around, once every four years, the least we Washingtonians can do is to put on our best bib and tucker and pull together for a few weeks. And, by and large, we get into the spirit of the thing and do just that. It's a nice feeling.

Another thing that inaugurals do for native Washingtonians, or so I believe, is to enable us to see our city once again with fresh eyes. People who live here grow somewhat immune to the monumental vistas of the national mall, the parks and great buildings. Many of us traverse these regions daily as we go about our business and after a while we cease to see their grandeur and grace, leaving those esthetic satisfactions to the millions of visitors our hometown attracts.

85

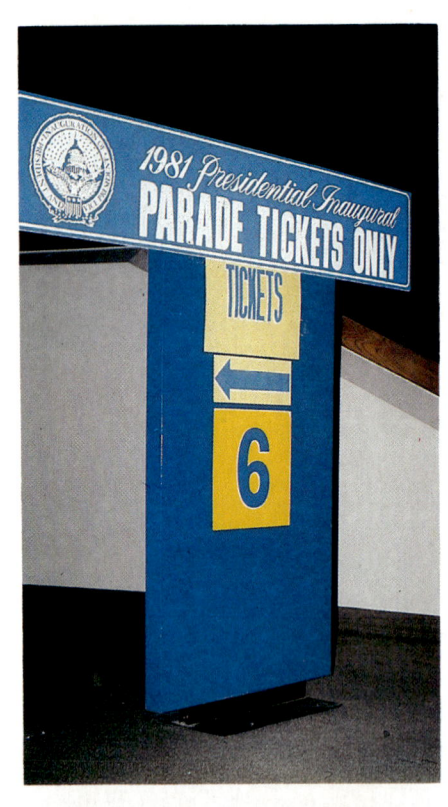

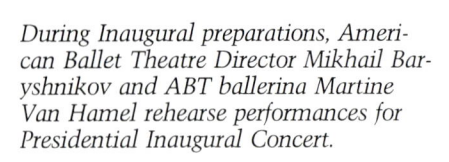

During Inaugural preparations, American Ballet Theatre Director Mikhail Baryshnikov and ABT ballerina Martine Van Hamel rehearse performances for Presidential Inaugural Concert.

But there is something about the inauguration that alerts our senses and restores our capacity to perceive the beauty of our surroundings. The festooned streets, the bunting, the flurry of visitors, the roar of helicopters overhead, the darting motorcades throughout the traffic, the air of expectancy, the sense of history somehow all combine to make us look again at the city's grand design as if for the first time. Then we too can sigh in appreciation of it and think how lucky we are to live here. That's a nice feeling, too.

It should be noted that none of this inaugural rigamarole is required by the Constitution. All it requires is that the new President recite those thirty-five little words which simply mean power and office is transferred from one individual to another. For this we turn the whole town topsy-turvy, but no Washingtonian among us would have it any other way.

87

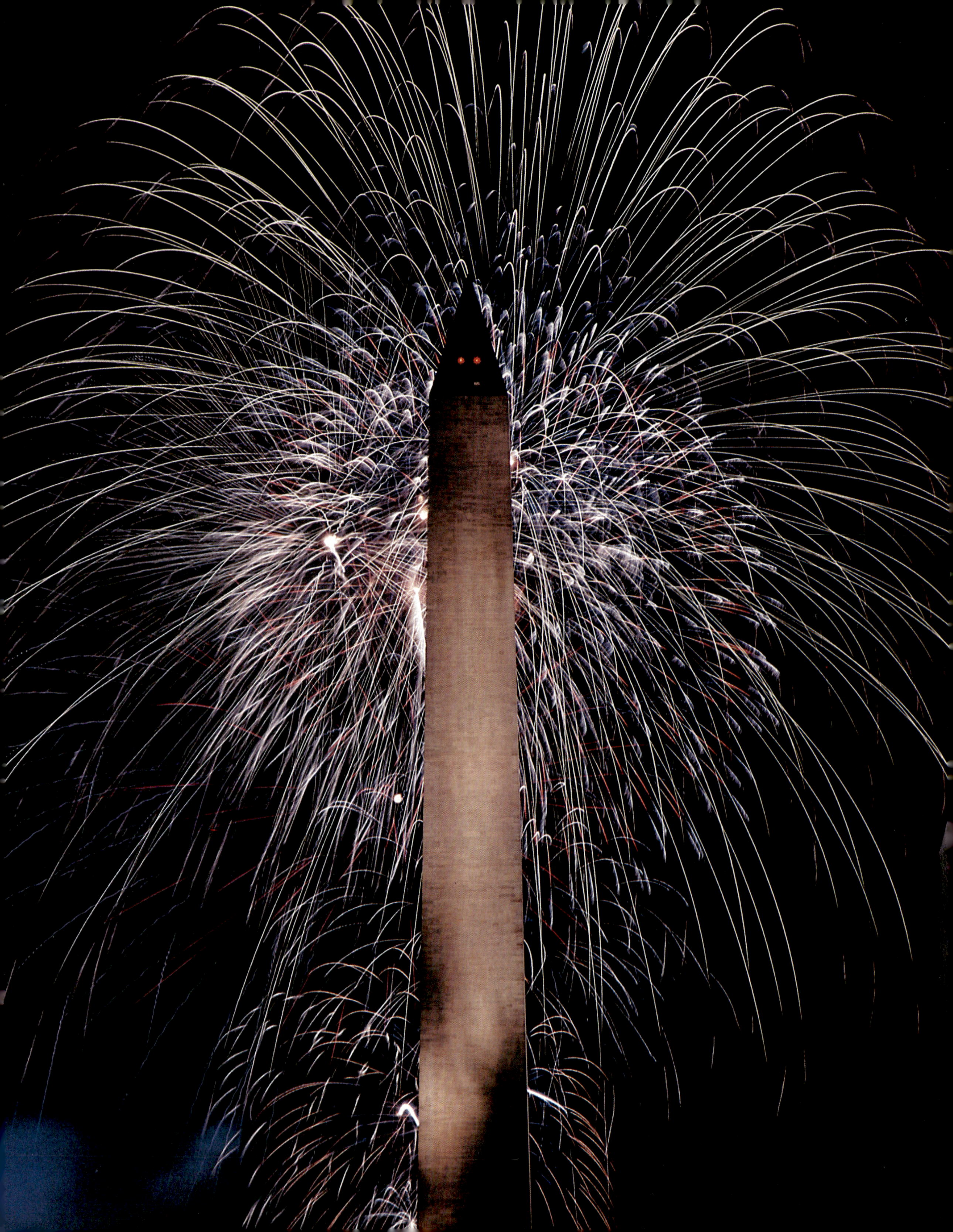

*Drama, Elegance and
National Euphoria
Usher In 'A Great New Beginning'*

The Inaugural Prelude

★

★

★

*I*nauguration Day, 1981, was to be an extraordinary day, even among inaugurations.

For who could have ever imagined that at literally the very moment the nation would be swearing in a new president—a man who had captured the hearts, minds and imagination of the American people—the agonizingly overdue finale to a national nightmare would end with the release of 52 Americans held hostage in Iran for 14½ months.

To many, no doubt, the day's events seemed totally unbelievable. Events were unfolding just too fast. As if the grandest inauguration ever, 300,000 flag-waving patriots, spine-tingling music, an exciting parade, breathtaking fireworks and elegant balls somehow weren't enough. There had to be more.

Little wonder, then, that many persons watching the incredible events of January 20, 1981, unfold

By G. Raymond Martin

before their very eyes in person and on television, felt they just might be watching an historic drama.

All the classic elements were there: Drama and excitement. The triumph of good over bad. And, of course, a happy ending.

That was Inauguration, 1981. A day when every sense in your body signalled that you were part of a great and wonderful emotional experience.

It was a great time for America . . . and a great time to be an American.

A brilliant sun was setting in the western skies as the U.S. Air Force jet carrying Ronald and Nancy Reagan from sunny California to their new home touched down at Andrews Air Force Base in Washington, D.C. on Thursday, January 15. A tumultuous, emotional adventure that not even the President-elect could imagine had begun.

Indeed, Reagan's time was no longer his only to determine. Already, he had been caught up in a whirlwind of events and activities that were to climax at noon on Tuesday, January 20, 1981, when

Mrs. Reagan receives roses from children participating in nationwide poster and essay contest on the Inaugural.

he would be sworn in as the 40th President of the United States.

Others were arriving, too. One group of Indiana Republicans came by rail in the private car once owned by banker J. P. Morgan. Moments after arriving on a flight from California, a young woman dressed only in a thin cotton dress and sandals inquired about the best place to buy a warm coat—fast! At two dozen hospitality booths at Washington airports and major hotels, cheerful volunteers handed out free maps, inaugural programs and handfuls of jelly beans, the new President's favorite candy, to the thousands of visitors who began swamping the capital city the weekend before Inauguration Day. Persons renting cars weren't at all interested in any of the import models; they wanted only those made in America.

A Taste of America

At Union Station, persons picking up reserved tickets for many of the Inaugural activities also could visit "A Taste of America," a lavish, varied—and free—taste-testers' delight that ran throughout the four days of pre-inaugural activities and pleased the palates of persons who picked up their tickets at will call booths.

The event dispensed hors d'oeuvre-sized samplings of special dishes and drinks from 38 of the nation's finest restaurants, 17 wineries and one brewery.

Participating restaurants had been gleaned from *Holiday* Magazine's Dining Awards List and from additional suggestions made by the program organizer and other "gourmets."

It was a gastronome's delight and one of the longest, largest and most varied open houses on record. "This is probably one of the most interesting and creative functions they've ever had at an Inaugural," said William Anton, a Detroit restaurateur and chief organizer of the event.

Gracious hosts and hostesses offered visitors a vast variety of delights: zesty spareribs and just-shucked oysters and clams on the half shell to steak tartare, exotic vegetables teriyaki, a fantastic pigeon en chartreause and exquisitely rich blacksmith's pie.

Wines from a number of the country's best vintners, including 14 of California's finest, and ample supplies of Stroh's beer also were served.

The food marathon's two snacking areas remained crowded throughout the celebration period, and at times, some exhibitors were forced to close their booths for periods just to replenish their supplies.

Cooking for the event was coordinated in two large kitchens at the nearby District of Columbia Courthouse and the Department of Energy, where 5,500 meals for government employees were being prepared simultaneously.

Throughout the event, a festive flair was provided by a strolling string quartet and, at times, a full orchestra that played in the so-called pit area of the train station, which had doubled as a National Visitors' Center during the Bicentennial celebrations.

"If the Inaugural Committee had to pay for this event, it would have cost them in excess of $200,000 minimum," organizer Anton noted during the foodfest, adding that restaurateurs had provided some of their best and most exciting dishes for sampling. As it turned out, it was a good thing these professionals knew their business. Each had been asked to provide a minimum 1,000 samples per day for the event, but most came well prepared with extras; the ones who hadn't quickly had extras flown in or arranged to buy additional supplies.

The event was among the first to greet inaugural visitors. By Saturday, news of the food extravaganza had circulated and lines were long. It was, nonetheless, one of the best (and most delicious) bargains in town.

A Spine-Tingling Opening Ceremony

On the Saturday night before Inauguration Day, an estimated 30,000 persons braved subfreezing, near-zero temperatures and icy winds to converge on the grounds of the Lincoln Memorial and the historic Mall area to witness the 1981 Inaugural Opening Ceremony.

From the heralding of trumpets performing "Fanfare Regalia" to the stellar finale, the beautifully choreographed patriotic production—the first ever in inaugural history—was all that it was promised to be.

Featured in the production, which was televised live simultaneously, were the U.S. Army Band and Herald Trumpets, under the command of Colonel Eugene W. Allen, and the 300-member Mormon Tabernacle Choir, directed by Gerald Ottley.

Host Efrem Zimbalist, Jr., who starred in "The FBI" television series, quoted from Reagan's Republican Convention acceptance speech and praised the President-elect for "reawakening the national pride."

The program began with a spectacular laser light show, in which all of the major monuments in Washington were linked together. The

The Mormon Tabernacle Choir, bundled up against the frigid air, opens the Inaugural with song at the Lincoln Memorial.

crowd "oohed and aahed" as the lasers sliced through the dark night like a battle scene out of a space movie.

After the Invocation, the Continental Color Guard, under the leadership of Staff Sergeant Phillip G. Young, presented the Colors.

The audience enthusiastically joined the U.S. Army Band and the Mormon Tabernacle Choir in the singing of "The Star Spangled Banner." As the words rang out in the frigid air, they brought tears to the eyes and a lump of pride to the throat:

". . what so proudly we hail,
By the twilight's last gleaming.
And the rockets' red glare,
The bombs bursting in air. . . ."

At those stirring words, a spectacular volley of red, white and blue fireworks lit up the sky behind the gleaming, floodlit memorial, as fountains of colored waters danced at either side of the stone edifice.

93

As the program proceeded, other distinguished guests, including Medal of Honor recipients, state governors, members of Congress and District of Columbia Mayor Marion Barry were introduced.

The Third U.S. Army Infantry, under the direction of Colonel Don Phillips, proudly paraded the flags of all 50 states.

As dramatic as the early program had been, its luster was measurably overshadowed by the introduction of President-elect and Mrs. Ronald Reagan and Vice President-elect and Mrs. George Bush, in what was their first official pre-Inaugural appearance. With a color guard attired in colonial garb preceding them, and the blare of trumpets and the roll of drums in the background, both couples stepped sprightly down the steps of the monument to take places of honor at the proceedings.

Neither man addressed the crowd; they didn't have to. It was enough for onlookers just to see and wildly cheer the two who so soon would accept the reins of government. At one point, the President-elect stepped out onto the extended stage platform fashioned in the shape of a huge blue-and-white eagle, and was immediately greeted with chants of "We love you, Ronnie; We love you, Ronnie," from the crowd. Reagan smiled broadly, cocked his head from side to side in now-familiar fashion and waved jubilantly.

The program continued with a musical tribute, beginning with a stirring rendition of Samuel Ward's "America the Beautiful" and including William Steffe's "Battle Hymn of the Republic" and John Philip

Sousa's "The Stars and Stripes Forever." A highlight of the musical tribute to the nation was the first performance of the specially created "Inaugural Grand March," commissioned just for the occasion.

"Thumbs Up, America," another original piece written for the Inaugural by former Secretary of the Navy J. William Middendorf, with lyrics by composer Sammy Cahn, was also an instant hit with the crowd.

The evening ended with a 14-minute laser light show and fireworks extravaganza, orchestrated by Osmond Productions and Disneyland creator Tommy Walker, that rivaled the best ever seen in the nation's capital, including those of the Bicentennial celebration of 1976.

Laser beams once again laced the sky between the Jefferson Memorial, the Capitol, the White House, the Washington Monument and the Lincoln Memorial, as different colors danced through the cascading waters spraying from both sides of the Reflecting Pool and behind the Lincoln Memorial.

More fireworks—12,000 aerial bursts in all—were exploded in just a few minutes than in last summer's entire Fourth of July display.

After the evening's events had concluded, many persons walked arm-in-arm up the icy steps of the Lincoln Memorial to gaze at the imposing statue of Abraham Lincoln, the nation's 16th president.

Floodlights turned upon the figure also illuminated Lincoln's Gettysburg Address and his Inaugural Speech, both of which are etched in the stone walls to either side of the statue.

It had been a momentous evening; indeed, an historic one. To many, the feeling of national pride was never greater.

95

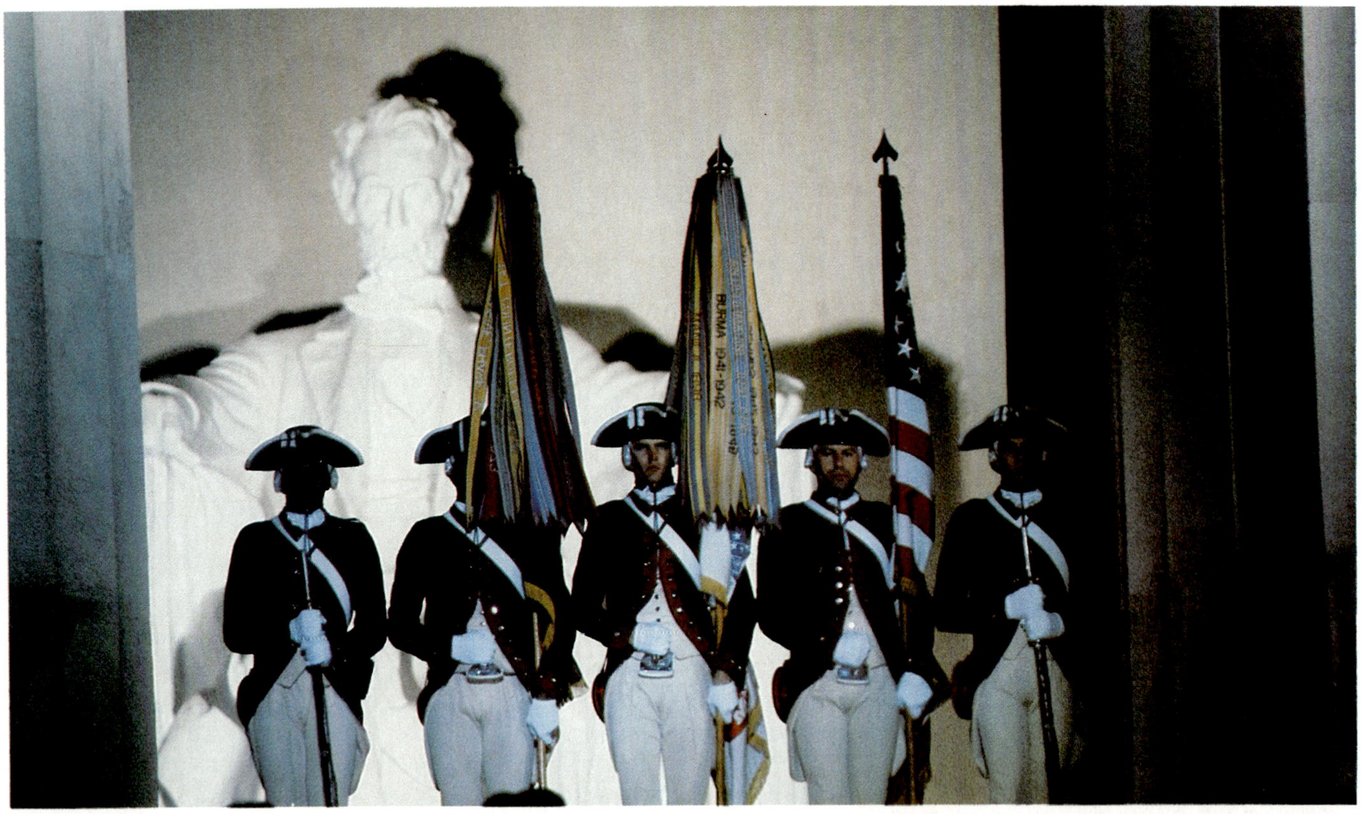

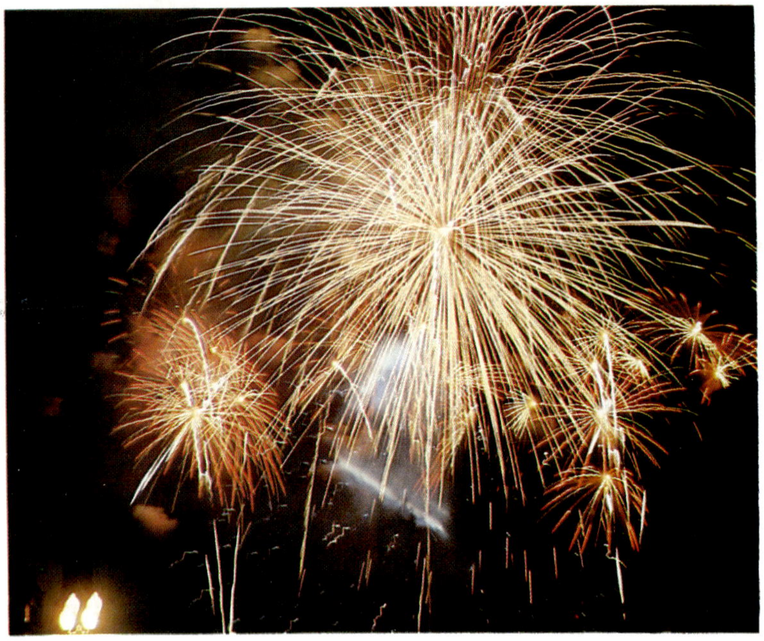

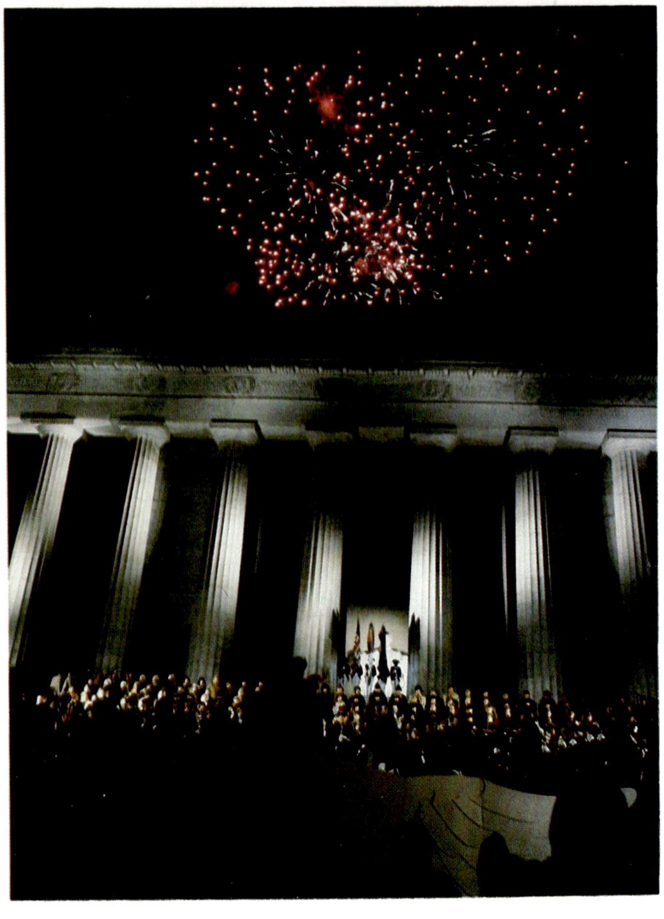

97

In the State Department Reception Room the Reagans join Co-Chairmen Robert K. Gray and Charles Z. Wick and Mary Jane Wick.

Left above, the President-elect with Erlenne Perkins and her daughter, Lynne Ashforth. Below, the Reagans greet Pamela Wick Michel during the Co-Chairman's Reception.

Co-Chairmen's Reception

Prior to the official public opening activities, Robert K. Gray and Charles Z. Wick, co-chairmen of the Inaugural Committee, had hosted a reception at the State Department in honor of top Reagan appointees, transition officials and key Reagan supporters.

The more than 500 guests invited to the affair sampled oysters, roast beef and strawberries, while keeping an eye on the video screens displaying the events taking place at the Lincoln Memorial.

"Oh boy," veteran newsman Walter Cronkite was moved to remark during the breathtaking evening. "With Bob Gray and Charlie Wick running it, this has to be one of the more spectacular inaugurations."

Another humorous anecdote was noted as the inaugural co-chairmen escorted the President-elect and Mrs. Reagan and the Bushes to the opening ceremony. Noting the cold of the evening, one of the guests teased Reagan by asking if he had come prepared by wearing thermal underwear. Leaning over and cupping his hand around his mouth with a conspiratorial air, Reagan replied, "Yes!"

Hugh O'Brian sharing an enjoyable moment with Mr. and Mrs. Walter Cronkite.

George Bush later returned to the reception cold but elated from the awe-inspiring and patriotic opening program. He summed up everyone's feelings when he noted: "I sure felt proud to be an American!"

With that event, inaugural festivities officially were under way, with thousands of area residents and visitors preparing to attend scores of official events and even more unofficial ones.

Americana Potpourri

There were many events from which to choose—from the unveiling of the new Reagan wax figure at a solemn ceremony conducted at the National Historical Wax Museum to a wide variety of concerts and special displays planned by each of the 10 museums that make up the Smithsonian Institution complex.

Each museum offered its own presentations of music, ranging from waltzes and two-steps of the Cajun people of Louisiana to performances featuring the work of contemporary composers and jazz and gospel artists.

Bluegrass, country and other forms of American popular music were represented, as were some musical selections popular with the ethnic minorities.

At the nook-and-crannied Museum of American History, crowds thrilled to the music of the Smithsonian Chamber Players, a barbershop quartet, the United States Army Chorus and a couple of jazz and bluegrass groups.

In the "We The People" hall on the second floor was a special inaugural exhibit of memorabilia of past inaugurations. "I Do Solemnly Swear" displayed old inaugural programs, buttons, admission tickets, invitations and jewelry. Among the display items were the table from which Abraham Lincoln took the oath of office and the Bible used by James Buchanan.

In another exhibit area, the inaugural gowns of the nation's first ladies drew large admiring crowds.

The 1981 "Official Inaugural Medal" was shown in a glass-enclosed exhibit in the Hall of Money and Medals, as were other medals from past inaugurals. The medal, one-and-a-quarter-inches of 14-karat gold, was struck by Medallic Art Co. of Danbury, Connecticut, from models prepared by Edward J. Fraughton of South Jordan, Utah.

On one side of the medal is shown the portrait of Reagan, while on the reverse side is depicted the West Front of the Capitol and the Reflecting Pool. The United States Seal also is shown in a small inset.

Since George Washington's time, buttons and, later, badges have been used, not only as mementos, but for identification of inaugural committee members. Medals later came into being and pieces bearing the portraits of such presidents as John Quincy Adams, Lincoln, Grant and others were unofficially produced.

At the Museum of Natural History, another popular gathering place for cultural events, Norvus Miller and Alvin Nessbith rocked the throngs in attendance with trombone and harmonica renderings of "Amazing Grace" and "When the Saints Go Marching In." The Army Blues combo, the Navy Commodores and other groups entertained listeners around the gigantic elephant that stands in the museum foyer. There also was a mixed fare of offerings, including barbershop quartets, jazz, Irish and Mexican music and bluegrass to thrill already buoyant audiences.

The other museums of the Smithsonian also participated. At the Air and Space Museum, for example, crowds listened to Cajun and Appalachian music, and do-si-do'd to the square dancing of the Ralph Case dancers. Ralph Case is the veteran caller who, in the late 40s, taught Margaret Truman how to square dance.

Museum visitors were treated to chamber music at the Museum of American Art, and in the Grand Salon of the Renwick Gallery, the Romantic Chamber Ensemble and the Smithsonian Chamber Ensemble entertained on 12 occasions over four days.

A Japanese Toho Koto concert and 20th Century Consort were enjoyed by large crowds at the Hirshhorn Museum and Sculpture Gardens. And at the National Gallery of Art, "The Republic" was presented, a patriotic cantata of music and documents of the American Revolution and the early days of the Republic.

And finally, in the National Portrait Gallery, visitors could see on display the handsome new portrait of Ronald Reagan, which hung prominently in the Hall of Presidents.

Visitors also used the occasion to take in many of the Washington area's art galleries. At the Kornblatt Gallery, for example, they marvelled at huge elephant heads made from split tire tubes and radiator-hose trunks.

Seventy-two pages of Leonardo da Vinci's famous "Codex Leicester" were on display at the Corcoran Gallery, thanks to the special arrangements of industrialist Armand Hammer, who had purchased the work in London the month before for $5.2 million. The "Codex," one of Leonardo's most famous notebooks, consists of voluminous notations scribbled in the author's famous "mirror" script, concerning the nature of water and other matters that attracted his astounding curiosity.

102

Mr. and Mrs. Ralph E. Becker, Vice Chairmen of Inaugural Cultural Events.

103

The Smithsonian museums burst into a flurry of activity during Inaugural week. Record crowds of over 200,000 visitors enjoyed the special exhibits and the countless cultural events. Top left the crowds at the Air and Space Museum listened to the music of the Pine Ridge Boys and Patsy of Mount Airy, North Carolina. The Ralph Case Square Dancers taught several groups the Virginia Reel under The Spirit of Saint Louis.

Top right Doctor Seffer of Chicago samples the ethnic fare at the Nationalities Reception.

Following page, top left, Mrs. Reagan greets Mrs. Mary Doremus a volunteer who worked on the Seniors and Handicapped Reception. Below, the Hispanic Americans honored Vice President George Bush at reception at the Hay Adams Hotel. The Los Quetzales dancers entertained the guests to the music of the Mariachis des los Americanas. That same day at the National City Christian Church, religious leaders and citizens met for an ecumenical convocation celebrating the Inauguration of the 40th president.

A Rousing Round Of Receptions

A number of official inaugural events also were planned to honor special groups of voters that helped elect Ronald Reagan president. Among those so honored with special receptions included groups of Hispanics, ethnics, seniors and handicapped, veterans and black voters.

One of the earliest receptions, in fact, was the Black Voters' Reception in honor of Samuel Pierce, the new Secretary of Housing and Urban Development and the ranking black appointment to date in the Reagan Administration.

Nearly 400 persons attended the festive event at the Sheraton-Carlton Hotel, where the distinguished guests included Vice President-elect George Bush; W. A. Walker, national chairman of the Black Voters for Reagan-Bush; Mayor Marion Barry of Washington, D.C., and Edwin Meese, counselor to the president.

105

The reception crackled with laughter after Pierce introduced Bush as "President-elect Bush." Bush did not complain about his introduction, however; only his limousine lag. "It's a terrible thing what they are doing to us in the next three days," he joked.

Sunday morning, the future first family left Blair House to visit their new parish in Northwest Washington. At the Presbyterian Center, the Reagans met the members of their new church and spent some time

106

The Reagans at the National Presbyterian Center with pastor, Dr. Louis Evans, and Rev. Donald Moomaw in background.

visiting with their new pastor, Dr. Louis Evans.

Members of the diplomatic community gathered at the beautiful Organization of American States for a reception and buffet brunch, to honor the new Secretary of State, Alexander Haig, and Secretary of Defense, Caspar Weinberger. George Bush offered the final toast to the international assembly, offering his wishes for continued world peace.

The Sunday afternoon traffic intensified as thousands of supporters tried to park on the residential streets surrounding the Sheraton Washington Hotel. Thirty-two governors of both parties were present at the Sheraton Washington Hotel to greet a throng of 15,000 well-wishers.

To accommodate the huge number of persons who turned out for the reception, committee organizers had divided the group into three and assigned each person a red, white or blue button to identify his or her group. Quipped one person: "It's like the old Chinese laundry saying: 'No tickee, no laundry.'"

The affair was attended by much pomp and circumstance. During a grand march of the governors, the U.S. Army Band struck up the "Triumphal March" from Verdi's "Aida." All through the event, introductions and announcements were made with trumpets blaring and drums rolling.

Special dignitaries included General of the Army Omar Bradley, the nation's only living, five-star general; former Texas Governor John Connally and actor Donald Defore.

The guests didn't seem to mind at all that they had spent $10 to see 32 governors and didn't get a thing to eat or drink. Joked one: "Well, what do you expect to get for $10 these days?"

A heavy dose of splendid nostalgia was in evidence at the "65 Years of Unforgettables" concert by Fred Waring and the 24-member Pennsylvanians at the DAR Constitution Hall.

The concert, which featured music ranging from classical works and songs of the Forties and Fifties to contemporary pop tunes of today, marked the close of a 100-concert, 24-state tour for the group.

The 80-year-old Waring, who often is called "The Man Who Taught America to Sing," was performing in his third Republican inauguration and clearly was having a good time. The group's rendition of the "Battle Hymn of the Republic," a piece which was to be heard often throughout the inaugural, was particularly stirring.

During the days preceding the inauguration, no fewer than 19 state societies hosted dinners for guests arriving from all over the country.

The functions were as varied as the states themselves, ranging from the Indiana State Society's black-tie dinner of filet mignon for 1,200 at the Sheraton Washington, to the "Black Tie and Boots" celebration of the Texas State Society, attended by

Guest of Honor General Omar Bradley, the nation's only living five-star general.

Maureen Reagan and her fiance, Dennis Revell, greet the crowds with Virginia Governor and Mrs. John Dalton at the Governor's Reception.

5,000 guests, where guests could dance to a mariachi band, make their own beef tacos and drink Texas beer.

A number of states threw somewhat less elaborate cocktail parties for the home-staters, while the tiny American Samoa Society threw a potluck get-together.

And there were private parties, dozens and dozens of them. One of the most elegant had to be the Los Angeles *Times Mirror* party in honor of Senator Howard Baker (R-Tenn.), the Senate's new majority leader. Tableclothes at the party were purple moiré, topped with red linen napkins and adorned with birds' nest baskets filled with red and purple anemones.

110

Concerts And Candlelight

After a day of receiving lines, traffic and a seemingly endless array of cultural events to attend, most visitors returned to their hotel rooms to dress up in gowns and cummerbunds for an unforgettable evening at the Kennedy Center. Upstairs, florists and caterers were transforming the scenic atrium into an elegant dance floor and dining area that, before the evening was over, would serve over 2,500 guests at a candlelight dinner.

Inaugural Concert Chairman Robert S. Carter and Karen Hart.

111

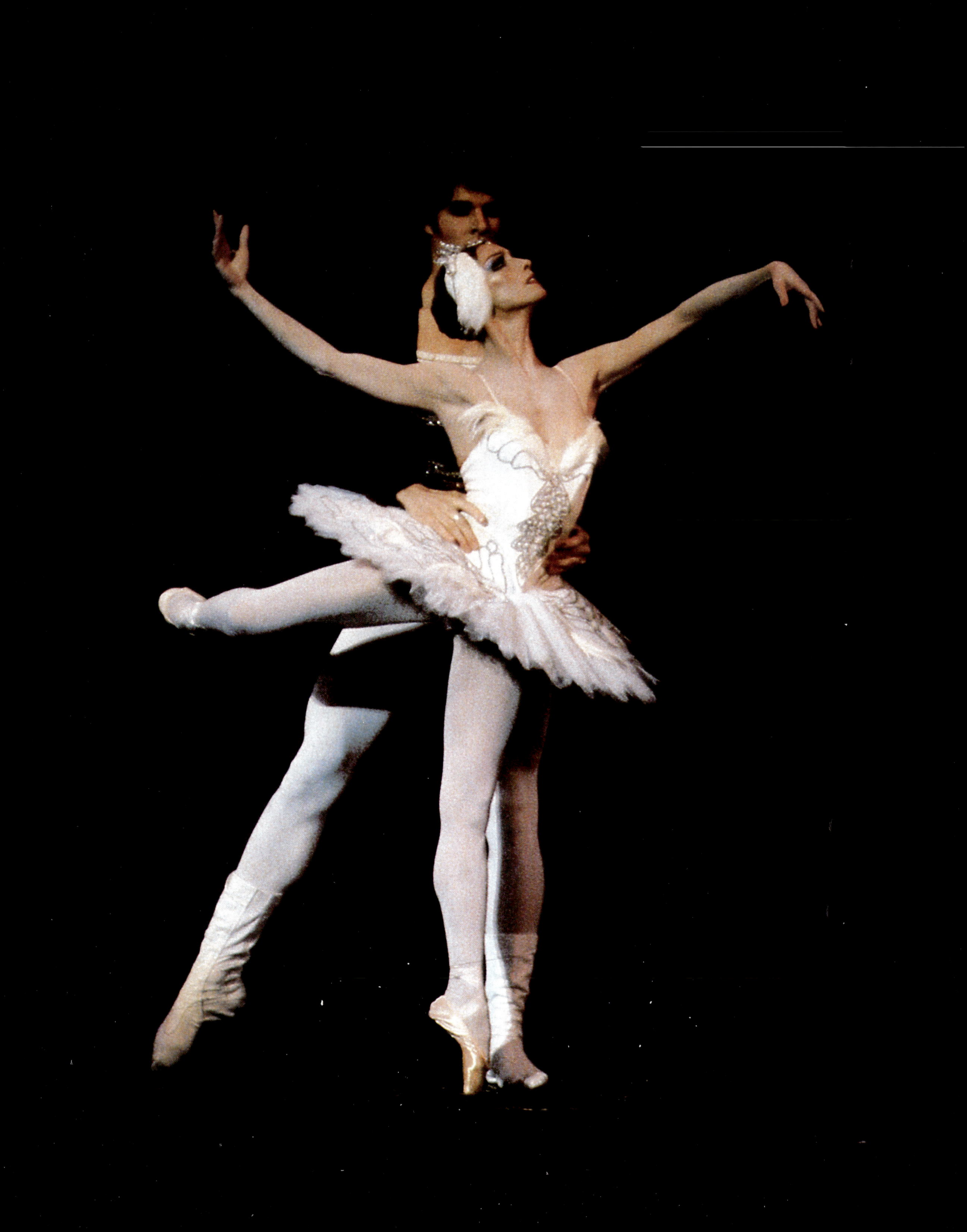

Downstairs, the activity was only beginning. Dancers and musicians had been rehearsing since early afternoon. Final touches were made on costumes and musical scores. The stages were swept, photographers arrived and bow ties were straightened.

At 7 p.m. the Presidential party arrived at the Eisenhower stage door. In the holding room they visited briefly with Robert S. Carter, the chairman of the three concerts, who introduced Martin Feinstein, producer of the evening's entertainment. The Reagans and Bushes went backstage where they stopped to thank the various artists for their generosity in performing for this unique inaugural concert.

And what extraordinary artists had assembled to honor the President-elect that evening. In the Opera House, Mikhail Baryshnikov, Martine Van Hamel and Marianna Tcherkassky performed American Ballet Theatre's innovative "Push Comes To Shove." Ms. Tcherkassky was partnered by Danilo Radojevic in the now famous ABT production of the "Nutcracker." Patricia McBride and Jacques D'Amboise danced to a George Balanchine interpretation of George Gershwin's haunting "The Man I Love." Two other world-renowned ABT dancers, Natalia Makarova and Patrick Bissell, danced the famous adagio from "Swan Lake." Suzanne Farrell and Peter Martins of the New York City Ballet completed the ballet section of the program with Tchaikovsky's "Pas de Deux."

After the Intermission, opera buffs were treated to a selection of arias from Verdi, Puccini and Mozart by

113

The Reagans and the Bushes enjoyed portions of all three concerts including ballet and opera, chamber music and the symphony.

American opera stars Grace Bumbry, Richard Stilwell, Roberta Peters, Warren Ellsworth, Karen Hunt, William Dansby, Jerry Hadley and Dana Krueger.

In the Eisenhower Theater, the Chamber Music Society of Lincoln Center offered the audience a rare instrumental performance by Lorin Maazel, who played Schubert's Sonatina in D Major, accompanied by Israela Margalit.

The Concert Hall crowds welcomed the Reagan party with a standing ovation. Then Mstislav Rostropovich struck up the National

Symphony Orchestra in a particularly stirring rendition of "The Star Spangled Banner." The orchestra was complemented by the Choral Arts Society and the Oratorio Society of Washington.

A particularly poignant moment occured when Rostropovich spotted the Presidential party about ready to leave their box. In a rousing encore he enthusiastically directed the orchestra in a breathtaking version of Sousa's "Stars and Stripes Forever."

After the chamber musicians and dancers had taken their final bow, many theatergoers stepped off the elevator onto the Kennedy Center terrace for the Candlelight Dinner. They were surprised to find a fully outfitted Old Guard Fife and Drum Corps serenading them with stirring revolutionary ballads as they stepped lightly through the arcade. Stopping a moment to find their seats among the sea of mint green tables decorated with hundreds of red roses, most diners moved into the canopied atrium where they waltzed to the music of the Army Strings and enjoyed a leisurely moment looking out over the frozen Potomac.

Dinner guests were served striped bass, fennel mousse with a delicate mustard dill sauce, medallions of veal, cherry tomato saute and snow peas. The place settings were designed especially for the occasion by the Boehm Porcelain Company. The entire dinner was rounded off by a festive Raspberry Bettina Florentina—created just for this inaugural repast.

Co-Chairman Robert K. Gray's table at Candlelight Dinner.

116

Mrs. Carol Price, Chairperson of the Candlelight Dinner, and her husband, Mr. Charles Price II.

White House Chief of Staff Mr. James Baker and his wife, Susan, arriving at Dinner.

Bonita Granville Wrather with Mr. and Mrs. Armand Deutsch.

Candlelight Dinner Chairperson Carol Price's table.

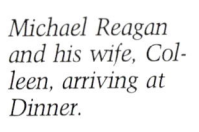

Michael Reagan and his wife, Colleen, arriving at Dinner.

Mr. and Mrs. Jimmy Stewart walk through the Old Guard Promenade.

Inaugural Co-Chairman Charles Z. Wick greets Hugh O'Brian and Robert Stack.

Counsellor to the President Edwin Meese III and his wife, Ursula, and their table above.

Inaugural Co-Chairman Robert K. Gray with Maureen Reagan.

119

Distinguished Ladies' And Vice President's Receptions

Monday's events included a Distinguished Ladies' Reception attended by more than 7,000 ladies who arrived by bus, limousine, private automobile and foot at the four theatres of the Kennedy Center.

As emcees Efrem Zimbalist, Jr., Robert Stack, Debby Boone and Hugh O'Brian welcomed the guests, crowds milled about in the long halls and the Grand Foyer, many sipping California champagne and taking pictures of one another.

Mrs. Reagan with Mrs. Bush and other distinguished ladies, Mrs. Anne Armstrong, Mrs. Carol Laxalt, and Mrs. Elizabeth Dole.

Mrs. Colleen Reagan and Maureen Reagan arriving at Kennedy Center for Distinguished Ladies' Reception.

Left, Mrs. Reagan with Distinguished Ladies, Mrs. Joy Baker and Mrs. Corrine Michel.

Nancy Reagan and Barbara Bush expressed thanks to the ladies for sharing in the inaugural activities, and thrilled more than a few by stopping to chat here and there for a few minutes.

Another major event was the Vice President's Reception at the Museum of American History in honor of precinct workers and county chairmen. Among the 17,000 guests of Vice President-elect and Mrs. George Bush were 1,500 VIPs, including Supreme Court Justices, congressmen, diplomats and government officials past and present.

Vice President-elect Bush wanted to shake everyone's hand, but had to be talked out of it when so many persons showed up that he would have had just a second and a half to shake every hand.

More than 130 members of the Bush family also were present, wearing big name tags and even bigger smiles. "They all look like George when they smile," one guest remarked.

At about the same time the Vice President's Reception was getting under way, a "Salute to America's Heritage" was drawing thousands of persons to the Health and Human Services Building.

The ethnic event featured the crafts, songs, folk dances and food of more than 35 nationalities.

The aroma of 1,000 bratwurst filled the building, as participants watched Japanese dancers, enjoyed Lithuanian ponckas (jelly doughnuts), admired Hungarian embroidery and swayed with swirling Bavarian folk dances.

"This is what grass roots is all about," said a committee worker. "It was 83.9 per cent of the ethnic community that voted for Reagan."

Meanwhile, under gray Washington skies, members of Carpenters Local 1110 swung their eight-pound hammers against the planks of the *real* Republican platforms, placing wooden boards on the green iron frames of bleachers in front of the White House. Nearby, General Services Administration carpenters were hammering away to finish the presidential reviewing stand and press box for the parade.

The Vice President-elect with his mother, Dorothy, and his son and daughter-in-law, Neil and Sharon.

Over on the Ellipse at the south side of the White House, a crew from the National Park Service began redecorating the National Christmas Tree in anticipation of the hostages' return, which even then was being negotiated. Except for the bright light on top of the tree, it had remained dark through the past two Christmas seasons as a reminder to all Americans of the hostages' lonely vigil.

At a dress rehearsal for the "All-Star Inaugural Gala" to be held later that same evening were several special guests who had been invited by Gala producer, Frank Sinatra. Among them were many of the relatives of the hostages. Invitations had been extended the previous week, before events made the release of the hostages seem imminent.

George Bush, Jr. and his wife, Laura, at the Vice President's Reception.

"I just thought, 'Why not come see Frank Sinatra?'" said Penne Laingen, wife of the U.S. Chargé d'affaires Bruce Laingen, the highest ranking of the hostages. "Of course, it helps take your mind off everything."

In a truly moving tribute, some of the stars joined in autographing 52 yellow napkins to be presented to each of the American hostages when their long ordeal finally ended. The yellow color originated from the popular song, "Tie a Yellow Ribbon 'Round the Old Oak Tree," a gesture a prisoner asks his loved one to make to remember him. Throughout the hostage ordeal and the inaugural, yellow ribbons of all sizes and shapes were seen billowing in the breeze throughout the nation.

123

All-Star Inaugural Gala

Clearly one of the most festive and long-awaited events of the inaugural period was the televised, celebrity-studded "All-Star Inaugural Gala" on Inauguration Eve.

An estimated 18,000 persons were bused from downtown hotels to the Capital Centre, a sports arena complex in Landover, Maryland, about 30 miles from downtown Washington, for the event.

Dubbed "Las Vegas on the Potomac," the Centre's Gala program featured such entertainment greats as Frank Sinatra, Johnny Carson (who served as emcee), Bob Hope, Jimmy Stewart, Ethel Merman, Rich Little, Grace Bumbry, Ben Vereen, Debby Boone, Donny and Marie Osmond, Charley Pride, Mel Tillis and others.

President-elect Reagan, Vice President-elect Bush and their wives were flown by helicopter to the Capital Centre, where they were escorted into the hall by Ol' Blue Eyes himself to the cheers of the audience.

The two couples took places of honor in blue, velour-covered wing chairs situated on raised platforms just off center stage. At the foot of Reagan's chair was a jar of red, white and blue jelly beans, with a note from Gala producer Frank Sinatra that read, "In case you get hungry...."

The entertainers felt no reticence about kidding the two guests of honor. Rich Little had Reagan roaring with laughter with his impressions of four presidents, including Reagan himself. The clever Reagan impression always began with a nod of the head and "Well..." the typical beginning to many of Reagan's impromptu remarks.

Johnny Carson also had fun with Reagan, saying that Reagan considers an economic emergency to be "when they run out of goose liver pâté at Bloomingdale's gourmet department."

125

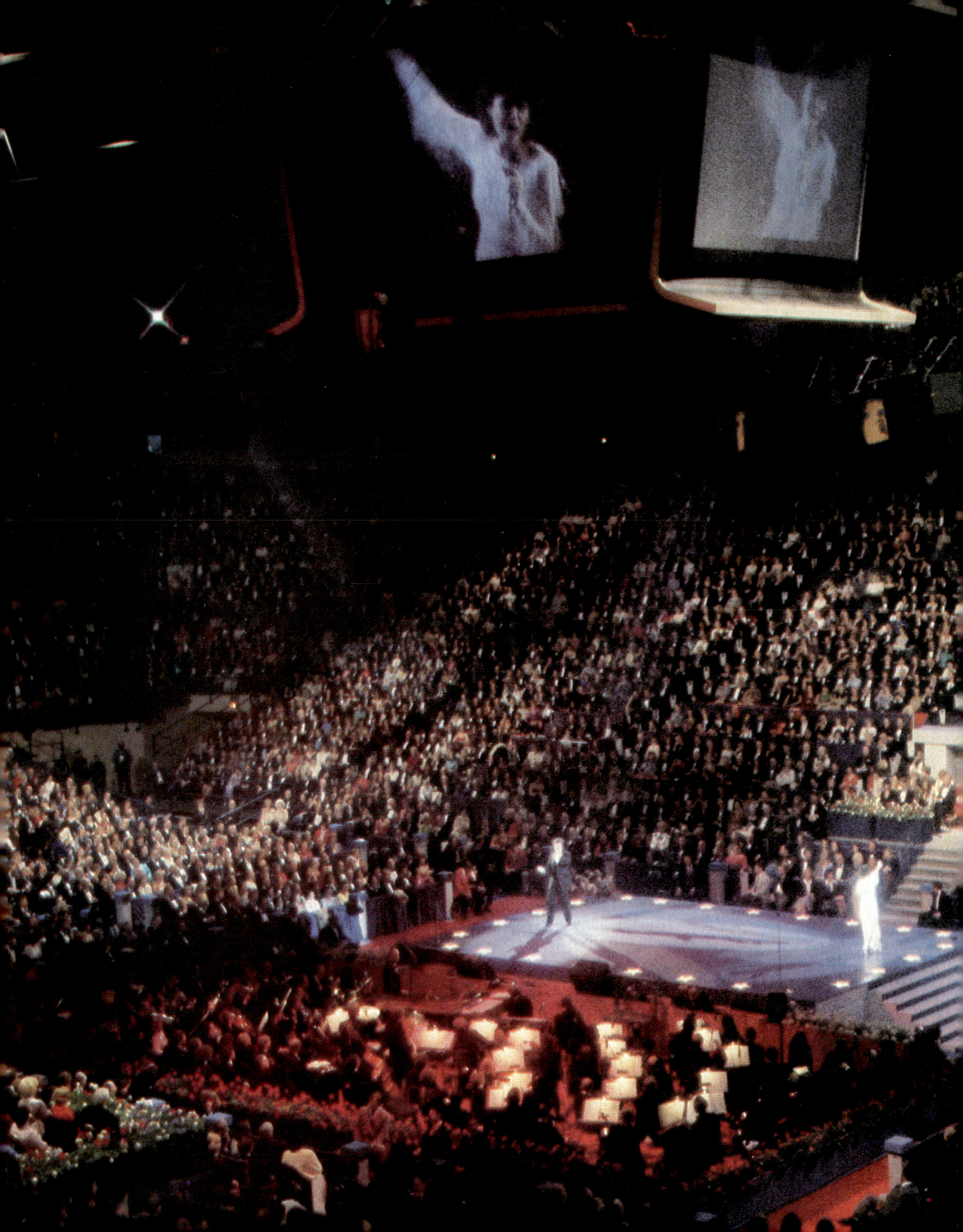

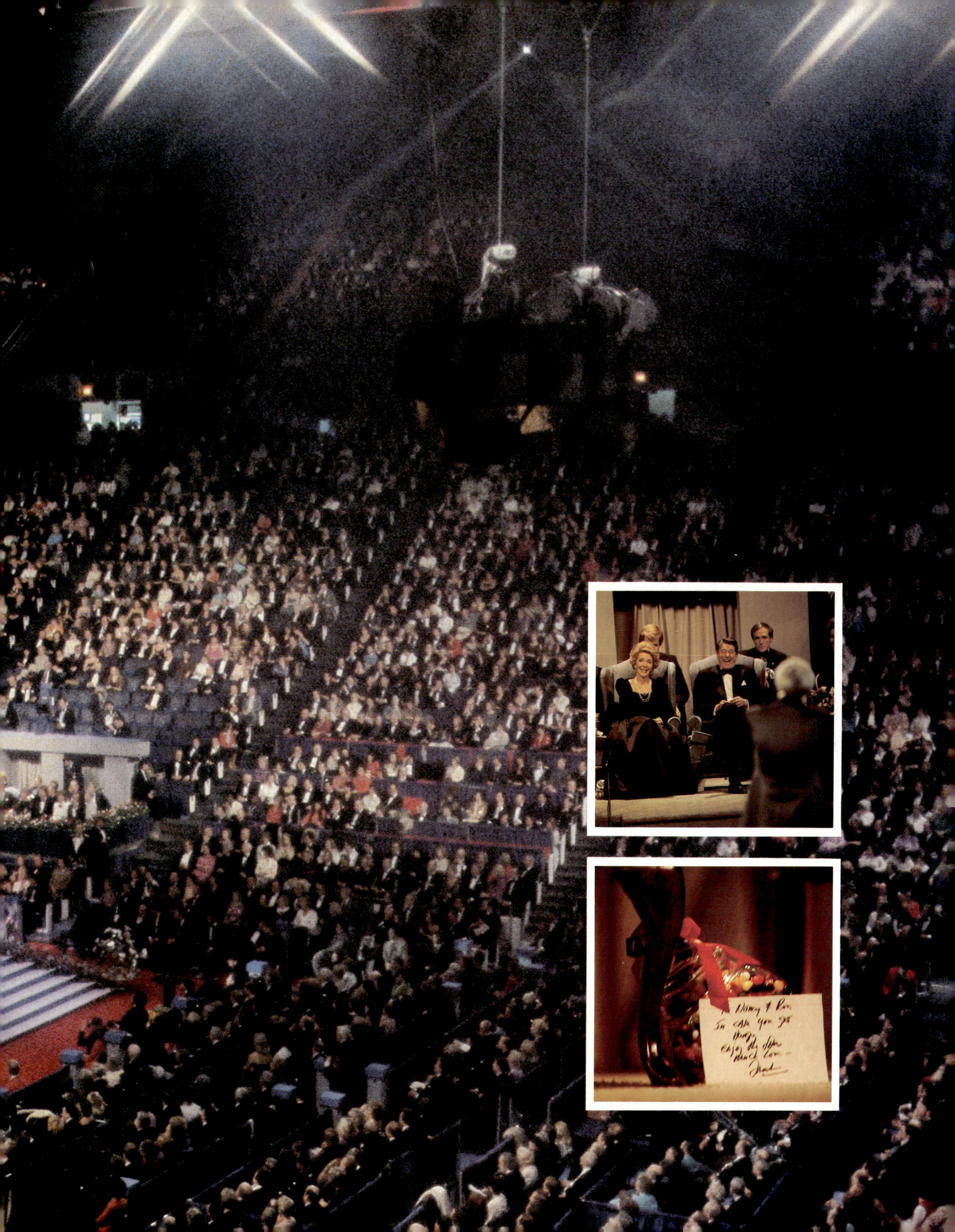
Nancy & Ron
Much Love –

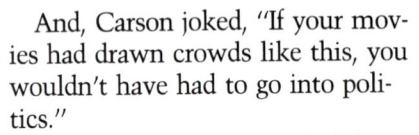

And, Carson joked, "If your movies had drawn crowds like this, you wouldn't have had to go into politics."

Vice-President-elect Bush didn't escape the comic's quips either. "I'm sorry, Mr. President," said Carson, "I didn't mean to ignore you, but you'd better get used to it." Before the Bushes stopped laughing, Carson added, "The vice president-elect sits in his office with an open airline ticket waiting for some foreign leader to die."

Sinatra's portion of the program included his rendition, with new lyrics, of his old standard, "Nancy with the Laughing Face," which he amended to "Nancy with the Reagan Face."

Ethel Merman's rendition of "Everything's Coming Up Roses" was particularly rousing. She drew cheers when she sang one line of the song, "Everything's coming up roses and jelly beans. . . ."

The Naval Academy Glee Club performed with expected precision and Grace Bumbry's singing of the operatic aria, "Vissi d'arte," and the song, "Natalie," were flawless.

The most moving ovation of the evening was for the 88-year-old five-star general, Omar Bradley, who was pushed to the center of the stage in a wheelchair by actor Jimmy Stewart, who paid a short tribute to "our new Commander-in-Chief." Following the tribute, Stewart snapped a salute at Reagan, who promptly returned the gesture.

Reagan lauded the stellar performance at its end by referring to the performers as "the greatest talents America could offer to any audience."

"During the past few days," he added, "I've been asked, 'Has it really sunk in?' Well, tonight, there was a point during the show when I leaned over to Nancy and said, 'It's sunk in.'"

The crowd cheered enthusiastically, just as it had during the performance itself at each mention of America, Reagan and the administration. The Reagans were clearly entertained.

Ron Reagan with his wife, Doria, and his sister, Patti enjoying the All-Star Gala.

In closing remarks, Reagan quoted writer Irvin S. Cobb, who praised show business people for "the pure pearl of tears, the gold of laughter, and the diamonds of stardust they spread on an otherwise dreary world."

129

Even as the Gala was getting under way, thousands of younger Reagan partisans jammed into DAR Constitution Hall for a Beach Boys concert in the President-elect's honor. The young people, average age around 21, had paid $40 apiece to attend the concert and the Youth Inaugural Ball the following evening.

Two of Bush's sons were in attendance, as was Susan Powell, Miss America, who appeared on stage in an electric-blue gown and sang "America the Beautiful."

Highlight of the evening was the appearance of the group everyone had been waiting for—the legendary Beach Boys. The group quickly had the audience on its feet as they played a number of old Beach Boys greats, which some in the crowd said never sounded better.

130

Among the songs performed well were such '60s classics as "California Girls" (their opener), "Surfin' U.S.A.," "409," "Help Me, Rhonda," and the soft and nostalgic "Surfer Girl." Drawn back on stage by thunderous ovations from the crowd, they performed two encores in which they sang their equally classic "Barbara Ann."

Backstage, later, the Beach Boys were enthusiastic about both their performance and the future. Announcing that they are personal friends of the Vice President-elect, bass guitarist Al Jardine had this to say: "I'm very optimistic about the future. We've gotta great team coming in. You gotta remember that running California is like running a country, so he's (President-elect Reagan) got the experience."

131

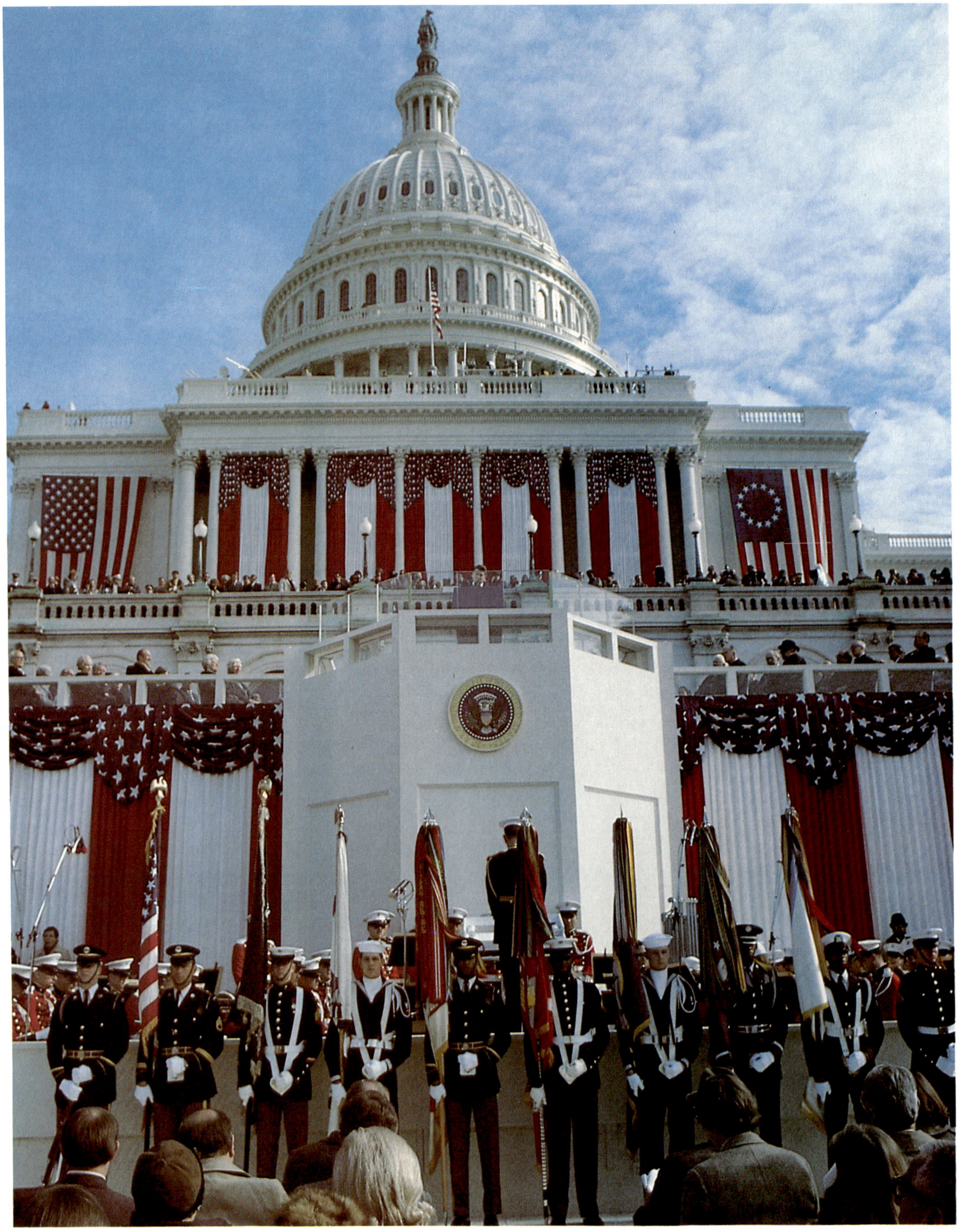

Inaugural Day 1981

★

★

★

As the sun rose on Inauguration Day, the air was crisp with anticipation. Although long-range forecasters had predicted a cold, rainy inauguration, like many in the past, temperatures quickly pushed into the mid-50s.

It was as if the Reagans had somehow managed to bring a little bottled sunshine all the way from California just for the occasion.

Washington was in both joyous and solemn moods. It was to be a day for celebrating and one of the most remarkable in the nation's history.

The Reagans had once again spent the night at Blair House, across the street from the White House. And, on this day, crowds began to assemble especially early, knowing that they soon would be attending a church service.

Inside the residence, a telephone rang at 8:31. It was President Carter calling. Last-minute snags that threatened to hold up the release of the hostages had been overcome, the President informed Reagan, and the release of the 52 Americans held captive seemed imminent.

By G. Raymond & Maureen Martin

The Reagans soon after departed for a private church service with family members and close friends at St. John's Episcopal Church, across Lafayette Square from the White House. From there, they returned briefly to Blair House and then called on President and Mrs. Carter at the White House for the traditional "Inaugural Coffee."

Back at the flag-draped West Front of the Capitol, the 24,574 reserved seats were filling quickly. It was the first time in history that the swearing-in would be conducted on this side of the Capitol, and judging from audience reaction, the decision was a very popular one.

From its high promenade, the inaugural party would have a sweeping view of the nation's capital and its celebrated monuments. Before them would lay Pennsylvania Avenue, the historic "Avenue of the Presidents," the scene of many moments of national joy and sorrow, of inaugural parades heralding new political leaders and funeral corteges mourning those that have passed. And beyond, the Potomac River and the land stretching out to the west.

More than two hours before the 11:30 swearing-in ceremony, an estimated 100,000 persons had gathered in the "preferred standing" areas on the Capitol lawn, with tens of thousands more getting situated at numerous other points off the Capitol grounds and along Pennsylvania Avenue. Although most persons could barely see the inaugural podium, much less make out the dignitaries that soon would be arriving, all nonetheless were there to be a part of history.

"This is what America is all about," remarked one elderly gentleman as he repositioned himself to soak up some sun, which had just begun to peek out from the clouds.

Another lady, eyeing the building crowd, said, "It looks like a bunch of people who want to get back to what America really means." And there were other comments: "This is it; this is what the country is all about," said one man. Remarked another, "Damn, it's great to be here!"

Maybe it was a Hamden, Connecticut, GOP precinct worker, though, who best summed it up: "This may be a once-in-a-lifetime thing."

Portable radios crackled with news of the hostages' transfer to Iran's Tehrabad Airport from their places of captivity. Panhandlers worked the crowds like entrepreneurs, one plainclothes detective in the crowd noted, and sidewalk vendors hawked everything from "Freedom" T-shirts to "I was in Washington for the Inaugural the day the hostages were released" buttons.

Most onlookers stood patiently, talked among themselves and listened to patriotic music played by the U.S. Marine Band.

"When I heard 'America the Beautiful,' " a man from Nanticoke, Pennsylvania remarked, reflecting on the enormity of the two impending events, "it gave me goosebumps. I looked out at all those people and I felt like I was part of history."

In the center of the standing room area in front of the Capitol, a young man leaned against a slatted fence that separated the invited dignitaries and guests from the masses of Americans, many of them dressed in blue jeans and parkas, who had come to see Reagan sworn in. "There's no fur coats on this side," he said, "but there's body heat. It's just great to be here."

At 11:15, as news circulated about the impending release of the hostages 8,000 miles away, the lights of the presidential motorcade carrying the Carters and Reagans to Capitol Hill could be seen winding slowly down Pennsylvania Avenue.

The scene on the swearing-in platform was a momentous one, indeed. After numerous dignitaries were seated, President and Mrs. Carter were introduced for the last time to the strains of "Hail to the Chief." On the way to his seat, the President was asked by a reporter if the

Above, Reverend Donald Moomaw gives the Inaugural benediction and Senator Mark O. Hatfield opens the ceremonies.

135

hostages were free yet. "Not yet," the President replied hastily, without pausing. "Not yet."

Senator Mark Hatfield, a Republican from Oregon and chairman of this year's Joint Congressional Committee on Inaugural Ceremonies, officially got the swearing-in ceremonies under way.

A light moment occurred when the senator asked all present to reach out their hands and join in the singing of the National Anthem. Murmurs of laughter erupted in the crowd, where most were packed in so tightly that they could barely move, much less extend their arms.

After the singing of "America," led by Michael Ryan, of the U.S. Marine Band, the Reagans' pastor, the Reverend Donald Moomaw of the Bel Air Presbyterian Church in Los Angeles, California, delivered the Invocation.

The vice presidential oath was administered to George Herbert Walker Bush, the nation's 43rd vice president, by Supreme Court Justice Potter Stewart, a college classmate of Bush's. Barbara Bush stood proudly and staunchly near her husband, as their five children and the new vice president's mother, Dorothy, watched.

After Bush acknowledged the loud applause and cheers of the crowd, another hymn, "Faith of Our Fathers," was played. Moments later, Chief Justice Warren Burger asked Ronald Reagan if he was prepared to take the constitutional oath, to which Reagan forthrightly replied, "I am."

Above left, Vice President George Bush places his hand on the family Bible and repeats the oath after Justice Potter Stewart.

'I Do Solemnly Swear...'

The two men stepped into the warm sunshine and Reagan placed his left hand on the family Bible, used and annotated by his late mother, Nelle. The Bible was opened to II Chronicles 7:14, which reads, "If my people, which are called by my name, shall humble themselves, and pray, and seek my face, and turn from their wicked ways; then will I hear from heaven, and will forgive their sin, and will heal their land."

Seated nearby were the Reagan children, Ron and his wife, Doria; Maureen and her fiance, Dennis Revell; Mike and his wife, Colleen, and daughter, Patti Davis. Also among the family members present were Reagan's brother, Neil, and Mrs. Reagan's mother and stepfather, Mr. and Mrs. Loyal Davis.

Standing between Chief Justice Burger and Reagan was the soon-to-be first lady, Nancy Reagan, who looked intensely into her husband's eyes as he repeated the Oath of Office:

"I, Ronald Reagan, do solemnly swear that I will faithfully execute the office of President of the United States, and will to the best of my ability, preserve, protect and defend the Constitution of the United States."

When the last words were said, the two men shook hands, the Reagans kissed and remarks of congratulations were exchanged on the platform. In an instant, it was over. Ronald Reagan had become the 40th President of the United States.

In the distance, a muffled 21-gun salute added an air of official dignity to the occasion.

The Diplomatic Corps gathered for the Inauguration.

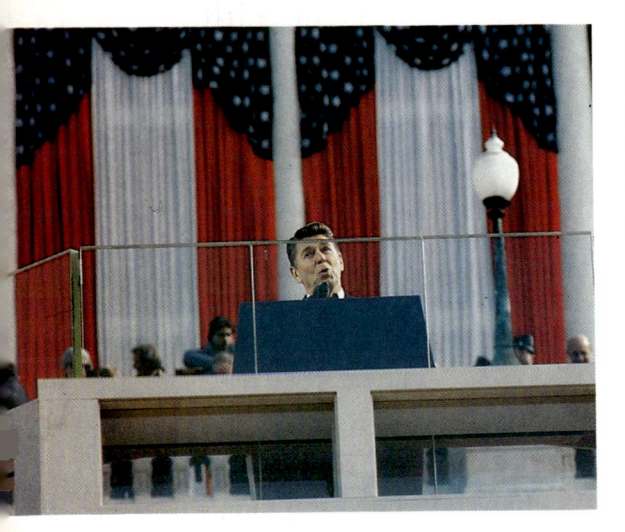

The assembled throng was delighted. "It's sort of an expression of joy," said a San Francisco lawyer. "Finally, something we've worked for has come to flourish. It's like a flower coming up in the spring."

"I am so proud to be an American," exclaimed a 58-year-old Denver resident, as she waved a tiny American flag. "I'm so proud to be an American."

The inaugural address originally had been written by Reagan on nine sheets of lined, yellow legal paper, partly in pencil and partly in ballpoint pen. Most of it, the President said later, had been written on a flight returning to California from Washington on January 8. The last page—the so-called "magic page"—was written a few days later.

Today, however, the address was printed in large type on half-sheets of paper in order that the President, who is nearsighted, could easily follow the text.

In his inaugural address, which was considered vintage Reagan, the new President first paid tribute to former President Jimmy Carter for

President Jimmy Carter congratulates the Reagans following the swearing-in.

Senator Hatfield offers his best wishes to the new President.

his "gracious cooperation in the transition process." Then Reagan singled out the largest problem of his incoming administration when he said the country is suffering from the longest and one of the worst sustained inflations in the national history; "one which threatens to shatter the lives of millions of our people."

Working out the nation's problems will require both those in and out of government to bear the burden, he said. "Our concern must be for a special interest group that has been too long neglected," he added. He specifically mentioned "the men and women who raise our food, patrol our streets, man our mines and factories, teach our children, keep our homes and heal us when we are sick—professionals, industrialists, shop keepers, clerks, cabbies and truck drivers."

"In short," he said, "they are 'We the people,' this breed called Americans."

"It is time for us to realize that we are too great a nation to limit ourselves to small dreams," Reagan

Above, in the Presidential Room at the Capitol, President Reagan signs his first Executive Order. In Statuary Hall, Vice President Bush offers his toast during the Congressional luncheon.

said, in one of his more memorable statements. "We're not, as some would have us believe, doomed to an inevitable decline....

"So, with all the creative energy at our command, let us begin an era of national renewal. Let us renew our determination, our courage and our strength. Let us renew our faith and our hope.

"We have every right to dream heroic dreams."

Following his 20-minute address, President Reagan acknowledged the applause of the onlookers as Juanita Booker, a Reagan supporter the new president had once met at a small town political gathering, sang a spirited rendition of the National Anthem. The ceremony concluded with a brief Benediction from Rev. Moomaw.

The speech was well received by the people, as it was in the nation's press the following day. "Ronald Reagan is down to earth," said a Republican convention delegate from Dodge City. "He'll bring the country back to its senses."

Above left, President Reagan gets the word "wheels up" confirming the American Hostages were on their way home. He offered a toast with the gathered dignitaries to announce the news to a waiting nation at left.

141

The brass plates on the back of each of the cabinet chairs are changed while the presidential party enjoys the military review.

"Reagan's speech was fantastic," said a government worker from San Antonio. "The man has the idea that we need to get government off our backs, that we need to defend ourselves. I think he can do it, and I'm going to help."

A young couple from Winnetka, Illinois, was even more impressed. "We're going to call our baby, Ronnie," they said, "because we want him to always remember that he was named for a great American."

And another person expressed it this way: "It's a chill that goes through you; all of a sudden you realize you are an American."

Departing the platform, the new President first visited the Senate chambers for greetings, and then moved into the adjoining Presidential Room. It was there that he carried out the first official acts of his presidency—imposing a federal hiring freeze and signing formal papers nominating his Cabinet. Both acts were carried out on the desk upon which Abraham Lincoln signed the Emancipation Proclamation.

The President then walked over to Statuary Hall to join approximately 100 congressmen, the Supreme Court and their spouses for a luncheon of walnut-stuffed chicken breasts.

Meanwhile, former President Jimmy Carter's motorcade moved slowly to Andrews Air Force Base. The National Anthem was played and a 21-gun salute was ordered before the plane carrying the Carter family home to Plains, Georgia, departed.

At the White House, a workman in the Cabinet Room was attaching a special presidential nameplate to the back of a new chair taller than all the rest, while other staffers quickly made the rest of the Executive Suite and first family quarters ready.

At about 2:20 p.m., President Reagan proposed a toast in which he gave the first official confirmation that the American hostages were on their way home from Iran, having departed the country aboard three Algerian 727 jetliners just minutes after the Inaugural oath-taking was concluded.

"Some 30 minutes ago," the President said, "the plane bearing our prisoners left Iranian airspace, and they're now free of Iran. So we can all drink to this one," he added, raising a glass of California wine.

143

The Inaugural Address Of The President

January 20, 1981

To a few of us here today this is a solemn and most momentous occasion. And, yet, in the history of our nation it is a commonplace occurrence.

The orderly transfer of authority as called for in the Constitution takes place as it has for almost two centuries and few of us stop to think how unique we really are. In the eyes of many in the world, this every-four-year ceremony we accept as normal is nothing less than a miracle.

Mr. President, I want our fellow citizens to know how much you did to carry on this tradition. By your gracious cooperation in the transition process you have shown a watching world that we are a united people pledged to maintaining a political system which guarantees individual liberty to a greater degree than any other. Thank you and your people for all your help in maintaining the continuity which is the hallmark of our Republic.

The business of our nation goes forward. These United States are confronted with an economic affliction of great proportions. We suffer from the longest and one of the worst sustained inflations in our national history which distorts our economic decisions, penalizes thrift and crushes the struggling young and the fixed-income elderly alike. It threatens to shatter the lives of millions of our people.

Idle industries have cast workers into unemployment causing human misery and personal indignity. Those who do work are denied a fair return for their labor by a tax system which penalizes successful achievement and keeps us from maintaining full productivity.

But great as our tax burden is, it has not kept pace with public spending. For decades we have piled deficit upon deficit, mortgaging our future and our children's future for the temporary convenience of the present. To continue this long trend is to guarantee tremendous social, cultural, political, and economic upheavals.

You and I, as individuals, can, by borrowing, live beyond our means for only a limited period of time. Why should we think that collectively, as a nation, we are not bound by that same limitation?

We must act today in order to preserve tomorrow. And let there be no misunderstanding—we are going to act beginning today.

The economic ills we suffer have come upon us over several decades. They will not go away in days, weeks, or months, but they will go away. They will go away because we as Americans have the capacity now, as we have had in the past, to do whatever needs to be done to preserve this last and greatest bastion of freedom.

In this present crisis, government is not the solution; it is the problem.

From time to time we have been tempted to believe that society has become too complex to be managed by self-rule, that government by an elite group is superior to government of, by and for the people. Well, if no one among us is capable of governing himself, then who among us has the capacity to govern someone else?

All of us together—in and out of government—must bear the burden. The solutions we seek must be equitable with no one group singled out to pay a higher price.

Our concern must be for a special interest group that has been too long neglected. It knows no sectional bounderies, crosses ethnic and racial divisions and political party lines. It is made up of men and women who raise our food, patrol our streets, man our mines and factories, teach our children, keep our homes and heal us when we're sick. They are professionals, industrialists, shop keepers, clerks, cabbies and truck drivers. They are, in short, "We the people."

Our objective must be a healthy, vigorous, growing economy that provides equal opportunities for all Americans with no barriers born of bigotry or discrimination. Putting America back to work means putting all Americans back to work. Ending inflation means freeing all Americans from the terror of runaway living costs. All must share in the productive work of this "new beginning," and all must share in the bounty of a revived economy. With the idealism and fair play which are the core of our strength, we can have a strong, prosperous America at peace with itself and the world.

As we begin, let us take inventory. We are a nation that has a government—not the other way around. And this makes us special among the nations of the earth. Our government has no power except that granted it by the people. It is time to check and reverse the growth of government which shows signs of having grown beyond the consent of the governed.

It will be my intention to curb the size and influence of the Federal establishment and to demand recognition of the distinction between the powers granted to the Federal government and those reserved to the states or to the people. All of us need to be reminded that the Federal government did not create the states; the states created the Federal government.

So there will be no misunderstanding, it is not my intention to do away with government. It is rather to make it work—work with us, not over us; to stand by our side, not ride on our back. Government can and must provide opportunity, not smother it; foster productivity, not stifle it.

If we look for the answer as to why for so many years we achieved so much, prospered as no other people on earth, it was because here in this land we unleashed the energy and individual genius of man to a greater extent than had ever been done before. Freedom and the dignity of the individual have been more available and assured here than in any other place on earth. The price for this freedom has at times been high, but we have never been unwilling to pay that price.

It is no coincidence that our present troubles parallel the intervention and intrusion in our lives that have resulted from unnecessary and excessive growth of government.

We are too great a nation to limit ourselves to small dreams. We are not, as some would have us believe, doomed to an inevitable decline. I do not believe in a fate that will fall on us no matter what we do. I do believe in a fate that will fall on us if we do nothing.

So, with all the creative energy at our command, let us begin an era of national renewal. Let us renew our determination, our courage, and our strength. Let us renew our faith and our hope. We have every right to dream heroic dreams.

Those who say we are in a time when there are no heroes just don't know where to look. You can see heroes every day going in and out of factory gates. Others, a handful in number, produce food enough to feed all of us and much of the world beyond.

You meet heroes across a counter—on both sides of that counter. There are entrepreneurs with faith in themselves and an idea who create new jobs, new wealth and opportunity. They are individuals and families whose taxes support the government and whose voluntary gifts support church, charity, culture, art, and education. Their patriotism is quiet but deep. Their values sustain our national life.

I have used the words "they" and "their" in speaking of these heroes. I could say "you" and "your" because I am addressing the heroes of whom I speak—you, the citizens of this blessed land. Your dreams, your hopes, your goals are going to be the dreams, the hopes and goals of this administration, so help me God.

We shall reflect the compassion that is so much a part of your makeup. How can we love our country and not love our countrymen? And loving them reach out a hand when they fall, heal them when they are sick and provide opportunity to make them self-sufficient so they will be equal in fact and not just in theory?

Can we solve the problems confronting us? The answer is an unequivocal and emphatic yes. To paraphrase Winston Churchill, I did not take the oath I have just taken with the intention of presiding over the dissolution of the world's strongest economy.

In the days ahead I will propose removing a number of the roadblocks that have slowed our economy and reduced productivity. Steps will be taken aimed at restoring the balance between the various levels of government. Progress will be slow—measured in inches and feet, not miles—but we will progress. It is time to reawaken this industrial giant, to get government back within its means, and to lighten our punitive tax burden. These will be our first priorities, and on these principles, there will be no compromise.

On the eve of our struggle for independence a man who might have been one of the greatest among the Founding Fathers if he hadn't given his life on Bunker Hill, Dr. Joseph Warren, President of the Massachusetts Congress, said to his fellow Americans, "Our country is in danger, but not to be despaired of . . . On you depend the fortunes of America. You are to decide the important question on which rest the happiness and liberty of millions yet unborn. Act worthy of yourselves."

I believe we the Americans of today are ready to act worthy of ourselves, ready to do what must be done to ensure happiness and liberty for ourselves, our children, and our children's children.

And as we renew ourselves here in our own land, we will be seen as having greater strength throughout the world. We will again be the exemplar of freedom and a beacon of hope for those who do not now have freedom.

To those neighbors and allies who share our ideal of freedom, we will strengthen our historic ties and assure them of our support and firm commitment. We will match loyalty with loyalty. We will strive for mutually beneficial relations. We will not use our friendship to impose on their sovereignty, for our own sovereignty is not for sale.

To the enemies of freedom, to those who are potential adversaries, they will be reminded that peace is the highest aspiration of the American people. We will negotiate for it, sacrifice for it; we will not surrender for it—now or ever.

Our forbearance should never be misunderstood. Our reluctance for conflict should not be misjudged as a failure of will. When action is required to preserve our national security, we will act. We will maintain sufficient strength to prevail if need be, knowing that if we do so we have the best chance of not having to use that strength.

Above all we must realize no weapon in the arsenals of the world is so formidable as the will and moral courage of free men and women. It is a weapon our adversaries in today's world do not have. It is a weapon that we as Americans do have. Let that be understood by those who practice terrorism and prey upon their neighbors.

I am told that tens of thousands of prayer meetings are being held on this day, and for that I am deeply grateful. We are a nation under God, and I believe God intended for us to be free. It would be fitting and good if each Inaugural day should be a day of prayer.

This is the first time in our history that this ceremony has been held on the West Front of the Capitol Building. Standing here, we face a magnificent vista, opening up on this city's special beauty and history. At the end of this open mall are those shrines to the giants on whose shoulders we stand.

Directly in front of me, the monument to a monumental man. George Washington, father of our country. A man of humility who came to greatness reluctantly. He led America out of revolutionary victory into infant nationhood.

Off to one side, the stately memorial to Thomas Jefferson. The Declaration of Independence flames with his eloquence.

And then beyond the reflecting pool, the dignified columns of the Lincoln Memorial. Whoever would understand in his heart the meaning of America will find it in the life of Abraham Lincoln.

Beyond these monuments to heroism is the Potomac River, and on the far shore the sloping hills of Arlington National Cemetery with its row upon row of simple white markers with crosses and Stars of David adding up to only a tiny fraction of the price that has been paid for our freedom.

Each one of those markers is a monument to the kind of hero I spoke of earlier. Their lives ended in places called Belleau Wood, The Argonne, Omaha Beach, Salerno and halfway round the world on Guadalcanal, Tarawa, Pork Chop Hill, The Chosin Reservoir, and in a hundred rice paddies and jungles of a place called Vietnam.

Under such a marker lies a young man—Martin Treptow—who left his job in a small town barber shop in 1917 to go to France with the famed Rainbow Division. There, on the Western front, he was killed trying to carry a message between battalions under heavy artillery fire.

We are told that on his body was found a diary. On the flyleaf under the heading, "My Pledge," he had written these words: "America must win this war. Therefore I will work, I will save, I will sacrifice, I will endure, I will fight cheerfully and do my utmost, as if the issue of the whole struggle depended on me alone."

The crisis we are facing today does not require the kind of sacrifice that Martin Treptow and so many thousands of others were called upon to make. It does, however, require our best effort, our work and our willingness to believe in ourselves and in our capacity to perform great deeds; that together and with God's help we can and will resolve the problems which confront us.

Why shouldn't we believe that? After all—we are Americans.

Begin The Celebrations!

While the most important event of the day was now history, the celebrating was just beginning. And on this day, there was much to celebrate.

The Inaugural Parade is one activity that can be shared and enjoyed by all the people who throng to the city on Inauguration day. Since the first inauguration, seven parades have been held in snow and 10 in rain, but always, the show has gone on.

Parades also have varied in length. Andrew Jackson vetoed a parade altogether and walked along a sidewalk with friends instead. By contrast, Benjamin Harrison's parade was so long in 1889 that darkness fell before it was over.

Inaugural planners early on decided that Ronald Reagan's parade would be a short one, of no more than one hour's duration. But events of the day threw those schedules off a little, resulting in the parade's delayed start.

Before the official start of the parade, the limousine motorcade bearing the new President and Vice President and their wives, the presidential party and members of Congress began the slow trip down Pennsylvania Avenue. The Reagans and Bushes waved victoriously from the open, sunroof tops of their limousines, thoroughly enjoying themselves.

Parents hoisted children onto their shoulders and thousands waved American flags and bobbed balloons as the motorcade went by. As word that the hostages were airborne spread through the crowd, small groups of persons along the parade route began chanting, "They are out; they are free."

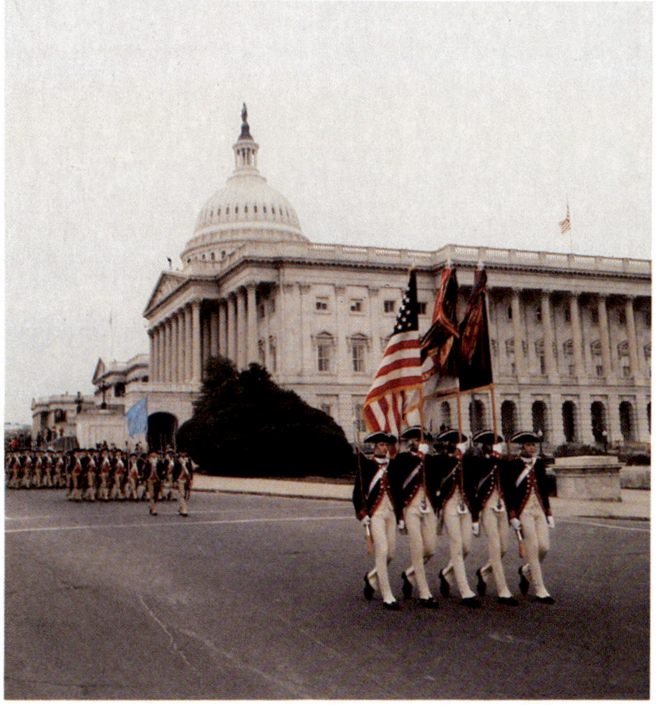

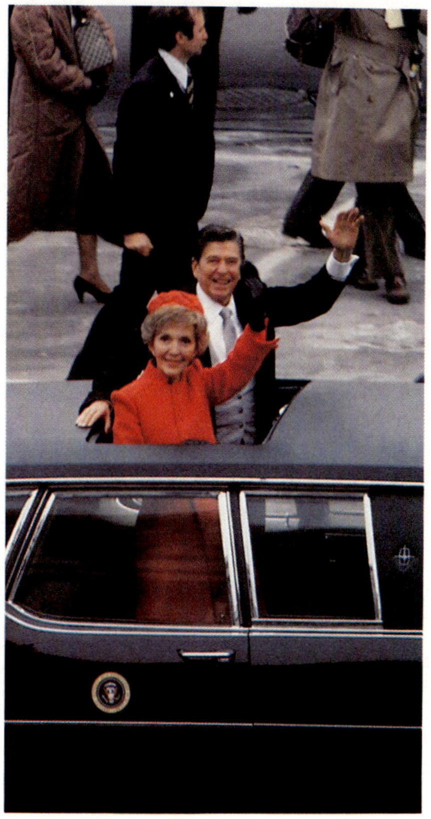

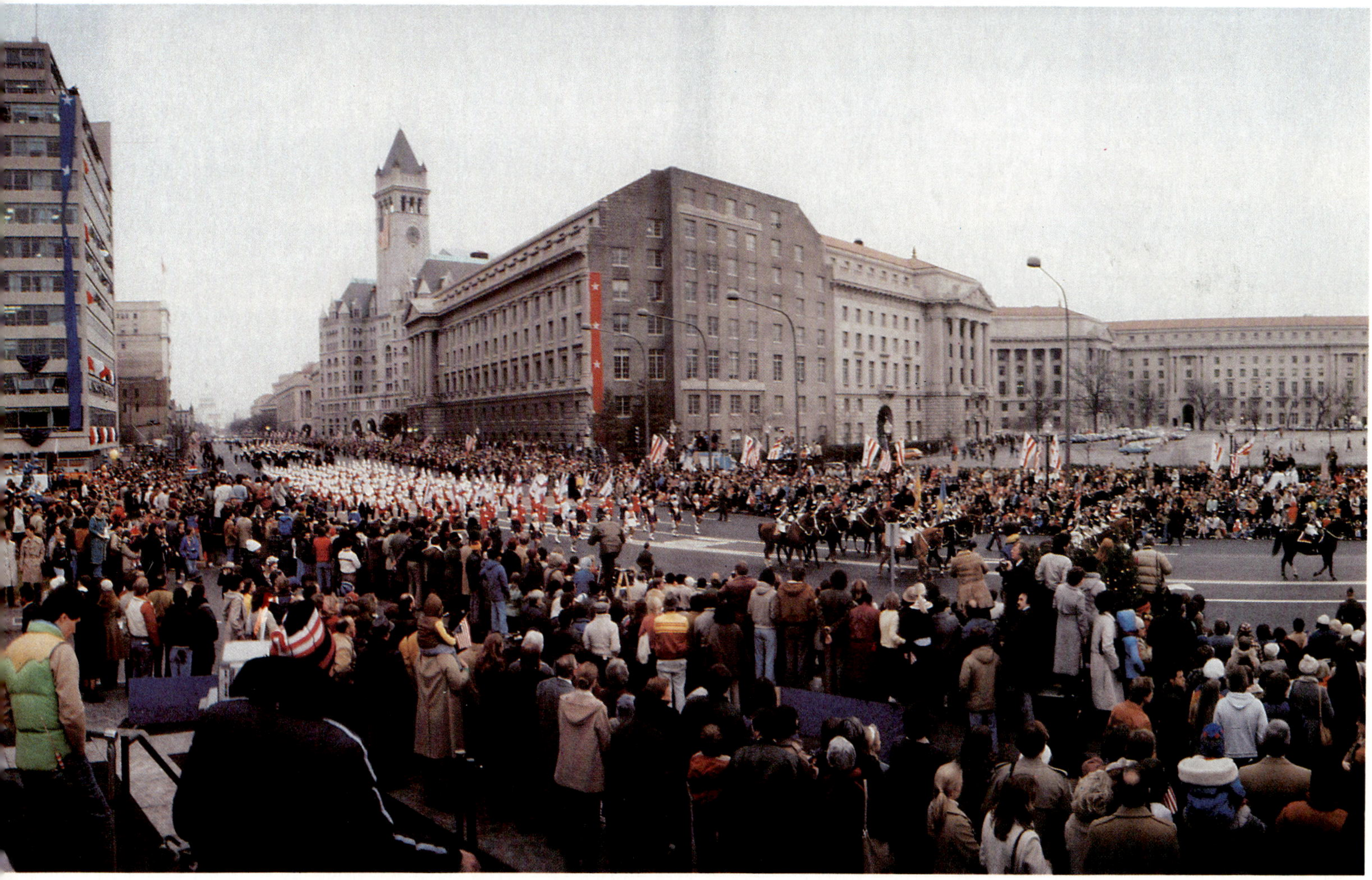

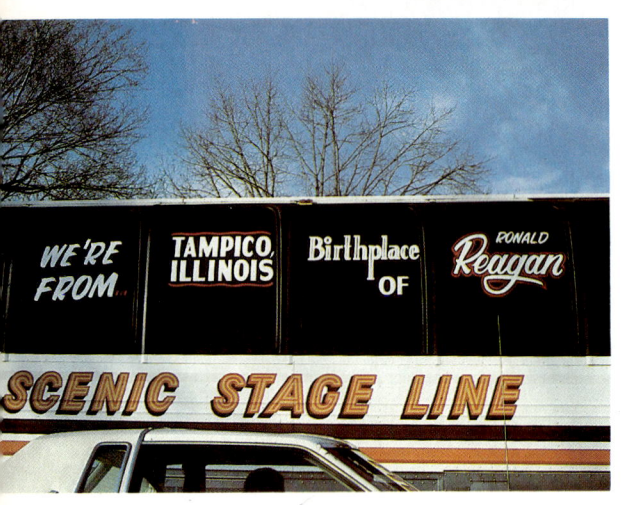

Among the well-wishers along the parade route were several groups of people from Reagan's hometown of Dixon, Illinois. A van from Dixon, dubbed "The Reagan Express," was parked at the corner of 12th St. and Pennsylvania Avenue.

One of the more heartwarming events of the afternoon came when Vice President Bush spotted in the crowd a sprightly 97-year-old named Lulu, whom he had first met at the Republican convention. The Vice President nearly fell out of his limousine as he waved at Lulu, called her name repeatedly and pointed her out to his wife. It was a very touching and endearing moment.

A tiny American flag handed to the Vice President by a child at 13th Street became the baton with which Bush conducted his chorus of applause and cheers.

Soon, the presidential party and other dignitaries were seated in a glass-enclosed reviewing stand in front of the White House. When the parade still hadn't gotten underway, a small group of spectators near the reviewing stand began singing "God Bless America," rather than complaining. Soon, a cluster of them were singing patriotic songs within earshot of the President.

Leading off the parade in a high-stepping manner was a spirited 10-year-old bay thoroughbred gelding named "Chili," upon which rode a U.S. Park Policeman who just happened to be a blacksmith by trade. The pair led a U-shaped formation of 23 mounted Park Police officers, including two women.

As the parade wound its way from the Capitol along the flag-draped Pennsylvania Avenue, more than 300,000 persons, many of whom stood up to 15 people deep in places, strained to get a better view. Several used red and white paper

148

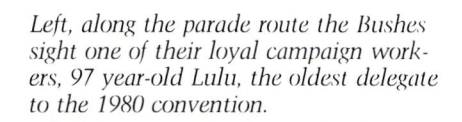

Left, along the parade route the Bushes sight one of their loyal campaign workers, 97 year-old Lulu, the oldest delegate to the 1980 convention.

periscopes to get a better look at the parade.

The parade included more than 8,000 marchers and musicians in 20 bands, 5,000 hot-air balloons, 25 Alaskan sled dogs (three of which had been stolen from their temporary kennels, and later returned in time for the parade), three floats, Indians, the 29-member Bill Williams Mountain Men group in buckskin britches and coonskin caps and color guards and marching units from each of the military services and their academies.

Most of the selections played were patriotic tunes like "This Is My Country," and "God Bless

149

America," and military songs, such as "Anchors Aweigh."

Crowds lining the streets broke into little jigs when the Marching Jukebox of Southern University tooted "Bourbon Street" and "Way Down Yonder in New Orleans." And partisan District of Columbia residents roared loudest for their own Cardoza High School Marching Band, one of the nation's finest.

As the Dixon, Illinois, High School Marching Band paraded by the reviewing stand, President Reagan stood at his seat and enthusiastically waved a cowboy hat.

An especially moving moment occurred when the Mormon Tabernacle Choir on a float stopped in front of the reviewing stand to sing a rousing version of "The Battle Hymn of the Republic." There wasn't a dry eye in the stands. Even the President was fighting back tears; a battle the first lady lost.

As the parade ended, the crowds dispersed. Many headed back up to Capitol Hill for more festivities.

151

152

The President's senior advisors share a special moment together after the day's activities. Left to right, Michael Deaver, James Baker, Edwin Meese, James Brady and Richard Allen.

Others, tired after a long and emotional day, much of it spent standing, were just anxious to get home. For the American Indians in the parade, it was off to a buffalo barbeque cookout on the Mall.

A decidedly more elegant evening was in store for the President, who left the reviewing stand with a small entourage and walked up to his new residence at 1600 Pennsylvania Avenue. Once inside the White House, the President sat behind his desk in the famed Oval Office and posed for photographers.

"I needed that to make this day perfect," he said.

The family portrait of the Reagans taken prior to the Inaugural Balls.

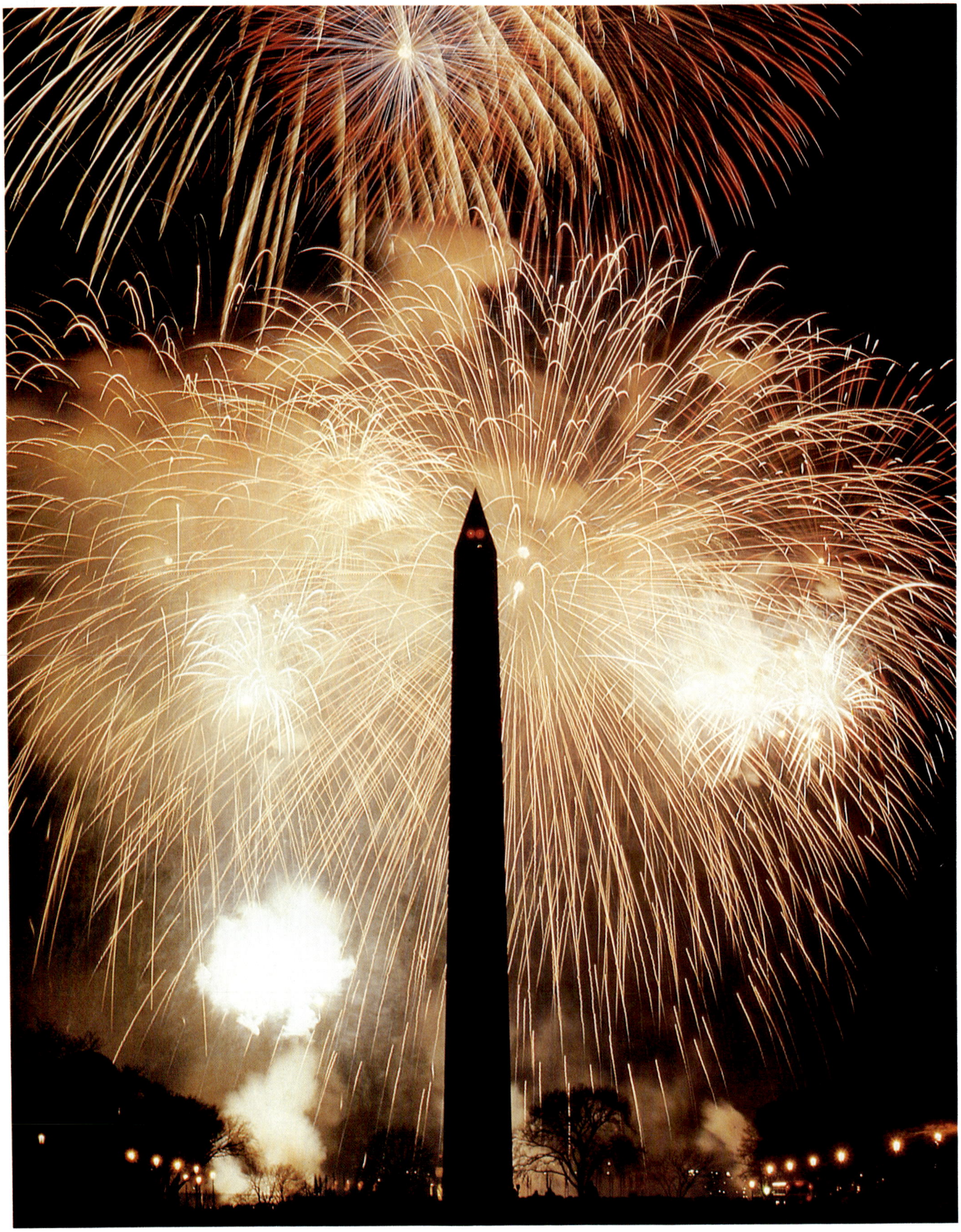

Festivities And Fireworks

Following the parade, many persons walked down to the West Front of the Capitol for an outdoor concert hosted by Willard Scott, the popular NBC "Today Show" weatherman.

Several in the crowd had clipped out a local newspaper notice about the concert, which included the lyrics for "Thumbs Up, America!" the inaugural theme song composed by J. William Middendorf, former secretary of the Navy. The first chorus of the lyrics, written by Sammy Cahn, president of the American Song Writers Hall of Fame, was sung with great spirit at the concert:

"Thumbs Up, America! We're still a mighty team,
Thumbs Up, America! Let's wave the star-spangled dream.
Thumbs Up, America! We've got the strength, the will.
Thumbs Up, America! The shining city on the hill..."

The Inaugural Day Sky Salute, hosted by writer George Plimpton, followed. The 15 minutes of fireworks were as intense as the wonderment of the estimated 50,000 persons on hand to witness the event. Thousands more within a few miles of the city could see the fireworks display lighting up the sky, from Capitol Hill over the Mall area down to the Lincoln Memorial and out over the Potomac River.

The display was organized by the famous Grucci family, which has been firing explosives for five generations. The head of the family was heard to say that having put on this display for a presidential inauguration, he could die happy, knowing that he had achieved one of the greatest moments of his career.

"Oh gosh, oh gosh," cried out one youngster, decked out in a snowsuit of bright green, trying to take in everything from the fireworks to the lasers playing off the national monuments in every direction.

"It's indescribable," said one man. Observed another, as he watched green and yellow fireworks illuminate the Capitol dome, "It's an emotional feeling that overpowers the senses."

The finale came with the eruption of a breathtaking silver crossfire at the steps of the Capitol, during the playing of "This Is My Country." To most persons, many of whom were moved to tears, the finale was a fitting conclusion to a truly tumultuous and historic day.

As quickly as the parade and fireworks ended, most of the 40,000 persons who were attending the nine official Inaugural Balls were dressing for the evening's dancing and celebrating.

At the American Legion's "Salute to Heroes" Ball, 203 of the nation's 272 living Medal of Honor recipients welcomed President and Mrs. Reagan to their first celebration.

The President related the story of a commanding officer who, as he lay dying, said, "There may be only one time in your life when you may be called on to do what has to be done. Do it or you will have the taste of ashes in your mouth the rest of your life."

"The men here tonight," the President concluded, "have no taste of ashes."

155

White Ties And Tales

Because President Reagan wanted to share the Inaugural Ball festivities with as many persons as possible, television cameras transmitted the ballroom music and scenes to more than 100 private balls across America in hotel ballrooms, civic centers and similar facilities. The "Conciergerie" in Paris had the distinction of hosting the first American inaugural ball ever to be held overseas.

The evening was everything and more than it was expected to be. The limousines, the white tie formal wear, beautiful gowns and furs, entertainers, celebrities and bright lights.

In the $2,000, 10-seat boxes, partygoers had chairs and space—near-priceless commodities in some of the more crowded balls—along with two bottles of Almaden Blanc de Blancs wine from California and a souvenir tray with the presidential seal. All guests received a souvenir set of gold blazer buttons with the Inaugural Seal depicted.

Above, William Buckley trades jokes with Bob Hope at the Kennedy Center Ball. Below, the festivities at the Air and Space Museum, and at right, the Kennedy Center Ball.

157

Above, revelers at the Veterans' Ball. Middle, Rich Little, Audrey Meadows Six and Jimmy Stewart at the Kennedy Center. The Pension Building Ball at right.

158

Never mind that many guests had to wait under threatening skies for up to an hour to get into the balls, or that the crowds made dancing almost impossible, or that drinks were served in plastic cups. The important thing was that you were there, and that's all that mattered.

The lights were bright on the 9,000 persons crowded into the Kennedy Center, where among the state delegations was that of California, the President's home state. Guests present included Jimmy Stewart, Bob Hope, Ed McMahon, Audrey Meadows and Dale Evans and Roy Rogers. Lou Rawls and Tony Bennett were among the entertainers, along with the Count Basie Orchestra.

At the Pension Building ball, the Reagans enjoyed their first dance of the evening. To the delight of partygoers, the Reagans danced cheek-to-cheek to the tune, "Moonlight Serenade," played by the Glenn Miller Orchestra.

The President apologized for having to leave so early, but said he and Mrs. Reagan had several more balls to attend before returning to their "public housing."

At the Museum of Natural History, they danced around the red-white-and-blue-draped pachyderm in the three-story rotunda. The noise did not prevent Cynthia Helms, wife of the former ambassador to Iran and head of the CIA, from keeping abreast of the hostage situation. She had brought a transistor radio in her purse.

Drinks were dispensed in the most unusual places in the museum: near the roach exhibit, next to the white polar bear and before a case of human skulls.

Patti Davis at the Kennedy Center Ball.

Above, Ron and Doria enjoy the festivities at the Natural History Museum with Mrs. Reagan and the President.

Woody Herman and his Thundering Herd serenade the President and his family. Above the Ball at the Museum of Natural History.

At the Museum of American History, the Tommy Dorsey band punched out old favorites from the big-band era, while over at the Air and Space Museum, Vice President and Mrs. Bush were being greeted with a laser light show and the "Star Wars" movie theme played by the Houston Pops Orchestra.

At the hotels, country entertainers Glen Campbell and Tanya Tucker sang a medley of songs at the Washington Hilton, while actor Charlton Heston and Michael Reagan, one of the president's sons, signed autographs.

John and Elizabeth Warner

Anthony Newly entertains the crowds at the Shoreham.

161

The Youth Ball at the Mayflower Hotel.

Ray Charles greeting the President.

The Pointer Sisters at Young Voters' Ball, with Ball Chairman Laurie McDaniel, Marueen Reagan and her fiance, Dennis Ravell.

Local satellite balls shared in the excitement of the evening by closed circuit television. Here local ballgoers in Cocoa Beach, Florida watch the President's first dance of the evening.

The Youth Ball at the Mayflower Hotel was described by some as having a college fraternity atmosphere. The group seemed to thoroughly enjoy the singing of the popular Pointer Sisters. Hostess for the evening was Dorothy Bush, the only daughter of the Vice President and Mrs. Bush. Among those in attendance were 80 students from Eureka College, near Peoria, Illinois, Ronald Reagan's alma mater.

Over at the Shoreham Hotel, there wasn't much dancing, but plenty of talk about fashions, the inaugural spectacle and the evening's music. The Peter Duchin Orchestra played a milange of tunes, ranging from Elvis Presley numbers to songs from the Broadway musical, "Annie."

The music of Harry James greeted those at the Sheraton Washington, which also was graced by the whooping and rollicking Texas delegation, there to wish a favorite son well as he began his work as vice president.

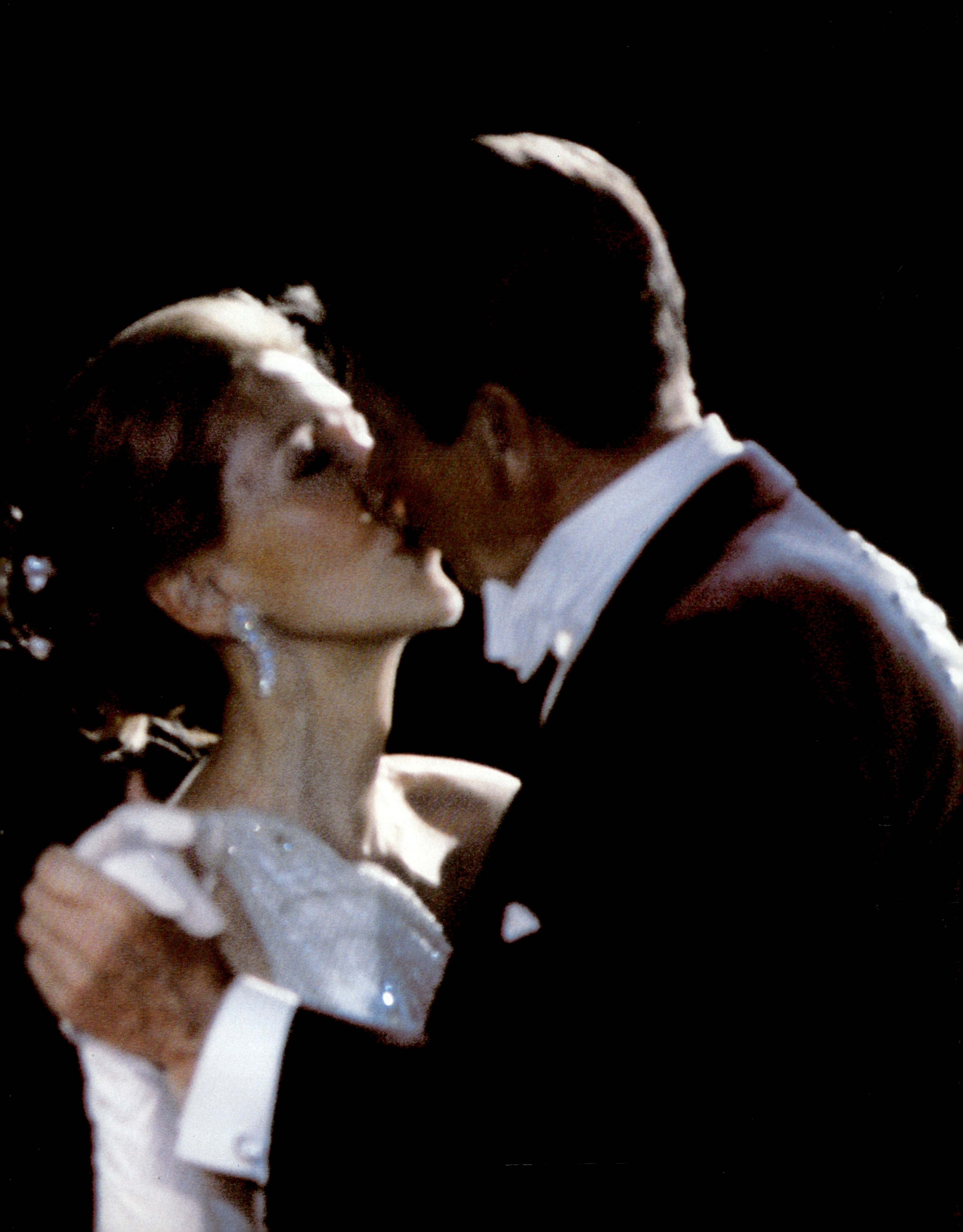

The National Tree that had remained dark for two Christmases, lights up with the news of the Hostages' return as the sky salute begins.

A Spirit Renewed

What a time it had been! During the inaugural events Americans found a new pride in America. Who won't remember the emotional moments when we heard the "Star Spangled Banner" and literally saw the "bombs" bursting in air in the form of brilliantly conceived fireworks at the Lincoln Memorial.

And the many entertaining events for all people going on all over our capital city. There were, in fact, more people-oriented and free events than any inaugural in history, making it truly an inaugural for everyone.

Not only was there something for everyone, but a great many "first"—from the Inauguration itself, held for the first time on the west steps of the Capitol to the first Opening Ceremony and the Sky Salute finale. Both were highlighted with the greatest fireworks displays Washington had ever seen.

Too quickly it was over—these culminating events that capped four days of festive inaugural gaiety. As the Reagan administration assumed the reins of government, it quickly put the celebrations behind and settled down to the hard work of running the country.

Over the seven days following the inaugural, the nation joyfully, jubilantly, enthusiastically and gratefully followed the 52 free Americans on their journey home, and stood ready to greet them when they arrived.

It was a time of new trust and confidence, and most of all, hope.

America remains strong, its people undaunted and more grateful, perhaps, for the freedom and democracy the nation safeguards so preciously.

It actually began to look as though the American people and their government would, indeed, make that "Great New Beginning"—together.

165

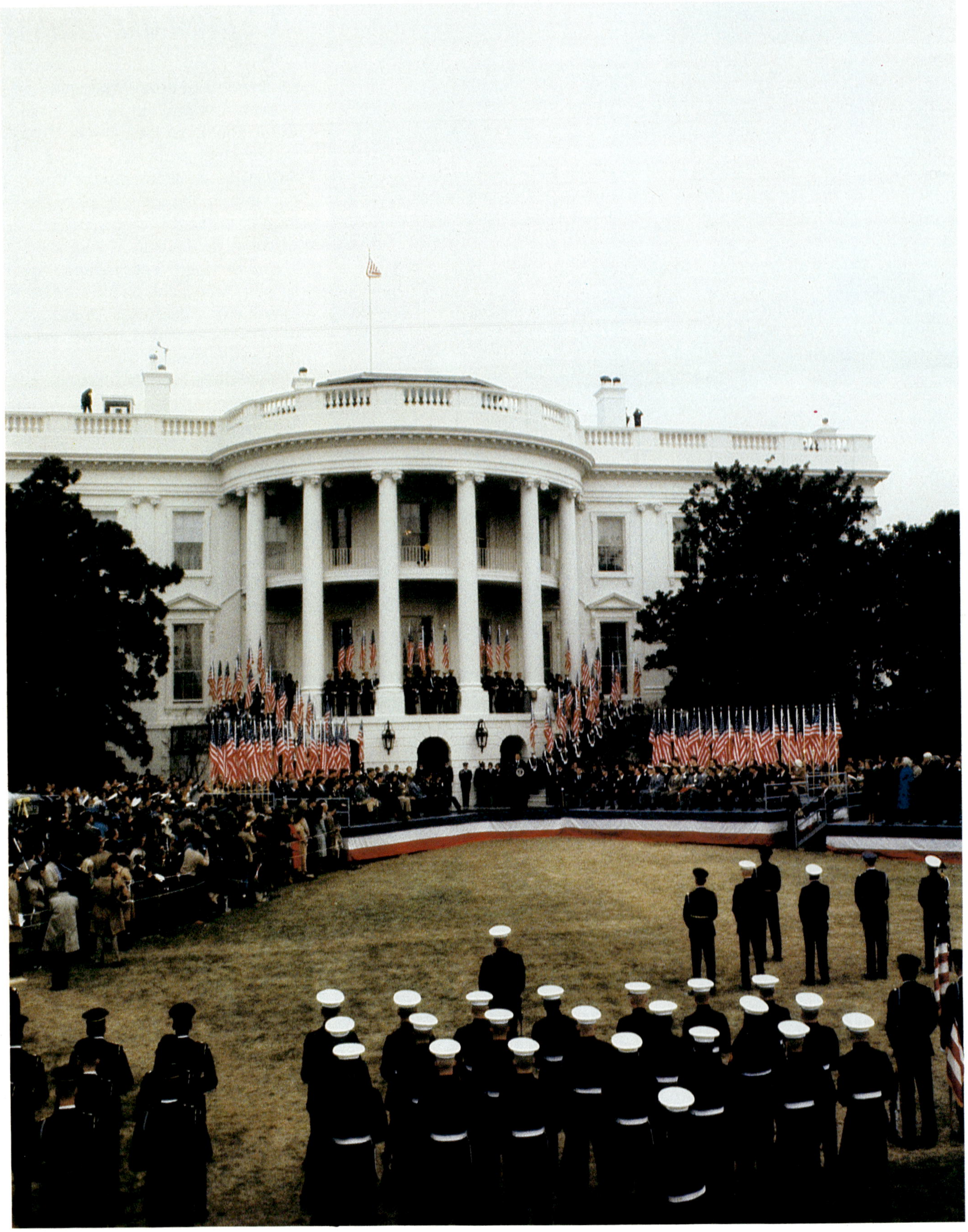

A Great New Beginning

By Landon Parvin

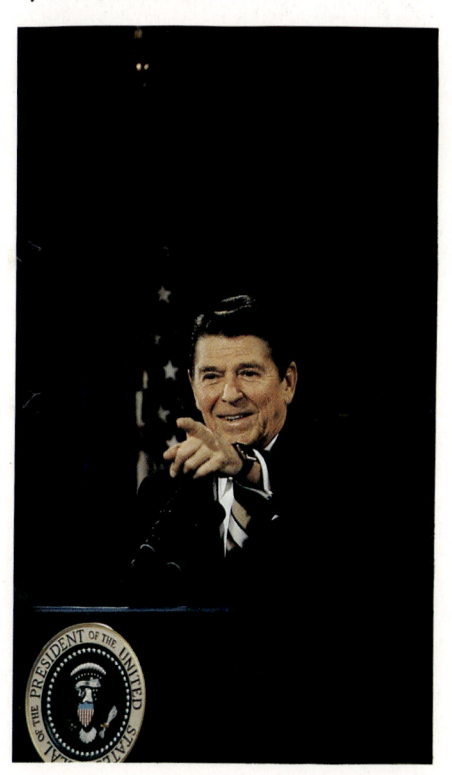

As President Ronald Wilson Reagan sat at his desk in the Oval Office for the first time, he must have speculated on what laws and proclamations he would sign there in the years ahead. He must have wondered what successes he would celebrate, what defeats he would endure, and what crises he would meet over that polished wooden surface.

And, in spite of the glare of television lights, the sound of self-winding cameras, and the commotion of reporters and aides, the President must have felt a momentary flicker of loneliness as he realized he alone in the United States was empowered to sit behind the imposing desk that separates private citizen from Commander-in-Chief.

The following days would show that the man fit the desk well.

Immediately, the President began stitching his political principles upon the quilt of government and sewing a new conceptual backing on the problems that face us. As part of his plan to deregulate America, he let fly a covey of executive orders, from the freezing of pending regulations to decontrolling oil prices. Vowing "swift and effective retribution" if American diplomats ever again were attacked, he welcomed home the hostages from their captivity in Iran, thus putting behind the nation a heartache which lasted 444 days. He met with Prime Minister Edward Seaga of Jamaica and President Chun Doo Hwan of South Korea, indicating to the international community that the word "ally" is once again in the U.S. lexicon of foreign affairs.

The President called a rapid succession of Cabinet meetings to get the wheels of his administration rolling with a smooth, ball-bearing acceleration. The major focus of these early meetings was the economy—the issue which the President said threatened to shatter the lives of our people; the issue, which more than any other, elected him to the highest office. Yet, in addition to grappling with the nation's perilous financial condition, the Cabinet sessions had another purpose. President Reagan was acquainting the Cabinet officers with his long-held commitment, developed while he was Governor of California, to a Cabinet style of governing. Through these initial meetings, he was priming the pump of Cabinet decision-making.

During his first weeks on the job, the President once again revealed his innate talents as a speaker, a persuader, a motivator. While schoolchildren of today may remember Abraham Lincoln as the Great Emancipator, schoolchildren of tomorrow may know Ronald Reagan as the Great Communicator.

As he lowered his hand from taking the oath of office, he raised his voice in an Inaugural Address that set forth clearly the aims of his presidency. In the weeks following he talked to Congressional leaders, black leaders, labor leaders, farm leaders, foreign leaders. He met with city fathers and right-to-life mothers. He held a press conference, unmatched in recent memory for its decorum and dignity. And he spoke compellingly to all Americans in a live broadcast outlining the economic precipice on which the nation teetered.

The President seemed to be taking the advice of the Apostle Paul: "For if the trumpet gives an uncertain sound, who shall prepare himself to battle?" President Reagan's messages were reassuring yet forceful. He was girding the nation for what one reporter called the "epic political struggle" to regain control of the federal government and its budget.

His first White House days were guided, as his entire term of office will be, by a simple conviction: government is the organized will of the people. To be truly representative, it must be based on the common sense of the common man.

Crowds clog the route from Andrews Air Force Base to the White House where President Reagan echoed the nation's relief that the American hostages are, at long last, home safely.

Former hostage Katherine Koob waves to the crowds from the bus at Andrews Air Force Base. Chargé d'Affaires Bruce Laingen receives the commemorative flag from the President as his colleagues look on.

The Scottish essayist Thomas Carlyle unwittingly distilled Ronald Reagan's political and economic beliefs when he wrote, "The work of an unknown good man is like a vein of water flowing hidden beneath the earth secretly making the ground green."

Ronald Reagan believes America is lush in liberty and verdant in opportunity because of her unknown good citizens. He called them heroes in his Inaugural Address. The President will rely on those unknown citizens in the years ahead more than he will rely on White House advisers with their steely, honed arguments or government experts with their stacks of computer printouts. These "ordinary" Americans will not submit complex reports on entitlement programs or discuss Southeast Asian affairs in the Cabinet Room, but their quiet values will provide unwaivering guidance to the man who shares their ideals.

In the early wintry weeks of the Reagan presidency, the nation sensed something genuinely different, even historic, was happening in Washington. Spring brought to the capital not only a change of seasons but a change in the business as usual attitude of the government. And as the cherry trees around the Tidal Basin blossomed, so did the people's hopes for a new beginning . . .

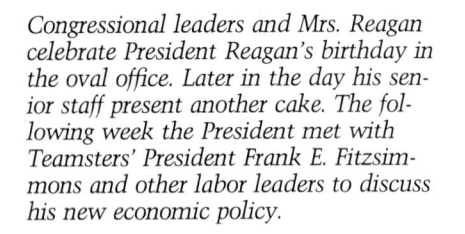

Congressional leaders and Mrs. Reagan celebrate President Reagan's birthday in the oval office. Later in the day his senior staff present another cake. The following week the President met with Teamsters' President Frank E. Fitzsimmons and other labor leaders to discuss his new economic policy.

The President meets with members of the press and answers a question during his first Cabinet meeting.

President Reagan and Vice President Bush talk with Secretary of State Alexander Haig and his wife, Patricia, during the State reception.

At left President and Mrs. Reagan stop for a moment on the South Portico with visiting Prime Minister Edward Seaga of Jamaica and his wife, Mitsy. Above, the President and Vice-President meet with Chun Doo Hwan, President of South Korea in the Oval Office.

The President

It would indeed be hyperbole if I claimed that, when I first interviewed Ronald Reagan in 1950, I felt I was in the presence of future greatness. But, on the other hand, I knew then I had met someone quite unusual—an extraordinarily intelligent and perceptive person, who knew what he was talking about.

Fade in to 1970. Reagan was now Governor of California. The scene was the San Jose airport. We were all awaiting the arrival of President Nixon for an election rally extolling the virtues of Senator George M. Murphy. Presidential One was late. The Governor, not one to waste time, repaired to a room where he began reworking his speech. For me, particularly, it was a fascinating sight. The actor of twenty years ago had become a superb politician.

And later that night, Reagan also proved to be a cool and collected leader. For the auditorium in which he and the President spoke, was surrounded by rock-throwing protestors. And Reagan, receiving reports of the alarming situation building up outside, took command of security measures. Unobtrusively. But firmly. Suffice it to say we all got out alive.

Coolness under fire may well be the dominant characteristic of the Reagan presidency. That was made obvious during the election campaign when Reagan refused to get rattled by momentary setbacks. When the polls showed him ostensibly losing momentum, Reagan stuck to his basic electoral strategy—and, needless to say, won big.

That same coolness was exhibited in his methodical selection of the team that will serve him in Cabinet and sub-Cabinet posts. Despite criticism of his pace from the media, the President-elect took his time picking men and women of outstanding ability.

President Reagan (how sweet it sounds!) has come a long way since I first met him. Based on by observations of him in the thirty years since, I know the Republic is in good hands. And that bodes well for the future of mankind.

By Victor Lasky

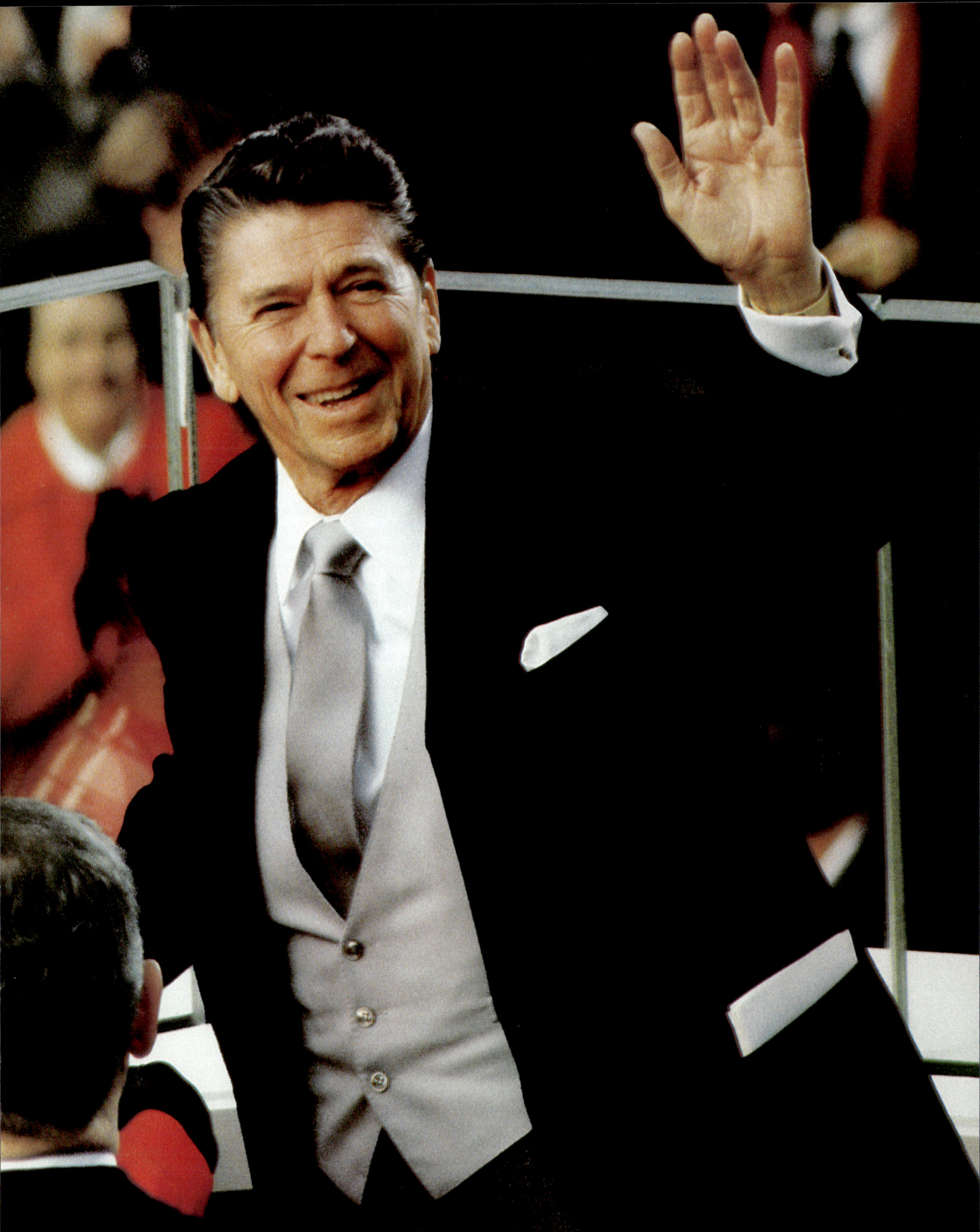

The 1981 Presidential Inaugural Committee

★ ★ ★

Co-Chairmen
ROBERT K. GRAY
CHARLES Z. WICK

Executive Directors
FREDERICK K. BIEBEL
W. GEORGE KERSEY
ROBERT G. McCUNE

Executive Advisor
MARY JANE WICK

Advisory Chairmen
THE HONORABLE GERALD R. FORD

THE HONORABLE WILLIAM J. CASEY   MR. MICHAEL K. DEAVER
MR. JUSTIN DART   MR. EDWIN MEESE, III
MR. HOLMES TUTTLE

Honorary Chairpersons

Mr. and Mrs. Robert H. Adams, Jr.	The Honorable and Mrs. Paul Laxalt
The Honorable Anne L. Armstrong	Mr. and Mrs. Fred Lennon
The Honorable and Mrs. James A. Baker, III	Mr. and Mrs. J. Willard Marriott
The Honorable and Mrs. Marion Barry	Mr. William J. McManus
Mr. and Mrs. Alfred Bloomingdale	The Honorable and Mrs. Maxwell Rabb
The Honorable and Mrs. William Brock	Mr. and Mrs. Henry Salvatori
Dr. and Mrs. W. Glenn Campbell	The Honorable and Mrs. William E. Simon
Mr. and Mrs. Joseph Coors	Mr. and Mrs. William French Smith
Mr. and Mrs. Theodore E. Cummings	Mr. and Mrs. James Stewart
The Honorable and Mrs. Raymond Donovan	Mr. and Mrs. Daniel Terra
The Honorable and Mrs. Thomas Evans	The Honorable and Mrs. Caspar Weinberger
Mr. and Mrs. Jaquelin H. Hume	Mr. and Mrs. William A. Wilson
Mr. and Mrs. Earle M. Jorgensen	Mr. and Mrs. Jack Wrather

OFFICE OF CO-CHAIRMAN GRAY
Special Asst.
Charles Crawford
Jerry Rapp
Paula Commers
Barbara Cook
Sally Goddard
James Jennings
Betsy Koons
Mark Moran
Landon Parvin
Leo Patterson
Annie Sonnabend
Peter Summerville
Marie Thessen
Sarah Watts
Susan West

OFFICE OF CO-CHAIRMAN WICK
Exec. Assistant
Karen K. Kwiatt
Frances R. Dickey
Sharon E. Jennings
Linda L. Lehmann
Capt. Peter Miller
A. Elizabeth Montgomery
Shirley R. Snyder

OFFICE OF THE CO-CHAIRMEN
Milton A. Rudin, Special Counsel/Entertainment
Mark Evans Austad, Special Advisor
Morgan Mason, Special Assistant/Entertainment
Gavin de Becker, Director, Special Services
Mrs. Goldie Arthur, Special Consultant/Entertainment
Stanley Kersten

HONORARY ADVISORY COMMITTEE
J. D. Allen
Richard V. Allen
Helen Marshall Boehm
Buckley Byers
Hon. and Mrs. William Clark
Dr. Willard Conger
Mr. and Mrs. Doyle Cotton
Lt. Gov. and Mrs. Mike Curb
Hon. Carl Curtis
Helene von Damm
Mrs. Justin Dart
Mr. and Mrs. Armand Deutsch
William H. Edwards
George Fritzinger
Jolyon Gissell
John Gnau
Josephine Good
Mr. and Mrs. Fred Gottfurcht
Mrs. Donald Gray
Mildred Hilson
W. Barron Hilton
Barbara Howell
Hon. Roman Hruska
Mr. and Mrs. Herbert Hutner
Mrs. Pat Jacobsen
James C. Jennings
Mr. and Mrs. Fred Lennon
Mr. and Mrs. Mervyn Le Roy
Mrs. Drew Lewis
Mr. and Mrs. Art Linkletter
Mr. and Mrs. Gordon Luce
General William Lyon
Mr. and Mrs. Glen McDaniel
Joseph M. McManus
Sen. Walter Mengdon, Jr.
Mrs. Duane F. Miller
Mrs. Pat Mosbacher
Mr. and Mrs. Gerald Oppenheimer
Mr. and Mrs. Franklin B. Pollock
Edmund T. Pratt, Jr.
Gilbert A. Robinson
Doray Saddler
Hon. Hugh Scott
Mr. and Mrs. Tony Scotti

Mr. and Mrs. Leonard Silverstein
Dr. and Mrs. Henry Singleton
Frederick W. Smith
Dr. and Mrs. Jules Stein
Mr. and Mrs. Geoffrey Swaebe
William Timmons
Jean Trousdale
Paul Trousdale
Mrs. John C. Tyler
Charles Tyson
Mr. and Mrs. Don Vannerson
John C. Whitehead
Mr. and Mrs. Meredith Willson
Richard B. Wirthlin
Clymer Wright
Jack Yogman

OFFICE OF THE CHAIRMEN FINANCE COMMITTEE
Chairman:
J. William Middendorf, II
Vice Chairmen:
William H. G. FitzGerald
David S. Smith
Treasurer:
Charles D. Daniel
Honorary Chairman:
J. Clifford Folger
Finance Director:
John Ricche
Assistant Finance Director:
Barbara Baroody
Executive Committee:
Leo M. Bernstein
David Broome
Charles E. Chamberlain
Anna C. Chennault
William J. Colley
John B. Conlan
Donald G. Conrad
Carl T. Curtis
Alex Dandy
Robert F. Dee
Fred L. Dixon
H. Robert Ferneau
Michael Doud Gill
Bill Hecht
Luther H. Hodges
Richard F. Hohlt
Charles R. Johnston, Jr.
Henry Kearns
John Krimsky
Bernard Lasker
Allan C. Levey
John Loeb, Jr.
James P. Low
Gordon Luce
William F. McSweeny
Jeremiah Milbank
Henry T. Mortimer
William H. O'Brien
George Olmsted
Thomas A. Pappas
John Ricche
Donald Rumsfeld
John Safer
B. Francis Saul, II
Richard M. Scaife
Gerard F. Schiappa
Edgar M. Skinner
David S. Smith
Charles W. Steadman
Richard Taylor
Dot Vannerson
Clifton Von Kann
Eleanor Williams

HONORARY FINANCE COMMITTEE
Mike Curb
George Scharffenberger
John C. Whitehead

NATIONAL FINANCE COMMITTEE REGIONAL CHAIRMEN
William A. Barnstead
Ralph E. Becker
Joe Coors
Mart T. Cox III
Kenneth H. Dahlberg
John S. Erthein
Kenneth R. Giddens
Harold R. Goldberg
Douglas W. Inglish
Henry Kearns
Charles J. Marshall
J. Willard Marriott, Jr.
William E. McCann
Jimmy Noe
Clyde B. Pinson
Paul H. Robinson
Jonathan W. Sloat
Edgar M. Skinner III
Mrs. Don Vannerson
Henry Zenzie
Armer E. White

FINE ARTS COMMITTEE
Pascal Regan, Chairman
Dr. Armand Hammer
J. William Middendorf, II
Hon. S. Dillon Ripley
David Kreeger
Carter Brown
Laughlin Phillips
Dr. Peter Marzio
John Kluge
Mrs. William French Smith
Joshua C. Taylor
Joseph H. Hirshhorn, Honorary Member

MANAGEMENT COORDINATION
Steve Coya
Edward F. R. Hearle
Michael M. Lent
Robert Mylls
Patti Watts
Jerome H. Werbel
Robin Whitney

LEGAL COMMITTEE
Chairman:
Robert W. Barker
Vice Chairman:
F. Elwood Davis
Joseph A. Cannon
Sterling W. Colton
Benjamin W. Cotten
Herbert L. Fenster
W. Stanfield Johnson
Clarence T. Kipps, Jr.
Herbert J. Miller, Jr.
F. Thomas Moran
John J. Ross
John Lewis Smith, III
Numa L. Smith, Jr.
Frank H. Strickler
Glen A. Wilkinson

EXECUTIVE STAFF
Dinah B. Argentieri
Francine P. Linde

GENERAL COUNSEL
Roger A. Clark

ASSOCIATE GENERAL COUNSEL
Herbert E. Marks

STAFF COUNSEL
Kemp R. Harshman
Jerry Solomon
Michelle Van Cleave

SPECIAL COUNSEL
Gordon C. Coffman
Alan P. Dye
Jonathan B. Hill

E. Sanderson Hoe
Leon T. Knauer
John M. Liftin
Robert A. Mangrum
Donald J. Mathison
Joseph M. McManus
Dale H. Oliver
Edward M. Prince
Raymond S. E. Pushkar
Gant Redmon
John E. Seeley
Leonard L. Silverstein
Paul J. Sinderbrand
Albert H. Turkus
Walter D. Vinyard

OFFICE OF THE TREASURER
William H. G. FitzGerald
David Amiot
Carolyn Austin
Jim Banks
Michael Barry
Barbara Baroody
David L. Bodenhamer
Patrice Boeke
Elliott R. Booth
Dorene Borquist
Susan H. Brands
Patricia Brockbank
Richard Burness, Sr.
Cary Carr
Joann Collins
Robert Comer
Francis A. Contino
Phillip Cunningham
Sara Ellsworth
John Evans
Larry E. Fell
Yoland Fields
Ben J. Fowicz
David B. Glass
Marshall Greene
Marcy L. Head
Kevin Igoe
Edward W. Kay
Richard Kendall
Dennis Kocik
Barbara Kostuk
George J. Kowais, Jr.
Donald T. Lynch
Josephine Martin
Mary McBride
John McCarthy
Jim McLaughlin
Set Momjian
Emmett G. Moore, Jr.
Joseph Moraglio
Paul Porter
Irene D. Raihle
Sandy Reilly
John Ricche
Cassandra Riley
Suzanne Scholte
Deanna Schreiber
Ruby Scragg
John Sears
Robbie Shultz
Ronald V. Sutherland
Andrew W. Swantak
Lisa Tharp
John Toole
Phillip Traina
John Viker-Smith
Evelyn Upshur
David Walters
Randolph Weber
Carol Williams
James Yatsko

INSURANCE
Chairman:
G. Dewey Arnold
Vice Chairman:
William G. Russell

ARCHIVES
Jerry L., Wallace
Sue Falb
Cindi Fox
John Roberts

GUARANTEE FUND
John Ricche

ARMED FORCES:
Major General Robert Arter, USA, Chairman
Brig. General Charles G. Prather, IV, USA, Deputy Chairman
Brig. General Harry T. Hagaman, USMC, Member
Rear Adm. Karl J. Bernstein, USN, Member
Brig. General Archer L. Durham, USAF, Member
Rear Adm. Harold W. Parker, USCG, Member
Sgt. Major Michael McCormick, USMC, AFIC Sgt. Major

JOINT EXECUTIVE COMMITTEE
Col. Charles H. Mayhew, USA, Chairman
Col. William Hammack, USMC, Member
Captain Donald H. Currier, USN, Member
Col. Wilbur D. Peterson, USAF, Member
Captain Thomas O'Hara, USCG, Member
Col. Marcia Rinkel, USA, Secretary

EXECUTIVE STAFF
Lt. Col. Alex Allen, USA
Lt. Col. David Fox, USA
Lt. Col. Lawrence Brooks, USA
Lt. Col. Donald Negley, USAF
Col. Robert T. Shellenberger, USAF
Col. Earl Ziebell, USA
Col. Jim Revels, USA
Lt. Col. Michael Dickerson, USA
Col. Hugh F. Eads, USA
Col. Richard Briggs, USA
Mr. Paul Miller

GOVERNORS, STATE & LOCAL OFFICIALS
Martin B. Dyer, Director
Terry Baker
Jan C. Bennett
Meade Camp
Karen L. Hodge
Fred Karger
Alisa M. Longworth
Jules F. Mermoud, Jr.
Chauncy L. Veatch III

COMMUNICATIONS
John Lengel, Director
Lee Troxler
John Roberts
Tom DeCair
Meryl Comer
Kimberley Borcherdt
Kim Tisdale
Laura Genero
Stratford Jones
Coral Schmidt
Lori Posin
Joyce Blair
Dixie Dodd
Douglas Leiker
Bruce Meadows
Doug Hart
Bobby Houser
Katie Holmes
Deborah Graham
Mark Rosenker
Ann McDonald
Richard Doubrava
Jerry Stromer
John Bailey
Elizabeth McCoulley
Katie O'Brien

Maxine Atwater
Victor Hurtado
Rick Ahern
Joyce Curry
Jim Hooley
Jim Moore
William C. Robinson
Gordon Seagrave
Robert R. Dahlgren

PRESS ADVISORY COMMITTEE
Nancy Thawley

OFFICES OF THE EXECUTIVE DIRECTORS
Frederick K. Biebel
Executive Director

EXECUTIVE STAFF
Otto J. Wolff, Deputy Director
Sonya Bell
Jane Chenoweth
Margie Crawford
Bill DiMambro
Marti Frucci
Noel Gross
Ann J. Guthrie
Jo McKenzie
Lynn Rhoads
Gill Sinonetti
Carolyn L. Tillotson
Jewell Wilks

W. George Kersey, Executive Director

EXECUTIVE STAFF
Ted Garrish, Deputy Director
Merle Brosius
Donna Eiron
Janet Gardner
Sallie A. Johnston
Mary Ann Knauss
Richard Walls

Robert G. McCune, Executive Director

EXECUTIVE STAFF
David Amiot
Dr. Monroe M. Bird
Mary S. Clippinger
William C. Clippinger, Jr.
Mervel Denton
Larry G. Kettlewell
William McManus
Wayne Peters
William Ward
Jeannette Winkel

CALLIGRAPHY
Marilyn McDaniel, Director
Trudee Albaugh
Russell Armentrout
Mimi Armstrong
Denice Becker
Ron Byrd
Dean Clavelli
Sandy Fox
Henry Frosch
Diane A. Hudock
Marilyn Jacanin
Marilyn Jeffrey
Fred L. Johnson, Jr.
Earl Kreins
Anne Lane
Lisa Leiter
Margaret D. Lewis
Rosemarie K. Lewis
Kathleen McCann
Louanne McKelvey
Shirley V. Merritt
Marilyn L. Mikesell
Emily Murray

Janet Murray
Avis Patterson
Diane W. Popper
Rosemary Roane
Valeta S. Rodier
George Selby
Helen F. Spotswood
Marilyn F. Spotswood

CORRESPONDENCE CONTROL
Louise G. Wheeler, Director
Mark Ashworth, Director Duplicating
Darlene M. Barkley
William Bolger
Mrs. William Bolger
Willie Carney
Nora Devlin
Major Douglas
Clyde F. Ensslin
Thomas Hillman
David Kirkman
Edna Knight
Dorothy McDaniels
Tanya Nesterczuk
Mark J. Robertson
Judy Stines
Adam Stolpen
J. F. Thomas
George Tyler
Paul Vancoverton
Greg Whiteman

FACILITIES
David J. Ryder, Director
Anne E. Allen
James F. Haight
F. Michael Tucker

FEDERAL PROTECTIVE SERVICES
Ronald S. Allen
Alphonzo Anderson
Ray J. Barnes
James A. Bell
Atlas H. Bivens
Lawrence A. Blackwell
George Bland
Edward T. Coby, Jr.
Ronald J. Coleman
James W. Crump
Clarence A. DeLaine
Samuel J. Dixon
William M. Dyer, Jr.
Frank M. Early
Irving Eleshire
Willie J. Epps
Otis J. Farrar
Director Federal Protective Service
Daisy R. Ford
James A. Gardiner
Deputy Chief General Services
Charlie B. Goodson
James E. Green
Albert W. Grier
Nicholas A. Harris
John G. Haynes
Charles F. High
James R. Hinnant
Raymond M. Jackson
John Jester
William P. Jeter
Calvin V. Johnson
James Jones
Sherman Kieth
Randy Lash
Clyde W. Lurry
Elwood E. Lyles
Jerry McGill
Charles E. McGowan
Ira Meyers
Ronald G. Miller
Ernest L. Moss
Chief Operational Services
Arthur E. Perpall
Tiab Rajah
Lewis Reeder
Robert Reynolds

Luther L. Rhodes
Phil Riedel
James E. Satterfield
John A. Scales
Reginald L. Thomas
Alvin Turner
McKinley Tyler
Osborne Ward
Robert W. Washington
Harold Waters
Wellington W. Waters
Douglas F. Watson
Russell West
Howard L. Williams

GENERAL SERVICES ADMINISTRATION
Daryl M. Dearman
Margaret A. Anthony
Jim Arthur
Ervin Auston
James Banks
William Banks
Mr. and Mrs. Charles Battle
Mary L. Beasley
Mr. and Mrs. James E. Beavers
John Bedner
Darrell E. Blaze
John O. Blazek
Joseph Bozzi
Vernon A. Brice
Arthur Brown, Jr.
Earl D. Catterton
Daltha M. Chick
Roy E. Clark
Johnnie Crawford, Jr.
Thomas T. Crumel
David A. Davis, Jr.
Doris A. Davis
Gres Dennison
Viola M. Drummond
Patricia Dutton
Michael Earl
Gloria J. Ellis
Jennifer Epps
Richard Estes
James A. Fisher
Kenneth E. Fisher
Thomas Fitzhugh
Robert Fromm
Leory Gantt
Alvin Guice
Virginia Guiles
Kenneth G. Hagerty
Jackie Hayes
Lloyd Herndon
Charles M. Higgs
Robert Hines
Eva P. Holley
Daryl Holloway
Gwen Jackson
James Jackson
Bernice D. Jamison
Gary Jefferson
Delcener Johnson
Mrs. Robert M. Johnson
James M. Jones, III
Virginia H. Jones
George V. Lampman
Mr. and Mrs. Edgar L. Lash
T. C. Leininger
Harvey L. Lewis
Harold Livingston
Joyce A. Lofty
Joseph Lowe
Essie Martin
Arthur Matthews
Paul V. Mattingly
Franklin H. McCoy
Michael D. McCray
Jean H. McDonald
Annie M. McDuffie
Caroll L. McGraw
Scott McKeon
Neil C. McPhaul
Ronnie Messersmith

Peter Miller
Lawrence Mitchell
Ronald Modkal
Jasper Murphy
Aljerry Myers, Jr.
Walter W. Norris
Ramond Outlaw
Bernice Owen
John Pagan
Herbert Payne
Michael C. Pellar
Logis Plater
Odell Price
Larry Purcell
Wesley Rose
Jasper L. Royal
Patrick Savoca
Stephen L. Seek
Millie J. Shadding
Harvey M. Shumaker
Mr. and Mrs. Charles G. Simmons
Joe R. Slade
Barbara A. Smith
Claire Soper
Albert C. Staley
Woodrow Swanson
Ruby Thorton
Rudolph Thorton
Mr. and Mrs. Edward D. Turner
John P. VanRoon
Eleanor R. Vaughn
Elnora R. Vaughn
Thomas Venable
Joseph Washington
Clarence Wagner, Jr.
J. L. Wallace
Eva L. Ware
Paul A. Warwick
Harold Watkins
Shawn Williams
Queen Womack
Evelyn Wood
Ms. Alma B. Young
Mr. and Mrs. Herbert C. Young, Jr.
Raymond C. Young, Jr.

INFORMATION SERVICES
Sarah Justine Estes Marks, Director
Susan Baker
Julianne Bakke
Marie Brookter
Alan J. Forst
Neville K. Gay
Hector Irastorza, Jr.
Harry A. Pace
John Carlo Papavaritis
Leo C. Patterson
Wilhelmina Rhodes
Kathryn E. Smith
Julia C. Varano
W. Gregory Wims

INVITATION CONTROL
Arthur J. Jackson, Jr., Director
Robbie Aiken
Philip C. Armstrong
Mark Ashworth
Mary Ann Baron
Kathie Bennett
Fran Boyd
Tom Buchanan
Ron Byrd
John H. Chen
Sally Christian
Scott Douglas
John Forster

Dave Gerth
Philip S. Hanson
Slade Hanson
Gladys Hook
John Jackson
Cathy Jacobson
Judy Jarrett
George L. Johnson, IV
Lynn Ksanznak
Debbie Kurilchyk
Gregory C. Larosa
Christy Lay
Ann K. Marshal
Ginnie Martinez
Ownie McBride
Joseph McCourt
Mike McCray
Leslie Mendal
Mary Meyers
Christopher D. Miller
Robert Moss
Lee Neff
Candy Ostrander
Cameron Quinn
Jennifer L. Rahn
Linda W. Reed
Allan C. Rodway
Murray J. Rossini
John Ryan
Tina Silverman
Cathie Smith
Sylvia Sniffin
A. Conover Spencer
Mike Sterlacci
Jon A. Stonebraker
Chicchina Stump
Francis P. Sullivan
Vivian K. Tabor
Samuel B. Taylor
J. Paige Torbert
James E. Tyvoll
James K. Van Slyke, III
David A. Williams
Ralph C. Wunder
Michael Ydiguras

EVENT FACILITIES
National Park Services
Manus J. Fish, Director
Elmer S. Atkins
George Berklacy
Georgia Ellard
Del Ennis
Gary Grimmett
Parker T. Hill
Karen Jackson
Skip Larson
James I. McDaniel
Robert Miller
William I. Newman
Gary Pierrucione
Richard G. Robbins
William F. Ruback
James Rubin
Jack Sands
William Saylor
Denny Sorah
Robert Stanton
Gary Treon

PERSONNEL
Kay Ford, Director
Jennie Reed
Michael Saltz
Abbie Weist

PURCHASING & PROCUREMENT
Robert J. Cohen, Director
James F. Browne
John W. Eakle
Michael Karem
Felisha E. Marcus
Stanley M. McGeehan, Jr.
Charles Miller
Thomas J. Morano
Lloyd R. Ricks
Florence Robinson
Linda Schnabl
Kimberly Vreeland

SECURITY
Robert Gubitosi, Director
Mary Beth Allen
Robert L. Athey
Larry Blanco
Maureen Brannigan
Ronald K. Bushnell
Arnold Coposky
Anne Dent
Patricia M. Gutierrez
Donnah Harrington
Michael Hodge
Bart G. Hess
Bernard W. Hite, Jr.
William C. Juran, III
Frank R. McKay
Susan A. Oliver
David J. Zachem

STATE COORDINATORS
Phil Armstrong
William A. Arseneau
Nelda L. Barton
Jean Birch
J. Michael Borden
Grace Boulton
Mrs. Orin G. Briggs
Patricia Bruns
Eleanor Clapp
Danny Cooper
Jack Courtemanche
Dr. Alfred B. Cramer
Artilia B. Cruz
Howard H. Dana, Jr.
James Davidson
Dr. Melvin H. Evans
John Fohl
Emory Folmar
Mario Gaztambide, Jr.
Clinton Graham
Randall Gregory
Lanny Griffith
Mrs. Noel L. Gross
Slade Hanson
Patricia Hurley
Nora Hussey
Timothy N. Hyde
Thomas A. Johnston
Kina'u B. Kamali'i
Phyllis Kincannon
Thomas J. Kirkpatrick
Mike Krauss
Fran Langholf
Lynn Lindley
Linda A. Long
Peter McCann
Kit Mehrtens
Mary Meyers
Lydia J. Miller
Dorotha Moore
Della Newman
Suzanne Nordbolm
Ann Pollis
Mrs. Jacque Ponder
Betty Lou T. Pyle
Jenny Rahn
Marynell D. Reece
Betty J. Renoel
Ranny Riecker
Helen W. Robbins
M. Sheila Roberge
Eileen C. Schouweiler
E. K. Stevens
Mary Stivers
Jim Stockdale
Mary Ann Sutton
Barbara Taylor
Gloria Tokar
Jim Van Slyke
Taber Ward
Julia H. Webber
Bee Whitmore
Eunice B. Whittlesey

TRANSPORTATION
Cindy Tapscott, Director
Michael Beatty
Tony Benedi
Ruth E. Berklund
Ann Bowen
Mrs. Chambers
Captain Day

Claire Dorrell
Norman Duncaon
Kathrine Ebert
Joseph English
Gary Engrebretson
Beth Goodrich
John Grinnell
Michael Gross
Mrs. Guest
Peter A. Hayes
Kenneth Hesford
Martha High
David J. Hovermale
Britt Hughes
H. Melvin Luken, IV
Mel Lukens
Rob Mahaffey
Bob Mann
Marge Mayo
John McClure
Dan Morris
Steve Musser
Joan B. Perrin
John P. Philbin
Mary Sawyer
Herbert Schmertz
Pat Segee
Marc Slavin
Mark Tapscott
Warren D. Toburen
Dennis Wacaster
Clark B. Wilson
Jay Witheridge
Ed Wolf
Shirley Wright

WILL CALL
Walter Gold, Director
Francis Acton
Leslie Adams
Louise Albia
Irving Aleshire
Doris A. Allen
Barbara Armstrong
Elizabeth D. Ash
Scott Ash
Carmella Baccari
Joyce Baker
Juanita Baker
Edward J. Banas
Euphenia P. Banas
Ann Barbar
Robert Barnett
Mrs. Robert Barnett
Stuart Barrett
May Batcher
Ann Beglin
Genevieve Behrens
Florence L. Berg
William M. Berg
Barbara Birra
Alice M. Black
Mildred Blandford
Fred Blumenthal
Kelly Bowles
Juanita Bradley
Paul Bradley
Parkes Brittain
Georgia Broadnex
Gilda Bronner
Barclay Brown
Norma Brown
Dr. Peggy Brown
Mary Burch
Margaret E. Burdick
Pamela Burge
Sandra B. Calhoun
Carolynda Campbell
Helene Campbell
Joyce Cappon
Daniel Casey
Daniel L. Casey
Janet Centola
Carline Cheatam
Candance A. Chimples
Michael A. Chrisanti
Gertrude Christiansom

Marjorie Clark
Shelley Clark
Maggie R. Clemmons
Lt. Col. Charles R. Clevela
Louise Cleveland
Nina R. Coin
Rita Conway
Vera Counihan
Kathy Covell
Ann M. Crews
Maurice J. Cullinane
Karlen A. Curtis
Elizabeth Dajany
Marilyn Davis
Jay Delehanty
Mayo Diantonio
Denise Dolan
Sally Dolan
Merci Drake
Merideth Duncan
Marilyn Eastwood
Col. Eric Eber
Peggy Eber
Patricia Economos
Nancy Egbert
Tina J. Eldridge
Veve Eldrdige
Conora Elliott
Robert Evans
Ellen Farley
Jill Fecci
Mary Ann Ferko
Andrea Fischer
Andrea Fisher
Dorothy Fletcher
Merle Fletcher
Frances Flikeid
John Flikeid
Unda Flood
Ed Florer
Laverne Florer
Iris Foggs
Lynette Foggs
Lloyd Forrester
Calvin C. Foster
Cornetta Freeman
Lee Fullmer
Patti Fullmer
Paul Furth
David Gannon
Susan Gannon
Cindy Gaumer
Beverly Geline
Adele George
Audrey Gibson
Alfred Giddings
Nira Giddings
John R. Gilmore
Rita Glauden
Penny E. Goddin
Walter Gold
Marlene Gordon
George Graeber
Mary Grant
Denise Grantham
Bruce Green
Thomas Greenland
Thomas A. Greenland
Elizabeth Greer
George B. Greer, Jr.
Billie Growney
Barbara Halbach
Mrs. John O. Harper
Sue Hawkins
Carole J. Hayes
Gary Hayes
Lianne Heiney
Estelle Henderson
Moselle Henderson
George Hieronymous
Heidi Hiltgen
Joan Hitchcok
Bobbie Hoffman
Richard Hohlt
Virginia Hook
Carol Hoover
Woody Horwell
Rose Howard
Joan Huneidi
Nancy Hunt
Nancy J. Ingalsbee
Carson Jackson

Ernestine Jackson
Nancy Jacobs
Ruth Jacobs
Ada Jacobson
Debbie Jarosz
Diane Jaskiewicz
Diane Johnson
Dorothy Johnson
Duane Johnson
Glenda J. Johnson
William Johnson
Yvonne Johnson
Shirley Jones
George Judge
Paul Kaye
Fran Keefe
Virginia Kellogg
Susanne Kelly
Edwin Kerschner
Richard Kessler
Jean Kirkwood
Nancy H. Knight
Rose Kreiser
Renee Kurdys
Beverly Lantry
Lyda V. Larkins
Lelyan Laye
Ruth Leader
Edgar Legum
Gordon Levi
Vivian Levin
Susie Lopes
Robert Luker
Del Malkie
Amelia Mancuso
Betty Martin
Sandra McAllister
Pat McCloy
Marion McDonald
Tom McGowan
Trudy McKimens
Jacqueline Meeks
Thomas Meeks
William Middlebrook
William Milburn
Twana Mims
Albert Mitchler
Albert E. Mitchler
Edgar Morgan
Mary Morgan
Allan Mulligan
Bill Murray
Jacob Myers
Orinda Nelson
Katie Newman
Carol Northamer
Naomi Nover
Virginia A. Oldham
Darlene Oliver
David Owens
Marjorie Owens
Francis Patterson
Claudine Paul
James Paul
James R. Paul
Don Pauley
Shirley Pearson
Louise Pease
Tina Peele
Maybelle Peter
Margo Petkus
Paul Phippo
Gary Pieruccioni
Ronnie Pittman
Simon Prema
Patrick G. Price, Jr.
Tula G. Prior
Peggy Quinn
Susan Rielley
Noel Ripple
Debra Roche
Allan Rodway
Neil Roland

Claire Romack
Francis Roos
Dorothy Rosenauer
Allen D. Rosse
Alice Roth
Merle Russ
Shelley Schramm
Rob Schuler
Judy Shaver
Clarence Shaw
Helen Siemaszko
Cindy Siko
Dorothy Simpson
Clinton C. Sisson
Shirley Smith
Fred Soldwedel
Alfonso Spera
Julette Stephens
Evelyn Stephens
Polley Storey
Edith Stratton
Lester B. Swink
Pamela Taylor
Anastassia Thamakas
Alice B. Thomas
James F. Thomas
Theresa Thomas
Robert Thompson
James Underwood
Louise Vaughn
Pat Veatch
Brenda Vumbaco
Pauline Wallace
Holly Wallins
Marie Watkins
Col. Martin Wender
Terre West
Florence Westphal
Tim Westphal
Denise Whitehour
Bernice J. Williams
Jackie Williams
Mary Williams
Eleanor Wilson
Zula Witcher
William Wolfe
Shirley Wood
Pete Wrobleski
Gloria Wynn
Rudy Yandrek
Tim Yingling
Charlotte Zettle
Ellen Ziebarth
Ruth Ziebarth
Pearl Zitmore
Ellen de Szunyuch

OFFICE OF THE EXECUTIVE ADVISOR

Executive Advisor:
Mary Jane Wick

EXECUTIVE ADVISOR STAFF
Karen Hart, Spec. Asst.
Dorothy Tyson, Spec. Asst.
James P. Bunnell
Marian Cook
Karen Felgner
Harriett Finkelstein
Patricia Hansen
Carol L. Lohman
Cathey Lozick
Edward Lozick
Virginia S. Milner
Annie Morris
Beverly Morsey
Beedy Ritchie

CONGRESSIONAL LIAISON
Corrine Michel, Director
Mildred G. Bighinatti
Jerry B. Clark
Alger C. Ellis
George L. Hooper
John Hvasta
Barbara J. McCaffrey
Barbara Meinen

Marjorie E. O'Donnell
Olga Simpson
Harrison F. Starn, Jr.
Mary Ann Zalowmis

DIPLOMATIC PROTOCOL
William R. Codus, Director
Bernice W. Behrens
Stephan Brown
Frederick W. Flott
Mary C. Garner
Mary E. Gibson
Mary M. McLaughlin
Ruth W. Warner

DISTINGUISHED GUEST LIAISON
Dorothy Tyson, Director

JUDICIARY
Patricia O'Connell, Director
James Enoch
Barbara E. Hanson
J. Paul Marshall
Thomas W. McKean
Carlton McLeod
Gerald E. Preston, Esq.
Bernice Robertson

THE PRESIDENT-ELECT FAMILY AND FRIENDS
June Walker, Director
Nona Snyder
Ann Davis
Jayne Davis
Susan Davis
Robyn Gordon
Anita Korten
Jeannie Lee
Ann Prather
Maria Vukusie

REAGAN-BUSH CAMPAIGN/ TRANSITION
Wendy Borcherdt, Co-Director
Marcia Hobbs, Co-Director
Ann Guthrie
Ann C. Vandevanter

THE VICE PRESIDENT-ELECT FAMILY AND FRIENDS
Jane Kenny, Director
Mary B. Ashmun
Grier Ballantine
William R. Braddock
James F. Carroll
Mrs. Joseph N. Cate, Jr.
Lt. Col. Dennis E. Damon
William R. Dunn
Francis X. Egan
John E. Fletcher
Marvin H. Floom
James P. Flowers
Lt. Col. Robert F. Gibson
Douglas C. Guiler
Peter R. Heimsath
Lt. Col. Jerry G. Henderson
Robert L. Herndon
Donnal Hiltbrunner
Kendall E. Jacobs
Victor Johnnides
Lawrence A. Kassin
Thomas W. Kaugher
Mark P. Keehan
William F. Kernan
Terry D. Labar
Terry N. Lewis
Junior D. Littlejohn
Ronald J. Lucas
Anthony T. Lupo
Bruce C. Lyon
Frederick McCorkle
Charles S. Mill
Richard L. Naughton
Larry Osborn
William Pedersen
Patricia Pewett
William A. Pittenger

John M. Razel
Bruce F. Roger
David A. Rolston
Tim Roper
Edward M. Rynne
David J. Seeley
Wilson A. Shatzer
Richard V. Sherwood
Terry G. Stull
Robert S. Tekell

ADVERTISING AND PROMOTION
Vice Chairman:
Mr. Barry Zorthian
General Business Manager—Advertising:
Mr. George Stringer
Director—Advertising:
Mr. Richard Krolik
Director—Inaugural Program:
Mr. Bob Sweeney
Director—Promotion:
Ms. Eleanor Callahan
Director—Concessions:
Mr. Ivan Scott
Drew Babb
Douglas M. Bibby
Deloss Blackburn
Duke Blackburn
Robert Brouse
Kermit O. Carpenter
Patricia Cormanez
Sheldon Dix, Jr.
Thomas Fazio, Sr.
Thomas Fazio, Jr.
Hunt Finley
Paul Gormsen
Gilbert Gosvenor
Eugene Hagburg
Dr. Armand Hammer
Chase Harrigan
Teryl Hirt
Teri Hirz
Kay J. Hughes
Edward A. McCoy
William F. McSweeney
John A. Meyers
Carol M. Musgrave
Howard E. Paine
Alice Parin
Richard Porter
George W. Renfro
Margie Rodovsky
Richard Rovsek
Leslie B. Seagrave
Dan Smith
Karyn S. Wellons
Victoria H. Winslow

INAUGURAL BALLS
Vice Chairpersons:
Mrs. William J. Casey
Mrs. Paul D. Laxalt
Honorary Co-chairpersons:
Sen. & Mrs. Robert J. Dole
Vice Chairman:
Mr. Gary Hunt
Ball Chairpersons:
Mr. & Mrs. John Alison
Mr. & Mrs. Robert Chambers
Miss Louise Gore
Mr. & Mrs. Edward C. Lozick
Dr. & Mrs. William Walsh
Mr. & Mrs. Carl Shipley
Mr. & Mrs. Joseph Coors
Colonel & Mrs. J. Hunter Drum, USA (Ret)
Director:
Mr. Peter Sorum
Tharp Ammon
Charles Bakaly
Matt Boland

Larry Butler
Sylvia Calloway
Dr. John L. Clay
Timothy Coyle
Robert V. Davison
Ken Donovan
Laurie DuMouchelle
Ronald G. Eberhardt
Jane I. Erkenbeck
Gilliain Green
Chris Hankin
Amy Harvey
Laurie Hefner
Barbara E. Higgins
Shelley A. Hoke
Bob Israel
Stephen Karolyi
Ann Kosco
Paula Kuzmich
Michael R. Lawler, Jr.
Andre LeTendre
Barbara Martin
Carol McCain
Lt. Kerwin E. Miller
Alan J. Moore
Joy B. Price
Bill Schereck
Mike Shahan
Diane Smigd
Jayn S. Stankowski
Diane Swift
Tim Swift
Donna Tuttle
Maryann L. Urban
Chandler Van Orman
Christ Vial
Kathleen S. Wild

INAUGURAL BALL IN EUROPE
Vice Co-Chairmen:
Mr. and Mrs. Leonard L. Silverstein
Co-Chairmen, Paris Ball:
Mr. Rodney Markley, Jr.
Mr. Erin Turnel

INAUGURAL BALLS IN STATES
Vice Chairman:
Charles T. Hagel
Aris T. Allen
Lisa Berger
Bill Biggers
James Bjornstad
Anne Boder
Beau Boulter
Richard Bowers
Sarah Boyce
Ken Brengle
Darwin J. Burke
Harry Button
Mary Combs
Marianne Crotty
John T. Dailey
J. Derr
Larry Dub
Maureen Dumas
Walter R. Dunlevy
Larry Ford
Thomas A. Fuentes
S. Charles Garofalo
Ron Giles
John Gorman
Colette Grinsted
Martha Gustavsen
Joan Havercroft
Myron Holen
William Hurd
Dean Jackson
Louise Johnson
Marie Kaigler-Reese
Sabina Kavanaugh
William R. Kearney
John T. Kehoe
Jack Kennelty
Karen S. King
Mark Larsen
Kay Ledbetter
Paula Lewellen
Kay Linton

Sharon Luba
Tom Lukas
Greg McGowan
Mike McKeever
Ethel McSweyn
Reed Mendelson
Melanie Miller
E. Z. Million
Mrs. Barney L. Morris
Jack Morris
William Murphy
Cliff Nettles
Carl F. Neu
Nicholas Norton
Commissioner Martha Olsen
Neil Penn
Ed Phelps
Dori Pye
Joe Ragland
Ellen Read
John E. Ritchey
Marge Ross
Robert Rovner
Harvey Sackett
Dr. Norman Scherman
Loren Schiebe
Barbara Schrang
James Sebesta
Susan Seguin
Dean Sims
Roger Singleton
Dave Smith
Lamar Smith
Richard D. Spence
Art Spencer
Mrs. Kyle Testerman
Dick Turner
Marie Vale
Bobbe Vargas
Harold E. Vogt
June Watkins
Corrine Weis
Glenn Wilson
Linda Woodruff

INAUGURAL CONCERT AND CANDLELIGHT DINNERS
Vice Chairperson:
Mrs. Holmes Tuttle
Honorary Co-Chairpersons of Candlelight Dinners and Concerts:
Dr. and Mrs. Lloyd Davis
Concert Committee Chairman:
Mr. Robert S. Carter
Vice-Chairpersons— Concert
Mrs. Fritz-Alan Korth
Mrs. Charles H. Price II
Producer:
Mr. Martin Feinstein
Concert Dinner Committee Chairperson:
Mrs. Charles H. Price II
Vice-Chairperson and Director—Dinner:
Nancy Harvey Steorts
Director—Concert:
Mr. Bob Gleason
William Aaron
April Adams
John A. Adams
Francis Aebi, Sr.
Josephine Anderson
Jules Armellini
Russell Armentrout
Wendy Batt
Susan C. Beaver
Mary Bendure
Cathryne R. Bennett
Matthew J. Boland
Warren G. Botz

Stephen Brown
Thom Buccieri
Barbara B. Buchanan
Edwin A. Buchanan
Lane E. Burnsed
Doug Campbell
Leslie R. Cashen
Jon Cincebox
Mrs. Jon Cincebox
Paul S. Clark
Nancy Clarke
James A. Clifton
Wm. Dewey Clower
Keith Conover
James K. Conzelman
Helen M. Cooper
Benjamin Cotten
Donald R. Cox
Bob Crandell
Dorothy Crosby
Charles F. Donahue
Jeff Ellis
William Enomoto
Victor H. Esch
E. Anthony Fessler
Mrs. E. Anthony Fessler
Helen Fiecke
Randolph A. Frank
Maria Gateau-Cumin
Anita Gauk
Bruce Gehlback
Laura Genero
Gene George
Gail Green
Carmichael Gully
Eileen R. Gurenian
Richard Hagstrom
Alan Hall
Gary Hancq
Karen Hart
Philip Hawley
Adolf Heck
Gary Heck
James A. Heime
Dean Hill
Robert T. Hoff
Edwin Hoffman
George Hooper
Edward W. Huffcut
Jim Hunter
Bernard Imming
Catherine D. Jacobsen
Jerry D. Jennings
Johnsen's Nursery
Robert B. Johnson
Helen Johnston
Bonnie A. Jones
Burton H. Kaplan
Tadaaki Kato
Judy Kaufman
David Keanealy
Dr. John Kenealy
Irene H. Kersten
Stanley R. Kersten
Larry G. Kettlewell
Irwin J. Kilday
Dick Kingman
Patricia M. Kirby
Ray Kitayama
Barbara A. Kratchman
Andrew J. Lapiska
Rae Leeth
Mark C. Lewis
Donald Livingston
Eugene Lundgren, Sr.
Eugene Lundgren, Jr.
Mrs. Eugene Lundgren, Sr.
Gary Madson
Mrs. Gary Madson
Jann Mahan
Harold Mahler

Arnie Malin
Richard Marcus
Greg Mathieson
Andy Matsui
Richard W. Matthews
Charles H. Mayhew
William D. McDonald
Joseph McGarry
Michael C. McGowan
James O. McGuire
Louise E. McKenzie
Wanda McKinney
Mrs. Mary J. Merrill
Ronad L. Merrill
Michael Miller
Robert Mondavi
Alexander Moore
Mark Murray
W. Mark Murray
Tosh Nakashima
Nakashima Family
David Ninomiya
Gene Nygro
Mrs. Michele Nygro
William F. O'Neal
Ron Obertello
Tom Oku
Conrad Pappas
Dennis I. Paul
Martin Peterson
E. E. Phillips
Wigmore Pierson
Max Pine
Thomas Porter
Mrs. S. Thomas Porter
Pam Powell
Victor A. Powell
Ella M. Quinn
Fred Radewagen
Linda Reynolds
Paul Ripley
Francis Rizzo
Michael J. Roberson
Donald Saddler
Roy Sakae
Erica Schmidt
Marion Scott
Michael N. Shahan
Yoshimi Shibata
Randy Simpson
Skip Skolnik
Jacob H. Smith
Ted Smithers
Gustave Springer
Marti J. Springfield
Mary Lou St. Louis
Donald J. Stallman
Francesca Steere
Deborah Steorts
Michael A. Sterlacci
Julie J. Stout
Bill Suyeyasu
Harvey G. Taylor
Peggy Taylor
Terry Taylor
Dorothy Temple
Mitchell L. Templeton
Roman Terleckyj
Arne Thirup
Paul R. Thomer
David Thompson
Carolyn L. Tillotson
Jennifer Tipton
Robert D. Trapp
James Trone
Kiyoko Uyeda
Chandler L. Van Orman
Don Vanni
James Wanko
Kathy Wild
F. L. Windholz
Dick Wright
David Young
Donald L. Young
Paul Young

VICE PRESIDENT'S RECEPTION
Vice Chairperson:
Mrs. Loret E. Ruppe

Honorary Chairpersons:
The Honorable Gerald R. Ford
Mrs. Prescott Bush
Mrs. Mildred Hilson
Mrs. Douglas MacArthur
The Honorable William G. Milliken
Mrs. Nelson A. Rockefeller
The Honorable Mary Louise Smith
Mr. Lowell Thomas, Sr.
Director:
Mr. David R. Scotton
Mrs. Harold E. Allen
Mary Ashmun
Joyce Baker
Mrs. Harry T. Carter
Pat Cate
John J. Coakley
Alice Cockerham
Terry M. Crosby
Peggy Depaoli
Theresa Elmore
Emily Ford
Mrs. R. D. Frazier
Tina Harrower
Betsy Hemminway
Diane Hendricks
Lois Hessler
Liz Howard
Joan M. Huneidi
Edith Izenberg
Ron Kaufman
Jane Kenny
Betty J. Leslie
Nancy Lilly
Tish Maher
Sally Novetzke
Pat Pewett
Jacqueline Phillips
Tricia Rodgers
Dean Ross
Dorothy Smithey
James Storey
Kate Tabor
Nancy Thawley
Mrs. Ross Vogel
Neal E. Wise
Gail Wray

GOVERNORS' RECEPTION
Vice Chairman:
Mr. Fred L. Dixon
Director:
Mr. R. Webster Chamberlin
Gwen A. Anderson
Alice M. Banks
Terry L. Baxter
Jan C. Bennett
Kim Blackwell
Nancy Bryant
John Christie
James K. Conzelman
Gary L. Curran
Mrs. Edward Deatherage
Mrs. Benjamin Evans
Harold Fangboner
Nathan L. Ferris
Elizabeth M. Fielding
Walter J. Haidar
James N. Juliana
Terrance G. Leonhardy
John Lyon
Henry M. Maggenti
Mrs. Ernest N. May
Mark McCullough
Paula E. McKinley
William J. McManus
Joanne K. Meredith
Gloria Miller
Elizabeth Moody
Nancy Nebeker
Suzy H. North
Mrs. Christopher G. Overton
Fred Radewagen

Delia T. Reddington
Lawrence J. Schoeps
Margaret Schweivert
Donald B. Stegner
James E. Stiner
Adam Stofpen
Cdr. Sperry C. Storm
Paul A. Theis
Robert I. Tuttle
Joseph P. Vaghi, III
Jacqueline A. Wakeling
Dr. Elaine Walter
Rita Walters
Mrs. Lee Wheelwright
James E. White
Mort Wilson

DISTINGUISHED LADIES RECEPTION
Vice Chairpersons:
Mrs. Guadalupe Hinckle
Mrs. Erlenne Perkins
Honorary Chairpersons:
Mrs. Gerald R. Ford
Mrs. Richard M. Nixon
Mrs. Lyndon B. Johnson
Mrs. Harry S. Truman
Co-Chairpersons:
Mrs. Howard H. Baker, Jr.
Mrs. Alfred Bloomingdale
Mrs. Warren E. Burger
Mrs. Robert C. Byrd
Mrs. Robert Michel
Mrs. Thomas P. O'Neill, Jr.
Director:
Ms. Kathryn Joseph
Linda L. Bartlett
Peggy Battle
Marie Denmark
Gail M. Donovan
Jacqulyn Endres
Charles Fagan
Charles L. Hildebrand
Janet B. Huber
James F. Hunter
Barbara Julian
Renee Robinson
Joyce Thomas

OPENING CEREMONIES
Vice Chairmen:
Mr. Thomas Walker
Mr. William L. Critchfield
Mr. Richard S. Andrews, Jr.
Honorary Chairmen:
Mr. Terry Jeffers
Mr. Howard Ruff
Director:
Mr. Ben Cotten

INAUGURAL DAY SKY SALUTE
Vice Chairman:
Mr. John Reagan "Tex" McCrary
Director:
Mr. Damian DuFour
Sandra Alley
Richard N. Bain
George Berclacy
Neil Blair
Skye Brainard
Bunny Brown
Jacilyn Brown
Roberta J. Browne
Wm. S. Canty
Cathy Chamberlain
W. Dewey Clower
Don Cohen
Monika K. Cranston
Dan Donahue
John Evans
Cliffeton Green
Lisa Harbach
Nina W. Henson
Capt. Robert Hines
Lt. Col. Larry E. Hofman
Harry T. Hubbard
Leo Hurst
Elizabeth Kahey
Mike Karen
Elizabeth Keahey

Charles B. Kemp
Robert E. Langston
Tammy Lanham
Paul Miller
Robert Miller
Ronald Miziker
Pat Nakasian
Yvonne Quirin
Peter Reiniger
Margaret Rogers
William Ruback
Jim Rubin
William Saylor
Col. Robert Schellenberger
Jerry Schiappa
Martin L. Struble
Peter W. Struble
Lt. Gary E. Treon
James Turner
Charles Weeks
Thomas M. Williams
John H. Witheridge, Jr.
Lucille Zlotek

CIVIC PARTICIPATION
Vice Chairman:
Michael Doud Gill
Co-Chairpersons:
Patricia Bruns
Director:
James Golden

CIVIC PARTICIPATION
Elizabeth J. Abbott
Francis G. Addison, III
Norman E. Adok
Andrew W. Allen
Andrew W. Allen, Jr.
Lois D. Allen
Lorenzo Allen
Patricia Alsabrook
Charles Alvarez
John W. Amatucci
The American Gas Association
Norbert Amsellem
Barbara Anderson
James Anderson
William Anton
Domenic Antonelli
Thomas W. Arata
Robert J. Armstrong
M. L. Au
James Bacon
J. Rafael Baltazar-Campos
Michael Baly, III
Robert L. Balzer
Charles R. Barker, Jr.
Arnold Barnett
Mrs. Arnold Barnett
T. D. Barre
James P. Barry
William M. Bartlett
Richard C. Beans
Norman Beebe
Robert A. Beer
David Bell
N. Bernstein Mgt. Inc.
Norman Bernstein
Stuart A. Bernstein
John Berry
Francisco D. Betancourt
Evelyn D. Bethel
Adrienne L. Biddle
Avis Birely
William C. Birely
Robert W. Black
Dr. David C. Blee
Dr. Nelson Blemley
Mrs. Nelson Blemley
Tim Bobbitt
Clyde Boden
Frederick J. Borrell
Michael Bost
Donald Bostwick

Anthony P. Bovello
Fred Bowis
Edward Bresler
H. William Brigfield, III
James B. Brockett
Anthony B. Brown
Barbara Brown
Larry Brown
Mrs. William Bruns
David Bruzga
John W. Bulloch, Jr.
Dr. Albert Bullock
Katja Bullock
Helen L. Burkett, DTM
Gale E. Busch
Mitchell L. Bush, Jr.
Ron T. Butler
Camera Graphics
Meade Camp
Angelo Campitelli
Louis P. Cannon
Lucy Carstate
Robert H. Carter, III
Anna Chennault
Donald G. Cherry
Joyce Chetty
V. S. Choslowsky
CIBI-Geigy Corporation
Ronald F. Cicioni
Warren Cikins
Ernest Clifton
E. H. Close
John S. Cockrell
Gwen Cody
Composition Systems, Inc.
Dorothy Condon
Robert Condon
James W. Cooke, Jr.
William Cooper
Barry Cooperstein
Carol Ann Coryell
Val Choslowsky
Anthony Cost
Doug Couto
Dewey Clower
Jeffrey B. Craven
Beverly Crawford
Steve Cubin
Maurice J. Cullinane
Rose Curamena
Curtis Chevrolet
Garry R. Curtis
Richard J. Daschbach
Thomas David
Edwin Davis
Mrs. Edwin Davis
F. Elwood Davis
Courtland W. Dawson
Joel Dawson
Joan De Cain
Donald De Franceally
Mrs. Donald De Franceally
Gaston DeBearn
Vincent F. DeCain
Harry DeFalco
George W. DeFranceaux
Thomas Dennison
Dr. Linton Deck
Jan Delsasso
Lois DeVecchio
Joseph DiBella
Vicky Dickinson
Joseph Dobal
Leonard B. Doggett
Robin A. DonRussello
Joseph L. Donnelly
Margaret Doubleday
Peggy P. Drane
Gus Duda
Walter Dunne
Wyatt Durrette
Curtis Dworken
William Eacho, Jr.
Barbara Ecabert

Charlotte Edmonds
William Ekeland
Michael Ellis
Shirley W. Evans
Mary Ann Ewers
Robert Ewers
Nancy Falck
C. Douglas Farmer
Mr. Featherstone
Thomas Fess
Mrs. Thomas Fess
Vladimir Fleischer
Robert H. Fogarty
Frank Gumpert Printing
Richard E. Frederick
Thurston Friend
Victoria Fulford
Marge D. Gannett
Robert M. Gardiner
Patrick J. Gartland
Roselie M. Genduso
John Gill
Van Gilmer
Carol Gilmore
Persia Golden
Sam Goldsmith, Jr.
Thomas Goode
Paul Gordon
Deborah L. Graham
John Graves
Robert Gray
Joan Gregoryk
Tim Grim
Lowell A. Grimaud
Gladys A. Gross
Grove, Jaskiewicz, Gilliam & Colbert
Harold H. Hall
Robert Hammerman
J. J. Hanley
James R. Hanson
James R. Hardy
Everett L. Harper
Lucille Harrington
Agaby Hayes
Webb C. Hayes, IV
Gloria Heckert
John D. Heckert
Edward J. Hefferman
Lawrence H. Henson
Edward W. Herbert
Lloyd Herman
Jack Herrity
John F. Herrity
Anne Heuer
Scott Heuer
Larry Higan, Jr.
Anne B. Hirschel
George E. Hnarakis
Gary Hoffman
Ruth Holland
William Holt
Thomas Hord
Herbert Hornberger
John B. Howerton
Jeffery L. Huffman
Richard E. Huhn
Charles R. Humber
Maryann Innis
Donald J. Jablonski
Andrew Jank
Angela Jannen
Barbara J. Jaskiewicz
Leonard Jaskiewicz
Rita Johns
Edward Johnson
Howard Johnson
Madeline Johnson
H. Daniel Jones
Mary K. Jones
Vernon Jones
Ann Kahn
Joyce A. Kaiser
Carlton Kammerer
Herman Kasper
Richard Kassatly
Hal A. Kauffman

Karen Keener
Roy B. Kelby
Bishop Samuel Kelsey
Patricia Kennedy
Lonnie Kishpaugh
Neal Knox
Leonard Kolodny
Norris J. Krone, Jr.
Mrs. Norris J. Krone, Jr.
Richard Kronheim
Theodore Kruczkowski
Rona F. La Prade
Daniel C. Lamke
Judith L. Lamke
Alexander C. Landsburg
William J. Lang
Isabel Lauka
Janis M. Lawrence
John W. Lawther
Mrs. John W. Lawther
Lorren D. Leadman
Dr. Allan J. Levey
Jose Linan
Robert Linowes
Richard L. Lobb
Marshall E. Lohr
Loral Company
Richard T. Loomis
James Low
Philip Lustine
Judith A. MacDonald
Robert MacDouglas
W. Gregor Mac Farlan
Timothy Malone
William Mann
Mrs. J. Willard Marriott
Phyllis B. Marriott
Patricia M. Marsh
Winston W. Marsh, Jr.
C. William Martin
Lawrence Martin
Maryland Cup Company
Mrs. Bobbie Mastrota
Mrs. Frances C. Mayle
Jerome Mazzuchi
William D. McAllister
George R. McBurl
Betty McCann
Catherine McCarron
Pierce McDonnell
Clarence McKee
Jean McKee
Richard S. McKernan
Thomas P. McLachlen
Edward McMillan
William McVicker
Frank Medico
Joseph Mendinghall
Dan Miller
Donna Miller
Marc Miller
Bobby Mitchell
Chris Mitchell
Joanie Mondscheim
Monsanto Company
Fredi Moody
Jerry Moore
Mark E. Moran
Laurie Moreci
Constance Morella
Patrick Mullins
Anthony S. Murray
Tony Murray
National Association of Newsletter Services, Inc.
Yvonne Nissen
F. Lee Noel
Mike Nolan
Michael E. Norris
Carol Northrup
Edward Nottage
Hugh O'Brian
Elkins Oliphant, II
Florence Ourisman
Brig Owens
Charles A. Peacock
Bob Peck Chevrolet
Robert Peck
Fred Pemberton
Patricia Perrcault
Mrs. George Petsche
Edwin L. Phelps

William Phenix
Martin Piecuch
Marshall Pittman
Jayne H. Plank
Anne Plaster
John Ponchock
Geri Porter
Potomac Electric Power Company
Martin W. Pracht
Larry Pratt
Marta G. Pregent
Jerry Pritchett
Richard A. Pulsiter
Walter Purdy
Robert Pyle
Richard T. Ragsdale, Jr.
Paul Ramey
Gwen G. Reiss
Daniel L. Rhoades
John W. Rhoads
C. I. Rice
Frank Rich
Charles T. Riel, Jr.
Joseph Rinaldi
J. Robert Ritenour
Ronald Robinson
Joseph A. Roche
Rockmont Chevrolet
Eugene Roesser
Mrs. Eugene Roesser
Diane Rolfe
Maureen Roloff
Robert M. Rosenthal
Rough Creek Oil, International
John Ruan
Joseph Ryan
Arthur A. Sabin
Sharon A. Sansone
Dale R. Schallhern
Dee Schmidt
Charee Schulman
Bernard Schwartz
Robin Ann Scussel
Donald Senick
Joanna Shaker
William Shaker
Lloyd Shand
Leslee P. Sherrill
Kathleen Shetler
Kathleen A. Shetler
Robert Shoemaker
Robert J. Smalls
Terry Smeltzer
E. Del Smith
Folecetas Smith
Herman Smith
Francis Snodgrass
Nelson Snyder
Jimmy Sotiropoulos
David H. Soule
Jonathan A. Soule
John Spies
Sport Chevrolet
Doris Stokes
Lisa Stollenberg
Stuart Stone
Harry Straus, Jr.
William Struck
Kay Sugahara
Thomas J. Tague
James C. Teague, Jr.
Charles J. Terio
The Marriott Corporation
The Tobacco Institute
Joan M. Thomas
Bradley Thompson
W. Reid Thompson
Salvatore Todaro
The Tommy Bryant Orchestra

Marie Travesky
John Tresvant
Laura W. Triest
Hugh F. Triggs
Moltugh Triggs
Gail Tseckares
Socrates Tseckares
Archilled Tuchtan
John R. Tydings
Sharon Urahatis
Leo Urbanske
Carmen Vas Quez
Martha Verrill
Eloy R. Villa
George Vogel
James Von Fleckenstein-Curie
Sandy Wallin
Ronald Walls
Barbara R. Walsh
Ed Walterbeek
James A. Wampler
Kung-Lee Wang
Chuck Warslay
Mary K. Weaver
Robert J. Webster
Ailcey Werber
William W. Werber
John West
Lorrine West
Martin R. West, Jr.
Jo Wiese
Cindy Wilkins
Frank Williams
Herbert M. Williams
Wilbert L. Williams
Paul Winick
Philip B. Wisman, Sr.
Ruth S. Wong
G. B. Wright
Levi Wright
Jean Yacovone
William J. Yanuzzi
Mrs. Thomas Ziebarth
Zuckert, Scoutt & Rasenberger

TASTE OF AMERICA
Julian Abio
John W. Amatucci
D. Paul Anthanas
William C. Anton
Jim Armstrong
Anthony Athanas, Jr.
Anthony Athanas
Michael R. Athlas
Ted Balestreri
Leah Barnett
Kelly Batie
Jim Beck
Amelia Bellows
Mitchell Benedict
George Berkowitz
Mark Berkowitz
Richard Berkowitz
Roger Berkowitz
John Berry
Frank G. Blandi
James Blandi
Walter Bodenweiser
Max Braverman
Rhonda Brittingham
Christine Britton
Stan Bromley
James Brooker
Stephen Brown
Raimond Buch
Jan Burmeister
Susanne Campbell
Valedia M. Casey
Leopoldo Chaidez
Margaret Chandler
Stephan Channer
Earl Chatterton
Michael P. Cliff
Linda Clugston
Harry Cohen
Lewis Cohen
Kathleen Comisar

Michael E. Comisar
Michael J. Comisar
Nathan Comisar
Craig Commons
Mimi Connelly
Cheryl Conners
Peter L. Cooper
Everett Cornilieus
Nicholas Coumanis
Barry Cox
Gino Croce
Susanna Crothers
Norma Cumby
Bert Cutino
Jan Delsasso
Carol E. DeLucca
Gregory J. DeLucca
Michael DeSando
Joseph Dennehy
Russell E. Dickenson
Zelande Douglas
Michael Doyle
Ron Dunham
Timothy Durney
Dennis Edelstein
Georgia Ellard
Delbert Ennis
Liz Erickson
Anne Essency
Jimmy Evans
Manuel Fernandez
Bruce Ferris
Donna Fiedler
Elliott A. Fine
Brooks Firestone
Catherine Firestone
Manus J. Fish
William Fontes
Russel Force
Paul Fox
Mark Fraker
Glen Frank
Nathaniel Frison
Robert Furek
Suzanne Furst
Giovanni Gabriele
Rosario Gabriele
Vincenzo Gabriele
Thomas Gaskin
David Gatta
Robert Giamo
Robert Giannetti
James Gibbons
Harry Ginden
Steve Ginsberg
John Giumarra
Larry Glatt
Nancy Goldberg
Judy Gollan
John L. Gomez
Mrs. Luz Gomez
Rudy Gonzales
Neale Goodman
Fran Gordenker
Jeffrey Gordon
Roland Gotti
Victor Gotti
Carl Green
Karl V. Green
Gisela Griffits
Michael Grisanti
Jay K. Gronlund
George Haidon
Oliver Hailey
Diane Hanke
John Harrison
Jeff Harshman
Gary Havrilla
Gary Heflin
John Henning
Parker T. Hill
Janet Hoffman
Ernst R. Hueter
Bruce Hunter
Gerry Jackson
Charles Jenz
Rita Johns
Gary Johnson
Harvey Kafsof
Howard Kauffman
Herbert Kaufman

179

Robert Kaye
James Keough
Ray Kern
John Kerry
David Key
Jean Kieffer
Karl Kilburg
Legh F. Knowles, Jr.
Gunilla Knutson
Ted Koumas
James Kring
Yves Labbe
Jean Lafont
Ranjeeb Lal
Joan Lancy
Ed Langus
G. Thomas Larkin
Isabelle Laucka
Gerard Le Grand
Steve Lee
Jack Leffaire
Theodore Leininger
Phillip J. Lenhoff
Gigi Leon
Jean Leon
Mai T. Leung
Charles Limoggio
Dennis Lindinger
Ed Lowe
Stanley Luckman
Marcia Maher
Bernard Malfait
Mike Malin
Alvin I. Malnik
Frank Mariella
Lawrence E. Marsolais
Giovani Martine
Carolyn A. Martini
Louis P. Martini
Mary K. Mathis
Jerome Mazzuchi
James McBride
John P. McClelland
Richard McClure
James McDaniel
Don McNeal
Thomas C. Michael
Jeff Miller
Michael O. Minning
Steve Mirassou
Marcie Mondavi
Robert Mondavi
Raymond M. Moran
Carol Morgan
J. Carole Morgan
C. A. Muer
Benjamin Munoz
C. W. Murchison
Rebecca Murphy
Joe Najjar
Merry Nelson
Amnuay Nethongkome
Yvonne Nissen
Edward Nottage
Beverly Nunez
Emilio Nunez
Helene L. O'Brien
Helen Obman
George Olto
Wallace E. Opdyke
Doug Pacheco
George C. Panayiotou
Nicholas C. Pannayiotou
Leon Pappas
Dennis Pasquini
Joe Patti
Joseph Pearcevault
Jack Peeples
Peter Pepdjonovic
Robert E. Petersen
H. Leon Pettway
Erwin Pfeil
Leonce Picot
Gary Pieruccioni
Perdimando Pietroni
Christian Planchon
Hon Jayne Plank
Marina Polvay
Molly Poynter

Valerie S. Presten
Bernadino Ramos
Nikolos Ramus
Chuck Rashwitz
June Reckert
William Reckert
John Rey
John Richmond
Brian Rielly
Juan C. Riveiro
Jacky Robert
May Roberts
Ronald Robinson
Natalie Ross
Oscar Royster
Dietmoir Salat
Fred Sargent
Kane Scheidt
Molly Schofield
H. M. Schramm, Jr.
Madeleine Schrichte
Horst Schulze
Bruce Schwartz
Robin A. Scussel
Don Sebastiani
Samuel J. Sebastiani
Dominic Serratore
Marv Shadman
H. M. Shumaker
Paul Simons
Ken Sipos
David Smith
J. C. Smith
Don Soffer
James Spak
Roland Speisser
Kathy Spielberg
Bob Staar
Arnold Stark
Noel Stein
Margaret Stern
Joni Stevens
Lisa G. Stoltenberg
Mrs. Harry Strauss, Jr.
Rodney D. Strong
Rosalie Sulfsted
James P. Sullivan
Patricia Sullivan
Joseph Swarthout
George Swerda
Sonya Swigert
Albert Taxin
Glenn Thomas
Remy Thomas
Erzsebet Thuleweit
Rainer Thuleweit
Harriett Toney
Tommy Toy
Eugenie Trone
Christine Vaccaro
Philip Vaccaro
Carlos Vasques
Martha Verrill
Don Victor
Jose Vilches
Gerard Vollieu
Hicks B. Waldron
Jimmy Weichman
John R. Weichman
Jan Wells
Eric Wente
Philip Wente
Marcy Whitman
Gerhart Wind
Wolfgang Winkler
Franklin Y. Yang
Jimmy Yeong
Larry Zambo
Jerry Zawideh
Ramsey Zawideh
Franz Znidar

PUBLIC SAFETY AND REVIEWING STANDS
Vice Chairman:
Mr. James H. Baker
Public Safety Committee Chairman:
Mr. Robert M. Moliter
Medical Committee Chairman:
Dr. William H. Cooper
Vice Chairman:
Dr. Mark A. Immergut
Robert W. Abel
Dr. John Albrigo
Walter Alfaro
Ann Almquist
Timothy Almquist
Capt. William Anastos
Terrance Baker
Phillip Ballagh
Craig Ballinger
David Baron
Laurie Bayer
William D. Beebe
Mary J. Berkeley
Barbara Blackshear
Veronica Blasic
Michael Bordner
Dr. Lawrence Bowles
Ann M. Briggs
Jacqueline R. Browne
Theresa Brzenski
Robert Burgess
Frank Buxton
Gregory Carey
Dr. Maurice J. Casey
Dr. William Chin-Lee
James Chinn
Joseph Chonock
Hugh A. Clarke
Dr. James Cobey
Larry Collier
Dr. Richard Conant
Deputy Chief Conner
Keith Conover
Arthur S. Cooper
Thelma Cooper
Kathy Cox
Robin Cuddy
Dr. Thomas Cullen
Gordon Dasher, Jr.
Alton Davis
Edgar Davis, III
John DeNobile
Elgin L. Deering
Kenneth Derrenbacker
Vincent Desiderio
Patricia Dieman
Robert Doherty
Michael Donahue
M. Phyllis Doriot
Bernice Duvall
Shirley Edwards
Maureen Elliott
Benjamin Endicott
Dr. Charles Epps
Dr. Roselyn P. Epps
Dr. Victor Esch
Scott Evenson
Jon Fiedler
Richard Folan
Mary A. Foster
Dr. Randolph A. Frank
Burton L. French
Isaac Fulwood
Anita Gauck
Katherine Gee
Flavia Giampietro
Marvin Gibson
Scott Gorton
Robert F. Graulich
Charleen Griemsman
Lt. William Grimes
Janice Haggerty
Douglas Hall
William S. Hamilton
Glenn Haney
John Harvey
Terrance Hassler
Ben Havilland
Kenneth Hawkins
Steven Heinowitz

Dr. Frederick B. Hendricks
Walter Herbert, Jr.
Howard Hersh
Iankford Hicks
Carl Hildebrand
Phyllis Hipshman
Edward Howard
Patrice Howell
Wayne Hummer
Bessi Hurtt
Dr. Gilbert E. Hurwitz
Karen Jackson
Charles Jacobi
Katherine L. James
Dorothy Janifer
Burtell Jefferson
Dr. Karl Jonas
Jel Kahn
Edward Kantor
Lois Kercher
John Kirby
Don Kirkwood
Elsie Kress
Frances Krizan
Dr. James Kunec
Harry Lancaster
John Lawrence
Deborah Leed
Rae Leetch
Dr. Joseph D. Lineham
Dr. Leon M. Liverett
Janet Lloyd
Barbara LoGrasso
Beatrice Lowery
David Ludeker
Glenn Luedtke
John A. Lundin
Earl Martin
Melinda M. Maury
Pleasant H. McBride, Jr.
Tim McBride
Teresa McCloskey
Tiny B. Medlock
Roger D. Middlekauff
Gerald Miller
Judith Miller
Vernon Mills
Dr. George H. Mitchell
Robert M. Moliter
Mary Moloney
Barbara Moyer
Cheryl Myers
Phillip Myers
Donald Nalls
Lena Napolitano
Kevin O'Connor
Sean O'Connor
Carolyn O'Hara
Elayne O'Loughlin
Patricia O'Malley
Conrad Pappas
Dr. Walter R. Perkins, Jr.
Lois Pilch
Gail Pittore
Mary Porter
Thomas Purcell
Capt. Joseph Quander
Thomas J. Reagan, Jr.
Joel Reich
Bill Reynolds
Norman Richardson
Kenneth J. Ritchey
Cynthia Robert
Cesar Rudzki
James Russell
Mary Sainsbury
Lucille Savage
Robert H. Scheerschmidt
David Schlegel
Evelyn Shears
Charles E. Sheetz
Edward Sherburne
Dr. Howard Silby
Eric Silfen
William Q. Sinnott
H. Wade Skiles

Dr. Susan Stanton
James Stillwell
Douglas Stutz
James Sumner
Roy C. Swab
David Swomley
Leoncia Tacungo
Robert Tallet
Peggy Taylor
Francis Teevan
Gail Tomlinson
Alfred Toone
Dr. James Trone
Jane Turner
Joshua Vayer
William Walker
Dr. Russell Wall
L. Lodge Weber
Dr. Jeffrey A. Weisberg
Barbara Whitaker
Sheila C. White
Christopher Wishard
Linda Wood
Nina Yarlovsky

INAUGURAL GALA COMMITTEE
Vice Chairman:
Mr. Raymond Caldiero
Honorary Co-Chairmen:
Mr. and Mrs. Michael Keith Deaver
Producer and Director:
Frank Sinatra
Chairman of Event:
Raymond Caldiero
Vice Chairman—Facilities:
Abe Pollin
Vice Chairman—Operations:
Juliette McLennan
Vice-Chairman—Transportation:
Robert Bannon
George Adams
F. James Ahlberg
Robert Aideinget
Elsie Anderson
Kathryne Barrett
Andy Berger
Melinda Bertram
Joseph H. Boyd, Jr.
Marilyn Bradley
James Brennan
John Campbell
Ron Clements
Nancy Coleman
Constance Conner
Brenda Cooley
Don Costa
Edward Cowling
Alice B. Cumberland
Frank d'Agostino
Art Dalton
Susan DeMarr
Jerry Donnellan
Ai Dotoli
Col. Robert J. Dunn
Chris Edwards
Gary Englestad
Vincent Falcone, Jr.
Robert Firth
Arthur C. Forster, Jr.
Joseph J. Gancie
James L. Hamilton III
Tanz Harris
Joe Hobson
Robert Hoff
Rochelle Holbrook
Veronica Jenkins
Gene Johnson
Madeline Johnson
Dan Jones

Paul Judge
Russ Kabeiseman
Robert Kiernan
Schlea E. Kolb
Hugh Lambert
Carl Larsen
Richard L. Lesher
Morgan Mason
Robert Marx
Ted McConnell
Deborah McFadden
Shelley McWhirther
Arnita Mongiovi
Robert Nelson
Terence O'Connor
Peter O'Reilly
Rene Poole
Noel Qualters
Amatha Radewagen
Fred Radewagen
Ray Rhinehart
David Rigby
Willard Robinson
Jim Rubin
John B. Shlaes
Walter R. Smalling
Talbott C. Smith
Barbara Soloman
Solters, Roskin, & Friedman, Inc.
David Stasko
Richard J. Steinee
Jorjett Strumme
Betty Swelt
Bob Targert
Mary Tarkington
Paul B. Twomey
Dorothy Uhlemann
Charles R. Van Horn
David Vandergriff
Burge Watkins
Margaret Whitehead
Roger Whyte
Joe Wisnewski
Joan Wolfe
Philip Yansinski
Larry Zack
Terry Zack

GALA TELEVISION COMMITTEE
Justin Dart
William FitzGerald
James W. Fuller
Virginia Milner
David A. "Sonny" Werblin

LICENSE PLATES
Vice Chairpersons:
Mr. Milton Mitler
Mrs. Peggy Meek Venable
Wandell Allegood
Bob Bander
Walter F. Barton
Bernard Beall
Robin J. Bell
Sanford F. Blau
Donald Bonin
Alan Botto
Richard Bremcamp
Thomas Bresnahan
Carl C. Briggs
Thomas Bundy
Wendell J. Chesser
Maureen Clark
Paul Courson
Pat Crowley
Bill Curley
Walter C. Davis
Noel Dawson
Robert J. Endres
Linda J. Flanagan
Charla Franklin
Roy F. Gaines
Paul J. Gerdon
Ann Gethner
Patricia Ginty
Lloyd Gordon
Mike Griffis
G. W. Hall

Martha Hamrick
Patricia A. Hansen
Marsha Helfand
Bob Hensler
Paul J. Herdon
Uel Hester, Jr.
Ken Hollingsworth
Jan R. Horne
Robert L. Hunnicutt
Madeleine E. Hunter
Pam Hunter
Warren E. Ihlenfeld
Danny Jacobson
Lemuel G. Johnson, Sr.
Richard Johnson
Colon Johnston
Elizabeth Jones
Doris E. Judd
Mal Kahn
J. Raymond Keany
Ann M. Keating
Sara Kimmel
Alfred A. King
William G. King
William H. Kirby
Matilda S. Kukulka
Richard E. Largill
Darrel W. Lownsberry
R. Lumenello
Rosetta M. Maggelet
Bob Martin
Bruce Matthews
George McGovern
Stanley W. McKievnan
Gerald L. Meyer
Steven L. Meyer
Lillian Mitler
Clara B. Moore
Maria S. Moore
Tim Moran
Adeeb J. Neam
Mary Ellen Nelson
Heath Newman
William Noel
Evan Nunn
Jacqueline M. O'Keefe
Don Parker
Bill Patten
Joyce Pavlitt
Kenneth Peach
Ana Maria Perez
K. Michael Plunkett
Charles A. Poole
Donald W. Poucher
Virginia Pride
Ray Reich
Charles Richardson
Leon Rippa
Charles L. Ross, Jr.
Bill Rowles
Chades L. Russ, Jr.
James K. Russell
Edward J. Sabatine
Richard Sanders
William S. Sawyer
Claudia A. Schaffner
Paul Selph
Sheila Shepard
Vincent Sikora
Angelina K. Smith
Charles Smith
Julia A. Smith
Stephen A. Smith
Bette Snider
A. Peter St. James
Cathy Stemple
Stanley W. Stephenson
David H. Stone
Sheldon Summerlin
Gayle Swofford
M. C. Tackley
Jeff Thompson
Melanie Thompson
Donnie Turner

William C. Van Arndel, III
Robert G. Walker
Bill C. Walls
Don Webb
John D. Wilson
Thomas Winter
Blanc T. Woody
Beth Yohe
Jeff Zufelt

SPECIAL GROUPS
Vice Chairman:
Mr. Bob Williams
Director:
Mr. John K. Wu
Martha L. Fraas
Alexander G. Gabriels
Donna Goodloe
Gloria Wilkinson

BLACKS
Director:
Angela Wright
Phyllis Berry-Myers
Mary Boone
Zelda Davis
Thelma Duggin
Frankie Scott
Eddie Smith
Dorothy Suber

HISPANICS
Co-Chairman:
Juan Woodroffe
Director:
Cathi Villalpando
Rene Ansalmo
Alex Armendaris
Ed Avila
Carlos Balido
Rick Bella
Carlos Benitez
Bernadette Brusco
Eduardo Caballero
Ricardo Capote
Al Cardenas
Charles W. Delgado
Pete Diaz, Jr.
H. Frank Dominguez
Percy Duran
Juan Guiterrez
Miguel A. Machiavello
Manuel R. Madrigal
Reynaldo P. Maduro
General Arturo D. Moreno
Philip Morris
Deborah E. Myers
David Ochoa
Isaac Olivares
Humberto Quinones
Republican Nat'l Hispanic Assembly
Dr. Ray Santos
Luis P. Terrazas
Gil Vasquez
Danny Villanueva
Henry Zuniga

NATIONALITIES
Director:
Steve Postupack
Ukrainian Women's League
American Turkish Society
Dan Andirch
Dee Ayers
Beth Bailey
Ildiko Berger
Alois Bruckbauer
Betty Bryant
Willard Burton
Tai Chi
Marie Cooley
Karl Edler
Edler Family
Martha Fraas
Cathy Freitag
Alfred Funk
Zandy Gabriels
Maria Gomez
Maria Gonzalez
Hargreaves Family

Hellenic Dancers of New Jersey
Betty Heyman
Hibben Family
Hal Hines
Hip Sing Association
Heinrich Hoffman
Dave Hoover
Ron Ikejiri
Japanese American Citizens League
Kalvelis Dancers of Baltimore, Md.
Richard Keesecker
Esther Kish
Richard Knutson
George Kontzias
Korean Folk Dancers
Lin Kung
Mike Leggett
Alice Letzler
Tony Lin
Willy Lin
Lin Kung Fu
Los Quetzales de Washington, D.C.
Mahina Polynesian Dancers
Alfred Moe
Jimmy Moose
Elvira Morgan
Loren Myers
Narod Balkan Dancers
Dr. Mima Nedelcovych
Northern Virginia Folk Festival
Norwegian Church Service
Norwegian Society
Richard Oakland
Harry Oh
Old Budapest Restaurant
Original Bavarian Dance Group
Christopher Pei
Electra Perros
Regina Petrutis
Mollie Poelsterl
Father Demitri Recachinas
Jhoon Rhee
Dave Rosenberg
Karl J. Rosenberg
Nancy Rosenberg
Schuhplattler und G.T.V.
Walter Sherron
Sons of Norway
St. Luke's Cr. of Serbian Sisters
Roma Starczewska
Sam Stulberg
Sara Stulberg
John Taba
Tai Kwon Do Group
Martha Terlicky
The Italian Cultural Society
Holly Trimble
Diana Tyler
Don Urner
Priscillia Urner
Harry Ways
Jim Weatherly
Mary B. Williams
Tom Williams
Nathan Wilson
David Zahirpour
Socrates Zolotas

RELIGIOUS
Director:
Robert J. Billings
Col. John T. Andrews
Lillian W. Andrews
Dr. Ben Armstrong
David Z. Ben-Ami
Qarm Braunstein
Gabriel Duffy

Philip D. Egert
Father Jerome Fasano
Dr. R. Herbert Fitzpatrick
Ernest R. Gibson
Dr. Samuel Goodloc Hines
Dr. William C. Howland, Jr.
Addah J. Hurst
Steve Kovach
Herzel Kranz
Sam McCullough
Nelson Meringola
William L. Miller
Forest D. Montgomery
Robert Pittenger
Jerry Regier
Phil Sheldon
Cleveland B. Sparrow, Sr.
Mrs. Bradley Thompson
Mrs. W. A. White

SENIOR CITIZENS AND HANDICAPPED
Director:
Jean C. Bergaust
Larry Allison
Robert Ardinger
Janet Bailey
Kathryne K. Barrett
Phillip C. Barton
Linda Botts
J. D. Byrd
Linda Champion
Gale Conard
George A. Conn
Roy Craig
John Davis
John E. Davis
Carol Deninger
Mary Doremus
B. Richmond Dudley
Flo Eley
Timothy R. Flannigan
Rudy Gawlik
Claire Gibson
Michael Hartman
Kathy Houghton
Steven Hikens
Lila Holdridge
Sharon Johnson
Virginia Lewis
Clara MacIntyre
Jerry Mager
George Murphy
Janice Nishimura
Carol Pace
Harald A. Reitan
Joseph Rosenstein
William B. Shepherd
Richard E. Sheppard
Grace B. Smith
Ray Sparks
C. Fred Stout
Marilynne Tilson
Dr. Robert Wehrli
General Ellis Wilhoyt

STATE SOCIETIES
Director:
Elizabeth A. Gordon
Rita Giordan
Ralph Golden
Marne E. Gordan
Richard D. Gordan
Bill Hambley
Gerald Love
Col. David Montplaisir
David Moulton
Dr. Takashi Noda
Louise L. Parker
Louis Priebe
Keith Rogers
Luther W. Shaw
Fred York

VETERANS
Director:
Don Clarke
Lloyd L. Burke
W. Grant Chandler
James D. Doughtie, DSC
Norman M. Gonsauis
Charles R. Jackson
Robert F. McAuliffe
Delores M. Otterson
Donald Sheldon
Don Skinder
Brian Whalen
Rufus Wilson
Flora L. Wood

YOUNG VOTERS
Chairman:
Paul E. Cotton
Virginia P. Breed
L. Mark Carron
Susan Clyne
Christine Conley
Dorothy Conley
Katherine A. Conley
Matthew Conley
John A. Daley
John Dendulk, Jr.
Dorothy A. Fletcher
Beverly Gelino
Deborah A. Harris
Steve D. Hersch
Cheryl Hobbs
Arthur Kober
Lisa C. Moore
Audrey E. Smith
Jack C. Straub
Juanita K. Taylor
Valdean M. Watson
Dorothy Wieber

YOUNG VOTORS BALL
Laurie McDaniel,
Chairman
Leah Anders
Elayne Arteberry
Scott Cairns
Patrick Christmas
Jim Davis
Nancy Davis
Doug Doyle
Gordon Fry
Andy Gralla
John Gratta
David Greenfield
Jill Harrington
Thomas O. Herrick
Howard Hirsh
Martha Janoschka
Meredith Johnson
Linda Kaiver
Ann Kalis
Jane Lewis
William McMaster
Michael Moore
John Raliegh
Donna L. Ring
Patricia Scanlon
John Scheff
Mary Jo Shelton
Dan Sullivan
Susan Towson
Debbie Valasiabas
Edward Weber
Elizabeth White
Sharon Wilkes
Geoff Wollacott

INAUGURAL PARADE
Vice Chairman:
Mr. Terry Chambers
Raymond W. Ainsworth
American Morgan Horse Association
John L. Baker
Morris Bales
Frank Barnes
Sandee Beaver
Dr. Elvin Blackwell
Carmen Blake
Jean Bowling
Christine Broderick

Robert J. Buzinski
John Cain
James D. Calabrese
John Caldon
Tom Cameron
Albert Castronovo
Thomas Chapman
G. Don Chevalier
Francis W. Cox
Mrs. Charles Crabtree
Jean Curtright
Thomas DeCain
James Delaney
Ken Demers
Russell Dickerson
Annette Doherty
Wilbur T. Farley
James Fisher
Stephen Foerster
Evelyn A. Foley
Fort Hood First Cavalry Division
Mike Gano
Col. Edmund Gautreau
James German
Robert Gill
Isaac Greggs
Raney Hall
William Hart
Bill Haughton
Ernest Hebson
Michael Hess
Keith Hinds
Dr. Jay Julian
Patty Kent
Paul Kneeland
Dr. William Lavery
Dr. Alan Levey
William W. Lilley
Charles Loeber
Walt Lovell
John Mars
Maureen McInerny
Peter Mehas
Robert Michaleski
Dennis Miller
General Richard A. Miller
Pale Moon
Ronald C. Morgen
Barbara Moroch
Theodore E. Namey
Lt. Lewis Neilson, Jr.
New York City Police
Gregory C. Page
George Parks
Glen Richter
George H. Ripley
Dr. Charles H. Samson
Mr. Schauer
Marsha Shepard
Susan Sirianni
John Snow
Col. Michael C. Stigers
Commissioner H. O. Sudholz
Paul Tibiri
Don Treadway
Lou E. Tsipis
United States Equestrian Team, Inc.
Darwin E. Walker
Beth Wentz
Jim Wilhelm

BUSINESS, INDUSTRY, AND SPECIAL EVENTS
Vice Chairman:
Mr. Jack Gertz
Director:
Mr. David Boyce
Rita Abrams
Joseph Adams
Aebi Nursery, Inc.
Fred Allen
Harold Allen
Myles Ambrose
Anthony Anderson

Mrs. John W. Angus, III
Jules Armellini
Dr. Camilla Auger
Jim Baldwin
Frank S. Besson, III
Bill Suyeyase
Delmar Birgfeld
William Bolger
Mrs. William Bolger
Samuel Bonsack
Daniel A. Botkiss
Warren G. Botz
Al Bourland
David Boyce
Bob Boyena
Homer A. Boynton
Francis Briscoe
Sy Brockway
Charles L. Brown
James Brown
Brown Williamson Tobacco Corp.
Mrs. Edwin A. Buchanan
Lane E. Burnsed Ferney
Ralph E. Burnsed Ferney
Phillip Caldwell
Wess Cantrell
Gabriel Carlin
R. Webster Chamberlain
Margret Chandler
A. Martin Clark
Don Clarke
John Cook
John Cooke
Don Cornett
Pat Crosby
Dick Cuneo
Ralph P. Davidson
Cartha DeLoach
Mike DeMita
Georgia L. Delyannis
Joseph D. DiCesare
Lt. Col. Michael A Dickerson
William Dorgan
Jim Drummond
Dottie Dunham
Ruth A. Dwyier
Martin Dyer
Delbert H. Ennis
Enomoto, Inc.
E. J. Enzor
Clark Erickson
Conroy Erickson
John R. Ewers
Mary Ann Ewers
James B. Farley
Federal Maritime Commission
Doyal Finley
Frank E. Fitzsimmons
W. V. Ford
Robin French
Robert Frerstein
Ralph Frey
GTE Info Centre
Patrick Galloway
Joseph H. Gamble
John Garst
Jack A. Gertz
Richard Gillis
Victor Gorlingski
Gail Green
Frank Grisanti
David Groutt
Rudy Grua
Frank Gumpert, Jr.
Michael P. Hagel
Richard Hagstrom
James Harford
Cecelia Harman
Lucille Harrington
Frances B. Havens

Philip Hawley
John Hechinger
Frank Henderson
Richard Herdman
Edwin K. Hoffman
John Hogan, Jr.
Charles Holland
Phil Hollywood
Peter Hubley
Carroll H. Hynson, Jr.
Lee Iacocca
Alan Imhoff
Bernard Imming
Charles H. Irving
Reef Ivey
Mr. Johnson
Chester Johnson
Bonnie Jones
Don Jones
Hal S. Jones
William Jones
Jim Juliana
K. Nakashima Nursery Co.
Fed Karger
Gary Katz
Paul Kelly
Donald Kendall
Patricia Kennedy
Michael Kfoury
Peter B. King
Dick Kingman
Joseph T. Kingrey
Ketayama Brothers
Horace Kornegay
George Kroloff
Lewis J. Krulwich
George H. Lawrence
Nicholas P. Lewnes
Carl Longley
Marion P. Love
Mary Ann Lundgren
Peter Macdonald
Richard Maher
Vincent M. Mahoney
Melvin L. Mallonee
Richard Marcus
Hall Martin
Jeff Martin
Matsui Nursery, Inc.
Joseph Maye
Lee McBride
Archie McCardle
John McClellan
Wm. McCollam, Jr.
R. Michael McCullough
W. J. McCune, Jr.
James I. McDaniels
Dorothy McDaniels
William D. McDonald
Joseph M. McGarry
Robert McMillian
Laramie McNamara
Robert E. Mercer
Reuben F. Mettler
Keith W. Meurlin
Gerald B. Meyers
Patricia Miles
Marc Miller
Montgomery Co. Chamber of Commerce
Ernest G. Moore
Gordon Morrison
Donald Moss
Mount Eden Nursery
William P. Mullane, Jr.
Joseph L. Murgo
Ann Murtaugh
Wm. Myers
Jerry Naidus
Katherine Niles
Ninomiya Nursery Co.
Winifred Noonan
Joe Novallis
Jim O'Brien
Ohio Conference of Teamsters
Oku Brothers
Barbara Oldjey
Olivetti Corporation
Operations Research, Inc. (ORI)
Carol H. Ostrow

Pajaro Valley Greenhouses, Inc.
Dennis I. Paul
Tony Paul
Stewart Pederson
Joseph Pendergrass
Doug Perry
Mr. E. E. Phillips
Gary Pieruccioni
Victor A. Powell Ferney
Ed Pueschel
John Puhola
Robert N. Pyle
R. J. Reynolds Tobacco Company
John Rains
Mrs. James Rebel
Dr. Martha Redden
Richard A. Reilly
Bill Roberts
Mark Robertson
William F. Rooney
Morris Rotman
Jean Rouchard
Virginia Schaefer
Nicholas J. Schaus
Joanna Shaker
Diane Sharff
Ernie Sharff
Betsy M. Shirley
Joseph Sico
Gilbert Simonetti, Jr.
Randy Simpson
Arthur J. Smith
Rodger B. Smith
Ron Smith
Ted Smithers
Society of American Florists
James Steiner
Joanne Stellar
Richard Stevens
Adam D. Stolpen
Dave Struck
Steve Stubicks
Terry Taylor
John Theil
W. Reid Thompson
Thompson Rose Co., Inc.
Dory Tiepel
Kevin Tighe
Florence E. Townsend
George Tyler
U. S. Tobacco Company
Paul Vancoverton
John Vincent
William Walker
James Wanko
Peter K. Warren
Watsonville Roses, Inc.
Patti Watts
Greg Whiteman
Robin Whitney
Edward J. Williams
Lilas Wiltshire
A. J. Winograd
Roger Winter
Nancy Yde
John Zorack, Esq.
Cartha de Loach

LABOR
Honorary Chairmen:
The Honorable Raymond Donovan
Frank E. Fitzsimmons
Co-Chairmen:
Shannon Wall
Jackie Presser
Vice Chairman:
Paul Locigno

Advisory Council
The Honorable Michael P. Balzano, Jr.
Jesse M. Calhoon
Douglas Fraser

Thomas Gleason
Norman Goldstein
N. Victor Goodman, Esq.
Senator Orrin Hatch
Lane Kirkland
The Honorable Betty Southard Murphy
Robert E. Poli
Ray Schoessling
The Honorable William Usery

Committee
M. E. Anderson
Richard Arango
Carroll T. Armstrong
Howard Bennett
Kenneth T. Blaylock
Peter Bommarito
John Bowers
Clarence E. Briggs
Sherman Brown
Ed Brubeck
Charles Byrnes
Jesse L. Carr
Philip Caruso
Robert A. Cassidy
Sam Church, Jr.
John H. Cleveland
Richard Collinson
Theodore R. Cozza
George Daly
Richard Daly
Dan F. Darrow
John DeConcini
James Duffy
William Fogle
Marlin Ford
Angelo Fosco
Harold Gibbons
Wayne E. Glenn
Robert F. Goss
Rocco Greco
John Green
Fred Gualtiere
Charles E. Haddock
Richard Hammond
Elwood Hampton
Frank X. Hanley
James Herman
Jack Higgins
Robert Holmes
Philip W. Horne, Jr.
John Joseph
Perry Joseph
Robert Kavalec
Jim Kinney
Gairald F. Kiser
Mitchel Ledet
Harold Leu
Richard Lewicki
Don Liddle
Rene Lioeanjie
Robert J. Lowen
Louis Lucci
Ken MacKay
Nicholas Manchuso
Morel Marshall
Lloyd Martin
Thomas Martinez
Frank J. Matula, Jr.
George Matz
Lloyd McBride
William J. McCarthy
W. Howard McClennan
Vincent McDonnell, Esq.
James McKinley
Robert E. Meyers
George E. Mock
Joseph Morgan
Frederick O'Neal
Frank Palumbo
Louis Parise

James F. Paterson
William Paterson
Louis F. Peick
Bill Perry
William Peterson
Salvatore Provenzano
S. Frank Rafferty
Andrew Rich
Charles Ryan
Don Rodgers
Nicholas Sansotta
Ray Schoessling
Maurice R. Schurr
Albert Shanker
John Sheehan
Talmage E. Simpkins
W. C. Smith
Nicholas Stinpanovich
Sam T. Stintsman
Andy Suckart
John J. Sweeney
W. W. Teague
Joseph Trerotola
Luther Watson
Arnie Weinmeister
Roy L. Williams
Jerry Wurf
William H. Wynn
Staff:
Mayo Antonio
Denise Balzano
Barbara Barnes
Roberta Browne
Alice Burroughs
Jane Craskery
Shirley Foote
Joyce Gacek
Debra King
Betty Leslie
Paul Locigno
Faith Loudon
Mike MacCarthy
Debbie Machen
Jane Mackay
Anne McCarthy
Robbie Motter
Erhelyn Nelson
Peg Niemcyyk
Bessie J. O'Connor
Cynthia Partin
Dianne E. Polaski
Ernie Shinemans
Edie Stratton
Jo M. Torpy
Kathleen P. Vogt
Carla de Creny

HOSPITALITY
Vice Chairperson:
Mrs. Jane Roberts De Graff
Co-Chairpersons:
Mrs. Harold D. Fangboner
Mrs. Noel Love Gross
Honorary Vice Chairpersons:
Mr. & Mrs. Robert H. Dedman
Director:
Mrs. Doriene Steeves
Ron Agron
Will Armstrong
Grier Ballantine
Francene Barber
Ted Barnett
Ms. Bateman
Mr. Brophy
Robert Brouwer
Mr. Burroughs
Sally Byington
Ellen Cantor
Mrs. Joseph Cate, Jr.
Mrs. Chapman
Mr. Clautier
Paul Clement
Anne Cline
Mr. Coddington
Dixie Conlon
Mrs. Dennison Coursen
Mr. Daley
Dexter Davis
Pamela DeGraff
Munseer Dean

Mr. Drury
Henry Fernandez
Mr. Fonda
Judith W. Frank
Geoff Garside
Mike Gilbert
Ruby Griffin
Jessie Hamilton
Harrison Hartman
Wayne Hartman
Carroll Henson
B. Hernandez
Mrs. Scott Heuer
Ms. Hudson
Julie Jaroshenko
Ozzie Jenkins
Nell Johnson
Carl Kent
Mr. Kinney
Frederick Kleisner
Helmut Knipp
Mr. Kober
Betty Long
Charles Luria
Elizabeth MacKregan
Judy Maggrett
Michelle Manire
Ann Marshall
Tom Marshall
Julie McCahill
Lynn McNeil
Augustus Melton
Stefan Merdinian
Barbara K. Moak
Mr. Moreno
Ruth B. Morgan
Mr. Moscatelli
George Mosse
Rose Narva
Richard Nelson
Paul O'Neil, Jr.
John E. Ogden
Mrs. S. Parker Oliphant
Bob Paris
Gary Payne
Joy G. Phillips
Jack Pollock
General E. P. Quesada
Jane Ring
Mrs. C. Jackson Ritchie, Jr.
Anne M. Rowe
Berman Rowland
Mary Ruhl
Mary A. Rutt
Lloyd E. Sampler, III
Mr. Sigler
William Smith
Mr. Stark
Linda A. Sterlacci
Derek Toms
David Vellis
Edward B. Williams
Gerald Wolsborn
Zandra Zafren

OUTDOOR CONCERT
Vice Chairman:
Mr. Myles T. Ambrose
Director:
Miss Amy Hardy
Kevin Ambrose
George Berklacy
Ed Bomsey
Tom Buchanan
Sammy Cahn
J. Raymond Carroll, P.E.
Ronald Childs
Wallace Clark
Richard J. Clement
Raymond S. Cole, Jr.
Gil Costa
Doug Craig
Daniel Danaher
Tom Decker
William Ensign
Wilbur T. Farley
Tony Gannon
Amy J. Hardy

Harvey Hubbell, IV
Mary Imhoff
Alan A. King
William Lundigran
Fred Malek
Ron Martinson
Colonel Earl Mays
Ralph W. Mills
Bob Mollitor
Bill Moore
Dennis Morgan
Daniel A. Nichols
Brendan T. O'Leary
Werner G. Passarge
Chief Powell
Susan Powell
Ronald C. Rogers
David Rowan
Paul Rowan
Sue A. Sandusky
Don Sarles
Ralph Schobitz
Willard Scott
Bonnie Seefeldt
Patrick Tyson
Barbara R. Wheeler
Daniel R. Wilson
Wilbert R. Wilson
John Zimmerman

INAUGURAL CULTURAL EVENTS
Vice Chairpersons:
Hon. & Mrs. Ralph E. Becker
Director:
Miss Susan P. Harrington
William W. Becker
Dorothy L. Johnson
Michael J. Moore
Joe Reed

SMITHSONIAN CULTURAL EVENTS
Dorothy Bistodeau
Rita Bobowski
Sarah Carr
Jay Chambers
Marie Cummings
Larry Deemer
Ken Derr
Peter Erikson
Julian T. Euell
Deana Fleming
Gary Floyd
Glenn Geiger
Tom Harney
Christian Hohenlohe
John F. Jameson
James Kellock
Tim Kidwell
Jeffrey LaRiche
B. C. May
James R. Morris
Diana Parker
Ralph C. Rinzler
S. Dillon Ripley
Alvin Rosenfeld
Daphne Shuttlesworth
Linda L. St. Thomas
Leslie Stein
Barbara Strong
Lawrence E. Taylor
James Weaver
Tom Wells
Lilas Wiltshire

INAUGURAL MEDALS
Chairman:
Senator Mark O. Hatfield
Ralph E. Becker
Bowers & Ruddy Galleries, Inc.
Dr. Darrell C. Crain
Tom Decker
Karleen Durrenberger

Edward J. Fraughton
Dr. Melville B. Grosvenor
H. Joseph Levine
Neil MacNeil
Medallic Arts Company
Elvira Stefanelli
Towle Silversmiths

CO-CHAIRMEN'S RECEPTION
Vice Chairpersons
Mrs. Anne Witty Sonnabend
Jerry Rapp
Jacqueline Grimes
Mary E. Quint

AIR TRANSPORT COMMITTEE
Vice Chairperson:
Dominic P. Renda

HOUSING
Vice Chairman:
Mr. James P. Low
Co-Vice Chairmen:
Mr. Austin G. Kenny
Mr. John Vickerman
Director:
Mr. Phillip Hollywood
Deputy Director:
Ms. Kae Rairdin
Robert Brittle
Ginger Bryant
Ursala K. Giordano
Theodore Hagans
Leonard Hickman
Ada Hubbard
S. Coleen Krantz
H. D. Lewis
Carlile B. Marshall
Ruth B. Morgan
Gail Riesch
Frances Rowan
James Sakas
Kathy Steele
Doriene M. Steeves
Frank Wade
Jeannie Weber

VOLUNTEER AND DONOR RECOGNITION
Vice Chairman:
Mr. Simon C. Fireman
Joe Freedman

VOLUNTEERS
Vice Chairman:
Mr. Ben Cotter
Co-Chairpersons:
Mr. & Mrs. Charles Bresler
Director:
Mrs. Louise L. Bundy
Deputy Director:
Mr. Artman Mandakas
Stephen N. Abrams
Ethel M. Acker
Francis Acton
Grace A. Adams
Leslie Adams
Stuart R. Adams
Claire L. Agoglia
Emmett B. Ahearn
Mila Albertson
Laurel C. Albrech
Wallace L. Alexander
Edward K. Alexanian
Esther Alford
Jodi Allen
Lucille M. Allen
Priscilla M. Allen
Patricia F. Alsobrook
Ida B. Altizer
Homeru Alvarez Castillo
Marge E. Anderson
Warren N. Anderson
Sharon A. Andrade
Gary N. Andreas
John T. Andrews, Jr.
Lillian W. Andrews

Sue W. Andrews
Kathy L. Applegate
Barbara Armstrong
Mary E. Armstrong
Nannette E. Arnott
Ruthann Aron
Chris L. Aronson
Naomi Arroyo
Dee Artim
Doreen D. Arzoonianian
Scott Ash
Sassy Ashbrook
Mo Ashby
Janet L. Ashcroft
Nita Astin
Fernando Astrogo
Maria S. Atkins
Carolyn F. Atkinson
Jean T. Atkinson
Patricia V. Atkinson
Maxine H. Atwater
Patricia J. Austin
Frances L. Aymar
Kay Badbezanchi
Vicki L. Bailey
Dorothy C. Baker
Larry M. Baker
Joan B. Baldino
Ruth B. Baldwin
May B. Ball
Edward J. Banas
Euphenia P. Banas
Wanda J. Banks-Schrock
Bruce N. Bant
Edward S. Baran
Ann Barbar
Francene Barber
Barbara Bargan
Carrol R. Bargan
Barbara C. Barnes
Mozelle M. Barnes
M. Louise Barnett
Robert B. Barnett
Eileen C. Barraclough
Donna L. Barron
Florence A. Barrow
Nancy K. Barrow
Herbert J. Bass
Vickie Bass
Mary Batcher
Carol L. Bates
George P. Bates
Mary E. Bates
Kathryn A. Bauer
Janice L. Baylor
Wilma Beahm
Barbara Beatty
Catherine Beaver
Jane C. Beaver
Janis Bebris
Theodore Bedwell
Ann Beglin
Genevieve Behrens
Nada H. Belcher
Rita K. Belechak
Dean G. Belmont
Antonio Benede
Virginia C. Benson
Wilmer K. Benson
Susan L. Benzer
Florence L. Berg
William N. Berg
Mary Lee Berger
Adele M. Berklund
Ruth E. Berklund
Harvey Berlin
Loretta M. Bernier
Rosemary A. Besenyei
Sharon Lee Biache
Colonel Billea
Mrs. Billea
Alice C. Birdseye
Sandra C. Birdsong
Gail B. Blachly

Alice M. Black
Hope Black
Lucy A. Black
Nancy Blackburn
Jeanne R. Blackman
Carmen Blake
Fran Blanco
Kathryn R. Blank
Margaret G. Blee
Arthur H. Blenkle
David S. Bloom
Dorothy A. Bloom
Ruth B. Bloom
Fred Blumenthal
Erma Bly Bowman
Gloria J. Boatright
Timothy G. Bobbitt
Sue A. Bockholt
Melanie Bogart
Karyn V. Bograkos
Margo K. Bohn
Patti Bokowski
Frank Bolden
Sara Jean Boney
Veronica Bonfanti
Jo Ann D. Bonsib
Les C. Borine
Michael J. Bost
Mary J. Botteon
Antony A. Botto
John B. Bottum
Betty J. Boucher
Patricia A. Boucher
Clara Bowell
Ann B. Bowen
May Bowen
Charles E. Bowie, Jr.
Joyce S. Bowles
Kelly Bowles
Sharon E. Boyle
Paul Bradley
Elizabeth Brainard
Shiela Brandt
Leslie J. Braun
Deanna Bray
Nan H. Brazell
Jean M. Brendlinger
Sally Ann Brien
Vivian Brogan
Gilda Bronner
Doris Brook
Barbara Brooks
Merle A. Brosius
Anita Brown
Barbara Brown
E. Jane Brown
Frederick T. Brown
James S. Brown
Karen Brown
Marguerite H. Brown
Norma I. Brown
Peggy Brown
Stacey Brown
Elizabeth C. Brune
Patricia A. Bruns
Ann G. Bruton
Carrie E. Bryant
Janice L. Buchan
Maureen C. Buck
Judi A. Buckalew
Mark Bueing
Heidi M. Bulich
Monica Bulich
Mary E. Bulloch
Albert E. Bullock
Louise L. Bundy
Mary Burch
Pamela Burge
David Burgess
Isabelle Burgess
Allyson A. Burke
Cathy Burke
Martha A. Burns
Helen E. Burnson
Alice H. Burroughs
Betty Jane Burson
Doris Burt
Zelma A. Burt
Edward C. Burtenshaw
Gale E. Bush
Darlene Bush
Pat Bush

Anna Francis Bussel
Phyllis C. Butcher
June W. Butters
Rachel A. Byers
David G. Byrd
Patricia Byrne
Phillip L. Cagle, Jr.
John A. Cain
Sandra Calhoun
Beverly Callihan
Michael Callihan
Rosa M. Calvert
F. Hamer Cambell, Jr.
Helen G. Campbell
Marck Campbell
Anne M. Campo
Henry F. Canby
Jean M. Canby
Janet L. Centola
Nancy Carlson
Eleanor M. Carr
Dorothea Carter
Alice E. Cash
David D. Centola, Jr.
David D. Centola
Janet L. Centola
Elizabeth W. Channel
Jesse F. Channel
Patricia L. Chapman
Cathryn M. Chase
Rita Chase
Carlen Cheatam
Shirley C. Cheeks
Susan Chen
Sheila A. Chenard
Mary Chenoweth
Rosemary K. Chesser
Elizabeth L. Chester
Cassie Chisolm
Erna B. Christian
Beverly Jane Christopher
Adrian Cisneros
Edith B. Clark
Juanita N. Clark
Judith A. Clark
M. Harrison Clark
Matthew Clark
Suzanne K. Clark
Suzanne M. Clarke
Marjorie Clash
Luella R. Clausnitzer
Sonie Clauson
Richard A. Claybrook, Jr.
Elizabeth F. Claypoole
Ruth J. Cleary
Richard J. Clementson
Charles R. Clevela
Louise Cleveland
Kaki Clifford
Susan G. Clyne
Evelyn M. Cobb
Stella Cohen
Thomas Cohen
Marjorie B. Colby
Lois M. Cole
Morris R. Coleman
Donald N. Collins
Mary M. Colmus
Merle P. Colson
David A. Conger
Connie G. Connor
Rita M. Connors
Susan Conroy
Rita H. Conway
Jenny Cooper
William B. Cooper

Linda Copeland
Doug Corbin
Doris C. Corbridge
Carolyn Cornils
Betsy A. Cotton
Mary Ruth Cotton
William R. Cotton
Josephine E. Couch
Vera Counihan
Carolyn Y. Coursen
Kathy Covell
Anne Cox
Judie L. Crabb
John M. Crayton
Michelle Cremona
Ann Marie Crews
Connie A. Crigler
Dorothy O. Crist
Lee A. Crombie
Darryl T. Crosby
Robert A. Crouch
Mrs. Leo B. Cuccias
Elizabeth W. Culp
Bert Cumby
Marilyn Cunningham
Robert Cunningham
Wildred B. Curley
Fay F. Curry
Karlen A. Curtis
Rita Curtis
William C. Dacanay
Virginia J. Dalton
John d'Amecourt
Robyn D. Dandy
Dee Daniels
Elizabeth Danjany
Elwyn L. Darden
Becky Davies
Betsy A. Davies
Emily R. Davies
Rebecca S. Davies
Esther G. Davis
Geraldine E. Davis
Isabell W. Davis
Marilyn Davis
Marion G. Davis
Pamela S. Davis
Vivian S. Davis
Sharon Davis-Holmes
Michel I. DeBakey
Michael E. DeBlasis
Pamela J. DeGraff
Peggy Anne DePaoli
Dolores C. DePasquale
Suzanne C. DePasquale
Aurelia A. DeRubis
John A. Dean
Sarah H. Dean
Carla deCreny
Alice T. Deisroth
Josephine G. Deitrick
Gloria Delaney
Jay Delehanty
Leland P. Delong
Georgia A. Delyannis
Karen Denfeld
Francie Denholm
Maria R. Denmark
Marie dePasquale
David S. Derricotte
Diane C. Detko
Eva M. Devine
Elizabeth A. Devinine
Alfred E. Diamond
Mayo Diantonio
Marie Dickerson
Pauline Dickerson
Willie J. Dickerson
Vicky S. Dickinson
Michelle Dillard
Virginia A. Dillard
Evelyn M. Distefano
Helen B. Dodge
Richard Doerner
Alice Dolan
Denise Dolan
Emory E. Donelson, Jr.

183

Jude Donovan
Mary G. Doran
Robin M. Doran
Helen Dorn
Margaret S. Dougherty
Denise Douglas
Scott K. Douglas
Brenda G. Dowling
Merci Drake
Joan D. Driscoll
Kimberly S. Driscoll
Pamela L. Drogo
Ann Drucker
Merrit Drucker
Nadine B. Drucker
Mary S. Duckworth
Susan Duerre
Linda A. Duffus
Robert A. Dumas, Sr.
Virginia D. Dunaway
William J. Dunbar
Meredith Duncan
Dorette V. Dunham
Robert J. Dunn
Robert P. Dunn
Neal Dunning
Margaret N. Dupke
Ann Y. Duvall
Terry D. Eagle
Paul Eastwood
Marilyn Eastwood
Eric Eber
Mrs. Eber
Mary E. Eckert
Janet E. Eckley
Themis Economos
Ahan Edalatapoor
Laura Edson
Jean G. Edwards
Sheila W. Edwards
Nancy Egbert
Jeanne W. Eggeman
Sandra K. Ehrenberg
Lynda Ehrlich
Glenn R. Eichensehr
Florence N. Eickhoff
Janice A. Eisenhardt
Jennifer Eisenhower
Sue Elder
Veve Eldridge
Mark H. Elenowitz
Flo Eley
Virginia H. Eliason
Carolyn B. Elliot
Conora Elliott
Lynn Ellowitz
Julie E. Emry
William Engert
Frances W. Enoch
Frank Enten
Harriet M. Epstein
Carol Esau
Kimberly J. Esmay
Emily S. Evanow
Laura F. Evans
Linda I. Everett
Diana Eyer
Margie K. Falk
Paula C Faraday
Ellen Farley
Lilly Farrish
George Fastuca
Irene Faulkner
Patricia A. Faulkner
Mary F. Featherstone
Boris Feinman
Carolyn M. Fell
David W. Fenstermaker
Cindy N. Ferguson
Donna Ferguson
Maryann Ferko
Aileen E. Ferrari
Eleanor F. Ferraro
Jill Ferre
Janie Ferurman
Eva R. Festa
Robin K. Ficker
Louise A. Fiegel
Harriet L. Finkelstein
Nancy J. Fischer
Jack Fishkin
Patricia J. Fitzgerald

Ann Flack
Ralph J. Fleron
Nadine Fletcher
Frances R. Flikeid
Lee Fllmer
Patti Fllmer
Anne R. Flocco
Dee Flood
Linda Flood
Ed Florer
Laverne Florer
Iris Foggs
Rose E. Follett
Renee L. Foote
Shirley Foote
Elizabeth M. Fore
Ann R. Forman
Jeanne Fortier
Nan Foster
Phyllis Foster
Della H. Foulks
Dawn M. Fowler
Patricia A. Fowler
Elizabeth M. Fox
Marianne Fox
Nancy Fox
Virginia Fox
Zena Franks
Marilyn C. Frazier
Claire E. Freeman
Cornetta R. Freeman
Gladys S. Freeman
Henrietta L. Freeman
Easter R. Freienmuth
Betty Sue French
Suzanne French
Thelma P. Frey
Lisa B. Friel
Ann M. Frommer
Vivienne M. Fulford
Paul Furth
Joyce V. Gacek
Judy N. Gadd
Kathleen R. Gagen
Donald A. Gale
Julie H. Gallimore
Edward R. Gallion
Argel Gallis
Nancy M. Gamber
David Gannon
Stacey E. Gannon
Susan Gannon
Joseph W. Gant
Mary Garner
Marshall H. Garrison
Sylvia Gash
Bobbie Jo Gaston
Virginia Gates
Mary A. Gattis
Cindy Gaumer
Courtney Gauntt
Beverly R. Geline
Rose M. Genduso
Adele W. George
Helen Gerdon
Beverly Gerig
Audrey Gibson
Alfred Giddings
Nira Giddings
Kevin J. Gilbert
Lauren R. Gilbert
Mark C. Gildea
Carol A. Giles
Mary M. Gill
Margaret E. Gillies
Dawn R. Gillogly
M. Susan Gillspie
Peter L. Gingrich
Emerald L. Giss
Lorna Gladstone
Cherry K. Glazer
Sanford A. Glazer
Scott A. Glazer
Rita Glowden
Penny Goddin
Mary J. Godefroy
Eileen J. Goggin

Sara M. Goins
Holly J. Goodman
Liza L. Gookin
Elizabeth A. Gordan
Carol Gordon
Mrs. Levi Gordon
Robyne Gordon
Terri M. Gore
John J. Gorski
V. Eileen Gould
George Graber
Frank E. Graham
Mary Grant
Julian Graubert
Donald L. Gray
Gwen Gray
Arlette Green
Bruce Green
Barbara Greenblatt
Ronald G. Greening
Elizabeth Greer
George Greer
David J. Grego
Shirley S. Grenadier
Elizabeth Gretzinger
Michael J. Grieco
Anne M. Griffith
Betty M. Griffith
Joey Griffith
Naomi Griffith
John Grinnell
Sally A. Groome
Billie Growney
Leslie A. Gruca
Betty J. Guarraia
Karella A. Gumppert
Kathie Gunderson
Margaret M. Guntharp
Eileen R. Gurenian
Marion G. Gustavson
William P. Guthrie
Hallie M. Guy
Valerie Haase
Marion J. Hafer
Ronald W. Hailey
Toni Haines
Barbara Halback
Doris M. Haley
David Hall
H. Douglas Hall
Sandra Halloran
Cavis B. Ham
Alexander Hamilton, III
Cora Hamilton
Virginia M. Hammell
Irene J. Hamsted
Jo M. Hanson
Joan A. Hardter
Arthur L. Harman
Dorothy H. Harmon
Janet H. Harms
Addie M. Harper
Mabel B. Harper
Carolyn B. Harris
Dorothy Harris
Judith B. Harris
Louise T. Harris
Cahrmaine Harrison
Howard J. Harrison
Allen P. Hart
Faye J. Hartfield
Sonia Havelka
Sue Hawkins
Judith M. Hay
Carole J. Hayes
Gary Hayes
Marie C. Hayes
Mary E. Hayslett
Donna Hazzard
Anne E. Heaney
Barbara Hedges
Mary M. Heffernan

Bradley Heiges
Virginia D. Heiman
Louise Heinly
Nora K. Heinrich
Lindsey C. Heisey
Mrs. L. L. Heiter
Carol E. Heller
Maureen B. Heller
Nancy Heller
Jean B. Hemphill
Charles F. Henderson
Mozelle Henderson
Sharol Henderson
David C. Hendley, Jr.
George A. Henning
Margaret M. Henry
Prudence K. Henry
Sylvia Hermann
Merci Hernandez
Dudley Herndon
Marika H. Herndon
Joyce Herring
Stephen D. Hersch
H. Lois Hessler
Mrs. Heuerman
Barbara M. Heyman
Ruth Hickey
George D. Hicks
George Hieromymus
Kevin Higgins
Martha W. High
Elline Hildebrandt
Betty Jo Hill
Gloria Hill
Kathy J. Hill
Anna Hillman
Timothy O. Hillman
Tom J. Hillman
Nan L. Hiltabidle
Heidi Hinchliff
Esther B. Hinchcliff
Richard Hinchcliff
Kieth Hinds
Carroll R. Hines
Mary J. Hines
Marciene Hirsch
Diane F. Hoag
Dorothy L. Hockman
Howard K. Hodges
Elsbeth S. Hoff
Suzanne Hoffman
Lilly G. Holdridge
James C. Holeman
Jo L. Holt
Betsy A. Honey
Virginia Hook
Margaret W. Hooker
Carol Hoover
Sally Hopper
Harriet Horbath
Susan K. Hori
Mildred Horne
Donna E. Horrom
Howard R. Horrom
Kathryn I. Hostetter
April A. Hovaner
Ann C. Hoverson
Charles R. Howard
Elizabeth A. Howard
Rose Howard
Leslie P. Howell
Rose Howerton
Nancy Hoyt
Janet S. Huber
Brad Hudson
Brenda Hudspeth
Debra L. Huelster
Edward R. Hughes
Eleanora H. Hughes
Rulison D. Hughes
Mary Ann Hundley
Ernestine A. Hunley
Nancy Hunt
William E. Hurt
Thomas R. Hutson
Charles S. Huttula
Susan Huttula
Kathy Hyatt
Andrew G. Hyde

Violet L. Hyre
Ernestine Jackson
John Jackson
Leata Jackson
Virginia E. Jackson
Mary C. Jacobs
Nancy Jacobs
Ruth Jacobs
Ada Jacobson
Cecil B. Jacobson
Thomas K. Jacobson
Carole A. Jacoby
Pauline W. Jacoby
Patricia L. Jager
Elsa M. James
Mary Alice James
Julie Jaroshenko
Debbie Jarosz
Joan F. Jarrett
Beth Jarzabski
Diane Jaskiewicz
Rosemary Jaskiewicz
Fred Jennings
Janet N. Jenson
Bobbie M. Johnson
Cernoia Johnson
Charon M. Johnson
Dianne Johnson
Eddie L. Johnson
Ethan W. Johnson
Jane W. Johnson
Jean H. Johnson
John E. Johnson
Johnnie Johnson
Livia Johnson
Olivia Johnson
Rebecca Y. Johnson
William Johnson
Lisa Johnston
Sattie A. Johnston
Syndey A. Jolliffe
Alma Jones
Ann M. Jones
Elizabeth M. Jones
Johnnie E. Jones
Roberta K. Jones
Shirley Jones
Starr Jones
Steven M. Jones
Virginia R. Jones
Jacqueline I. Jordan
Mimi Jordan
Kathryn K. Joyce
George F. Judge
Darlene H. Kane
Nancy Kaplan
Shaukat Karimi
Orestes N. Karousatus
Barbara J. Kaye
Paul J. Kaye
Virginia F. Keany
Meg Keech
Francis M. Keefe
Gail C. Keeney
Iura Kellar
Paul M. Kellerman
Janice L. Kellett
Virginia W. Kellogg
Ann W. Kelly
Eileen P. Kelly
Karen L. Kelly
Susanne W. Kelly
Virginia S. Kelly
Janice Kempa
Mary Claire Kendall
Christine Y. Kenyon
Leslie J. Kerman
Elizabeth H. Kern
Belinda J. Kesner
Betina R. Kesner
Bonita J. Kesner
M. Jane Kesner
Raymond N. Kesner
Madeline Key
Winifred J. Kidwell
Karen H. Kilday

Annabelle Kindred
Arthur J. King
Lisa L. King
Barbara L. Kingdom
Marian W. Kirkley
Jean W. Kirkwood
Joan F. Kisber
Evelyn Kischefski
Helen L. Klassen
Nancy Kloepfer
Donna E. Knight
Jane Koche
Mary Frances Koerner
Marilyn Koestler
Roberta L. Kohl
Kathleen A. Kohler
Albert Kohrn
Barbara F. Kohrn
Mary Kathryn Kolodny
Aurelia Korte
Doris Kostishak
Carolyn Kovener
Jan Kramer
Marjorie Kraning
Avita Kratville
Julius Krause
Erik R. Kreins
Rose L. Kreiser
Mae G. Krill
Mark Krotosk
Theodore P. Kruezkowski
Randolph Kruger
Elda A. Krupa
Doria A. Kruse
Margaret M. Kucera
Paul J. Kucera
Anna B. Kuhne
Louis Kumro
Marion Kunce
David S. Kurke
Cvia Kutner
Deborah S. Laccy
Robert H. Lacey, III
Art W. Lahr
John M. Lamont
Nathaniel R. Landry
Lois J. Lange
Gillian Langill
Richard E. Langill
Vivian Langill
Jo Lankenau
Beverly Lantry
Janet S. Lapolla
Lyda V. Larkins
Joanne F. Lathrop
Martha D. Lathrop
Dawn Latta
Isabelle A. Laucka
Fernand A. Lavallee
Mary G. Lawler
Jacqueline L. Lawrence
Malcolm Lawrence
Patricia B. Lawrence
Lelyan Laye
Lee M. Lazareck
Mary J. LeBlanc
Cathy A. LeLacheur
Robert M. Leahy
Vivian Lebin
Michelle Lee
Patricia A. Lee
Rowena K. Lee
Stanley M. Legenc
Frances E. Lehmann

Joan G. Leiner
Cindy Leitner
Peter Leitner
Amy B. Lessig
Eilien Levington
Sherman Levy
Mary Anne L. Lewis
Thelma V. Lind
Nancy Lindhoff
Gladys K. Lisanby
Lora J. Lisle
Roy Littlefield
Adele M. Livesey
Laury Anne Lobel
Maurice Lockhart
Lois H. Lockyer
Emma 'Daisy' Logan
Betty H. Long
Marta Long
Sandra J. Longnecker
Marisa Longo
Israel Lopez
Luz Lopez
Mary Louise Lopez
Faith M. Loudon
Elvin Louk
Ernest W. Love
Morgan Love
Dorothy M. Lovett
Gary J. Lovett
Darrel W. Lownsberry
Ann B. Lucas
Barbara S. Lukens
Herbert M. Lundien
Mary Lutton
Helen O. Lynch
Virginia Lynch
Willa Lyon
Janet L. Lyons
Judith E. Lyons
John C. MacArthur, III
Michael MacCarthy
Dorothy MacDonald
Barbara A. MacIntosh
Debra A. Machen
Prudence C. Mackall
Bernadette C. Mackay
Maureen C. Mackay
Donna E. Madronal
Athene Maganias
Captain Leslie Magee
Rosetta M. Maggelet
Beulah Magruder
Juanita Maguire
Elaine Mahoney
Adam E. Maier
Dorothy M. Maki
Esther Mallory
Alyce C. Manausa
Eva E. Manchester
Dorothy B. Maneri
Katherine M. Manning
Kathryn A. Manning
Santal B. Manos
Rose Mansker
Philip J. Manzio
Donna M. Manzolillo
Margaret M. Marchese
Carole S. Marck
Tamara L. Markoff
Marilyn Markowitz
Mary Markuski
JoAnn Marriott
Joseph Marshall, III
Weezie Marston
Gloria Martel
Betty Martin
Mary K. Martin
Robert W. Martini
Nadinea M. Mason
Krishan Matheur
Ann Mathieu
Lorna L. Mattern

Dorothy J. Matteson
Marjorie N. Matthews
Mary Jane Matthews
Sharon K. Matthias
Jane M. Mattingly
Marion W. Mattingly
Vincent F. Maturi
Barbara M. Mayle
Brenda Mayo
Marjorie N. Mayo
Linda McAndrew
Bertha H. McBreen
Mary R. McBride
Nancy R. McCabe
Silvia H. McCarney
Martha J. McClellan
J. L. McColl
Mrs. J. L. McColl
Janet L. McConnell
Jeannine A. McConnell
Margaret S. McCormack
Donald B. McCoy
Joan T. McCoy
Mary McCutchan
Margaret A. McDonald
William V. McFarland
Sheila McGill
Betty R. McGinnis
Maria D. McGlamery
Sally A. McGrady
Katherine F. McHugh
Kim M. McKean
David L. McKee
Jack F. McKenna
Trudy McKimene
David McKowsky
Mary N. McLaughlin
H. Edwina McLean
Mary A. McLean
Shirley S. McLeod
Sandra McLindon
Regina M. McMahan
Charlotte McManamen
Paul J. McManamen
Sally K. McMurray
Jean E. McNair
Judy I. McNally
Ronald J. McNamara
Edith A. Mead
Cecile S. Mecca
Judith F. Mecsics
Anita Medico
Marsha E. Meidling
George F. Meierhofer
Betty L. Meredith
Jacqueline Merrill
Sandra J. Merryman
Colette L. Mesich
Sandie L. Messina
Wilma Meyer
Mary Michael
Sandy Michaels
Bernadette Michalski
Cora Middlebrook
William Middlebrook
Grace A. Miglio
Ernie Migoya
John Miller, Jr.
Loret C. Miller
Mary Ellen Miller
Virginia S. Miller
Maxine Mills
Twana Mims
Nancy S. Mion
Maude W. Misenheimer
Martha Mispireta
Paula W. Mitchell
Lillian S. Mitler
Matthew E. Mitler
Ann S. Mizerak
Barbara Moak
Samantha Moffly
Douglas M. Mohney
Jacqueline E. Moison
Irene Molyneux
Kimberly Monahan
Debbie Moncton

Lorraine M. Monnier
Rebecca P. Montgomery
Thelma Montgomery
Anne Moore
Mae J. Moore
Marguerite A. Moore
Mitzi B. Moran
Susan E. Morey
Elizabeth D. Morin
Keith A. Morken
Charles L. Morris
Geordie Morris
James B. Morris
Nancy J. Morris
Virginia G. Morse
Patricia Moschell
Betty Mott
Evelyn Mueller
Laura Mullen
Victor E. Muniec
Michele M. Munson
Lydia H. Murdock
Valeria N. Muroza
Mary E. Murphy
Mary Anne Murphy
Patrick W. Murphy
Irene Murray
Janet C. Murray
William R. Murray
Doloras J. Muth
Dolores Muth
Lori L. Naatjes
Constance F. Narro
Sara Y. Nash
Thomas J. Naulty, Jr.
Annissia Neal
Ayoka Neal
Marianne Nebel
Carol S. Neitz
Theresa Nelsen
Ben W. Nelson
Ethelyn Nelson
Jessie H. Nelson
Orinda Nelson
Stephen A. Nemeth
Sylvia Nemeth
Carol Nertz
Larry Nesbit
Eugene L. Newman
Katie Newman
James B. Newton, III
Joanne L. Nichols
Joanne W. Nickerson
Phyllis Niebur
Margaret Ann Niemczyk
Maggie Nightingale
Betty R. Nilles
Martha Anne Nolan
Susan K. Nolte
Kelly A. Noonan
Vivian Y. Norfleet
Jean A. North
Carol Northamer
Robert A. O'Bannon
Mary O'Brien
Mary C. O'Coner
Shirley O'Conner
Bessie J. O'Connor
Charles D. O'Connor
Mary T. O'Keefe
B. J. O'Shei
M. Brent Oldham
Virginia A. Oldham
Ernest Olivas
Darlene Oliver
Kathleen F. Oliver
Laura Ann Olsen
Elaine L. Olson
Karl G. Olson
Ruby R. Olson
Sydney Olson
Margaret Orend
David Orgel
Anne P. Orleans
Donna B. Otten
Henry E. Otten
Herta E. Ouellette
Debra F. Outlaw
Sandra Overton
David Owens
Marjorie E. Owens
Mark Oxley

J. K. Pacheco
Doris Paddison
Dorothy B. Page
Willard H. Page
Bridge Palta
M. Jeanine Pappous
Martha J. Pappous
Mrs. Barrington Parker
Vivienne H. Parker
Betty H. Parkinson
Linda M. Parks
Carolyn C. Parris
Anne C. Parrish
Cynthia J. Partim
Carol J. Partridge
Leslie Pater
Lois M. Paterson
David A. Patten
Francis C. Patterson
Paula A. Patterson
Claudine Paul
Susan D. Paxton
Ewell W. Payne
Thada G. Payne
M. Walker Pearce
Shirley Pearson
Louise Pease
Margaret M. Peel
Willie M. Pelham
Dina Penny
Goddin Penny
Barbara Perkens
Alice M. Perkinson
David G. Perlman
Jean A. Peter
Kitty Peter
Patricia A. Peters
Jean B. Petersen
Donald B. Peterson
Jeff Peterson
Michael J. Peterson
Winnifred M. Peterson
Milica R. Petzak
Ruth Phelan
William E. Phenix
Mary Ann Phillips
Vaughn T. Phillips
Paul Phipps
Louise Pinckernell
Ronnie Pittman
Peggy P. Pixley
Dom H. Pizzo
Fannie Plain
Howard A. Plattner
Mary J. Pohlers
Dianne E. Polaski
Elaine L. Polaski
Carolyn W. Pollin
Elizabeth W. Pollio
Carol A. Pope
Gordon A. Potter
Pamela M. Potter
Stephanie Potts
Ann O. Prather
Thomas E. Pratt
Carol Ann Preshlock
Beverley Price
Patrick G. Price, Jr.
Virginia C. Pride
Marjorie Principato
Tula G. Prior
Mark Propp
Josephine Pulvari
Peggy Quin
Jeanne H. Quinn
Mary E. Quint
Barbara J. Rabak
Emily Rache

Robert A. Radano
Frances B. Rademacher
Kathleen K. Rahman
Barbara G. Ramo
Betsy A. Raposa
Lucy W. Rasco
Mary C. Ratkus
Katherine P. Ratliff
Larry E. Ray
Julie K. Rayfield
Elizabeth C. Redfield
James W. Redfield
Indra Redin
Mary E. Redington
Irma M. Reed
John Reed
Laura E. Reed
Sherry Reed
Virginia J. Reed
Winifred V. Reed
Bridget E. Reilly
Joe Reinkemeyer
Maydalen J. Renfrow
Joann B. Renner
Michael Rentschler
Virginia M. Rettgers
Terry Reyman
Judith A. Rheubottom
Caroline C. Rhodes
Josephine A. Rhodes
Meredith Richards
Hazel M. Richardson
Vanessa Richardson
Gabrielle Richmond
Clare K. Richter
Carol R. Rickard
Sadie S. Riddle
Susan Rielley
Jean H. Riley
Virginia W. Rinehart
Noel Ripple
Tena Rips
Caroline Rishel
Vaughan Rivers-Bulkeley
Maria Riviera
Nancy E. Riviere
Kathryn R. Roarty
Mary Robenhymer
Bernice M. Robertson
Cynthia Robinson
Ellen E. Robinson
Deborah Roche
Betty S. Rock
Girard Rodgers, Jr.
John Rodriguez
Elizabeth L. Roesser
Jean Roesser
David F. Roland
Claire Romack
Francis Roos
Becky L. Rose
Bertha R. Rose
Kathy Rosenaver
Amy K. Ross
BevAnne Ross
Charles Ross, Jr.
James H. Ross
Mary C. Ross
Sarah C. Ross
Virginia C. Ross
Alice Roth
Clara R. Row
Sandy D. Royal
Patricia B. Ruda
Jean M. Rude
Rick R. Ruscak
Betty Russell
E. Ward Russell
Evelyn Russell
Katheran Russell
Mary Ann Rutt
Naomi C. Ruz
Dolores T. Ryan
Florence Safrit

Kerrin E. Salamone
Elaine Salisbury
Roberta F. Sandberg
Eleanor W. Sandford
Marcia G. Sandground
Brian Sanford
Andrew C. Sankin
Joan A. Santaiti
Mary F. Santonastasso
Marc S. Satrazemis
Betty W. Saunders
Joe W. Saunders
Sally A. Saunders
Don Saylak
Timothy D. Schaefer
Janice L. Schar
Sally S. Schiffer
Jo J. Schlank
Linda O. Schlesinger
Ben P. Schmutter
Pearl Schramm
Stanley W. Schroeder
Robert Schuler
Myra L. Schutzer
John Schwaiger
Elaine R. Schwartz
Leona M. Schwarzmann
Robert H. Schwarzmann
Joan H. Scarby
Judy Sechrest
Ed Segal
Carole Seidel
Jason A. Seidel
Ethel Sendlak
James T. Sensei
Mary Rose Sensel
Veronica M. Serratore
Wanda Lee Seward
Mary Lee Sexton
Eleanor Shapiro
Mary Ann Shapiro
Linda M. Sharkey
Judy Shaver
Clarence Shaw, Sr.
Mary R. Shea
William L. Shea
Cindy Shefferman
Sheila A. Shephard
David E. Shepherd, Jr.
Anita R. Shimer
Ernestine H. Shineman
Linda Shovlin
Sara G. Shriner
Glennda R. Shriver
Virginia P. Shufflebarger
Mark P. Siciliano
Renay E. Sieger
Edwin Sievers
Patricia L. Siggins
Marilyn Silver
Norma L. Simmons
Kathryn A. Simms
Sally S. Simms
Benjamin Simon
Donna Simon
Prema Simon
Pauline C. Simonsen
Bea B. Simpson
Dorothy Simpson
Mary Simpson
Laurie Sims
Kelly K. Sinclair
Beth M. Singley
JoAnne Sinnott
Grace D. Sisson
Gail P. Size
Virginia C. Slifer
Lucille L. Sloan
Bridget M. Smiley
Addison L. Smith
Brent M. Smith
Kim Smith
Leigh Smith
Madalyn Smith
Patricia A. Smith
Peg H. Smith
Sandra D. Smith
Sharon Smith
Shirley Smith
Todd A. Smith
Edward Snyder, Jr.
Hazel Snyder

185

Nancy Snyder
Nona M. Snyder
Paul P. Snyder
William R. Snyder
Nancy Sohl
Fred Soldwedel
Beatrice A. Sommovigo
Jacqueline T. Sorrells
Donna F. Sorrill
Fay B. Sorrill
Jessie H. Spangenberg
John P. Sparano
Fran Sparshott
Flora Spencer
Geoffrey K. Spencer
Agnes B. Spera
Alphonso Spera
John G. Spies
Brendan C. Stack, Jr.
Joanne Stalker
Beverly Standridge
Rhonda Stanley
Radmila Staples
Marie Starn
Emma N. Starr
Wini Steadley
Neva M. Stearns
Janet W. Steed
Donna Steele

Arlene C. Steffens
Larry Stein
Mary Kay Stein
Catherine Stemple
Juliettte Stephens
Beth A. Sterenfeld
Evelyn Stevens
R. Janice Stevens
George A. Stevenson
Jocelyn Stevenson
Deborah H. Stewart
Donald E. J. Stewart
John A. Stewart
Nora Stewart
Patrick Stewart
Peter Stewart
Sam Stokes
Estelle M. Stolz
Ginette L. Stone
Earl M. Storm
Edith L. Stratton
Priscilla B. Stringer
James W. Strong
Doreen A. Strothman
Rosemary J. Stroud
David Stuart
Wilma R. Stucker
Vala J. Stults
Todd R. Substad
Richard Sutter
Jeanne M. Sutton
Linda Swacina
Betty L. Swett
Rosanne D. Szabados
Susan Szulman
David Taflan
Ora Belle Tamm
Quinn Tamm
Mary Tarkir
Dannie P. Tarman
Helen V. Tate
Brooke B. Taylor
Jane Taylor
Madge Taylor
Constance Teele
Eva S. Teleki
Mary A. Tevington
Peggy L. Tevis
Lucille Thilke
Alice Thomas
Ann L. Thomas
Betty S. Thomas

Christopher P. Thomas
David M. Thomas
Dorie Thomas
James P. Thomas
Theresa Thomas
Anne W. Thompson
Dawn G. Thompson
Donald W. Thompson
M. Bradley Thompson
Cheryl Thorpe
Kimberly A. Timmons
Winifred H. Tindal
Nancy T. Tisdale
Richard C. Tonnar, Jr.
Jo Ann Torpy
Robert C. Tourek
Jean Tower
Kay H. Towers
Susan E. Trees
Carolyn Troupe
Fred W. Troutman
Anne Tuccinardi
Dominick Tuccinardi
Mary C. Tucker
Jane Tuggle
Galina Tunick-Rosniansk
Rose L. Turner
Anne C. Turton
Ruth N. Tyler
Neil W. Tyra
Angela J. Tyvoll
Betsy Ann Uhl
Irene T. Uhl
Nancy Ultz
Mildred F. Underwood
Anne Uno
Tad Uno
Evelyn T. Upshaw
Ann C. Van Devanter
Terri Van Loon
Marjorie G. Van Meter
Thomas J. Vande Sande
Ted F. Varano
Kamal N. Vaswani
Margaret H. Veach
Pat C. Veatch
Alexander Velaj
Robin S. Vierbuchen
Chiquita R. Vines
Mark A. Voelker
Ann Vogel
Robert E. Vosger
Ann V. Voss
Brenda J. Vumbaco
Diane L. Wadkovsky
Janis J. Wakelin
Christine P. Walker
Diane E. Walker
Greyson Walker
Jean Walker
Pauline Wallace
Holly Wallins
Erin E. Walsh
Kimberly J. Warendorf
Ellen H. Warfield
Irene M. Wasserman
Rachael M. Wasserman
Kenneth R. Waterbury
Violet A. Watka
Dorothy L. Watkins
Frances A. Watkins
Judalon Watson
Betsy Wattis
Caroline Watts
Jeffrey A. Watts
Linda G. Watts
Steven E. Watts
Lynn C. Webb
Peter W. Webb
William E. Webbert
Spencer Webster
Angela Weichert
Jane E. Weigel
Carole A. Weinberg
Doris C. Weinley
Carol L. Weinman
Sandra J. Weiss

Terry Weldon
Jeanette Wells
Betty D. Welsh
Martin Wender
Mary Lou Wentzel
Frank M. Wessely
Dale E. West
Terry West
Tom Westfall
Florence L. Westphal
Sylvia M. Weymer
Carleen D. Wheeler
Donald Wheeler
Elizabeth White
Eloise C. White
Linda E. White
Mamie J. White
Mary M. White
Susanne E. White
Denise Whitelow
John Whitney
Dorothy H. Wieber
Patricia S. Wiggins
Margaret M. Wild
Cherie L. Wilderotter
Winston A. Wilkinson
Sheryl William
Brenda L. Williams
Jackie Williams
Mary L. Williams
Robert E. Williams
Ronnie Williams
Rose E. Williams
Sandy Williams
Juanita J. Wilmer
Eleanor Wilson
Marjorie R. Wilson
Muriel E. Wilson
Susie Wilson
Linda R. Winer
Gloria Winn
Nadine Winter
Ruth Wise
Zulo O. Witcher
Mildred R. Witzig
Barbara E. Wixon
Marian F. Wixon
Vera Wixon
Ginger S. Wolf
Barbara Wolff
Lydia A. Wong
Allan Wood
Clarice R. Woodley
Marjorie W. Woods
Anita W. Wright
Gretchen L. Wright
Jackie Wright
Mary L. Wright
Pete Wrobleski
Mary P. Wunderlich
Rudy Yandreck
Peter J. Yanello
Carole Ann Yaskovich
Harold Yaskovich
Janis A. Yaskovich
Stephen T. Yelverton
Tim Yingling
James R. Yohe
Sandra Zaldana
Janine Zanecki
Mary E. Zayac
Charlotte Zettl
Mark T. Ziebarth
Ruth Ziebarth
Pearl Zitmore
Margaret A. Zorthian
Sylvia Zoslow
Anne V. Zuckerman
Sharon Zukoski

MILITARY
Military & Social Aides:
Gerry Abrams, USCG
Charles Akstin, USMC
Joseph G. Amaral, USCG
Robert Anson, USN
Charlie Arms
William R. Armstrong, USCG
Joseph Arroyo, USMC
Bruce C. Bade, USN
Larry Balok, USCG

Richard Beaver, USCG
Bedinger, USN
Henry Beebe, USAF
Bersticker, USN
Jerry Bever, USN
Richard S. Bizar, USAF
Ronald Blake, USAF
Larry Bockman, USMC
Bill Boozer, USA
Larry Bostic, USN
Gerald Bottorff, USAF
Stanley Boyd, USAF
Eugene Brindle, USMC
Dwight C. Broga, USCG
Don Brown, USAF
Eber Brown, USA
Todd Bruner, USN
Jerome J. Burke, USN
Darrel D. Burton
Robert Bush, USA
Skipp Calvert, USN
Terry Cannon, USMC
Brant M. Carter, USN
Louis Casale, USCG
John Chipman, USAF
Felix Ciarlo, USA
John Clements, USAF
James C. Clow, USCG
Cordis Colburn, USA
Robert O. Corey, USN
Garrett Cowsert, USA
Charlie Cox, Jr.
Eugene Cragg, USN
Larry S. Craig, USAF
Steve Crittenden, USMC
Thomas Cruser, USN
Robert A. Danforth, USCG
Kerry Davidson, USN
James H. Davis, USMC
Robert Davis, USAF
Nicholas DeCarlo, USN
Chuck Debellevue, USAF
Mike Dewitt, USCG
Dietrich, USAF
Charles Dittmar, USMC
Tom Driskill, USA
William R. Dunn, USA
Robert Durst
Sam Ebbeson, USA
James Eden, USAF
David C. Edman, USN
Theodore J. Ehlers, USN
Kevin J. Eldridge, USCG
Robert Ellard, USCG
John Elle, USAF
David Evans, USMC
Lorin Evans, USAF
Oliver Evans, USN
John Ferrillo, USAF
Richard Fields, USA
Pat Finneran, USMC
R. Flaherty, USMC
John E. Fletcher, USA
John J. Folan, USMC
Thomas Fox, USAF
Dennis M. Frank, USN
Steve Freiherr, USMC
Richard Fuller, USAF
Ernest F. Gale, USN
H. Gardner, USMC
Joseph Gawlick
Howard Gehring, USCG
Fredric R. Gill, USCG
Fred Greene, USA
Jeffrey Grimes
Thomas J. Haas, USCG
Jackie Hagan, USMC

Gary Hagen, USAF
John Hammer, USN
Carol Hemphill, USA
Jim Hickman, USA
Don Hirsch, USMC
Gerald Hirsch, USN
Neil Holben, USN
Grat Horn, USAF
Patrick Howard, USMC
Thomas Hruskocy, USAF
Seth Hudging, USA
Justin Hughes, USA
Henry Huntsberry, USA
Gerry Ingalsbe, USAF
Wendell Irby, USAF
Kendall E. Jacobs, USA
James Jacobson, USN
Vaughn Johnson, USAF
Marsha Johnson-Evans, USN
Jeffrey Jones, USA
Pete A. Joseph, USCG
Paul Kanive, USN
Mark P. Keehan, USA
Terry Kemp, USAF
Kenneth Key, USAF
Bill Keys
Chuck King, USCG
Ed King, USCG
Jon King, USCG
Mark N. Klett, USN
Rosalyn Knapp, USAF
Richard Krueger, USAF
Charles Kubic, USN
Greg Kuzniewski, USMC
William E. Lansing, USN
Ted Lewis
Lance Lord, USAF
Marshall B. Lundberg, USN
David Lyon, USCG
Robert Makinen, USAF
Stewart Marsh, USCG
Gregory Marshall, USN
William Masciangelo, USMC
Bill May, USCG
Gerald May, USAF
John Mazach, USN
John McCabe, USAF
Walter S. McCabe, USN
Lewis McFarland, USA
Nicholas V. McKenna, USN
Charles Meadows, USMC
Fred Mellor, USAF
Glenn Messerli, USAF
William Metzger, USN
Dennis L. Miller, USN
Neil Mitchell, USMC
James Morris, USAF
Roger D. Mowery, USCG
Denny Murphy, USAF
Timothy A. Murphy, USN
Ben Newlin, USCG
Bill Newsom
Kenneth Nocito, USAF
Kenneth M. Norris, USCG
Thomas Nunes, USCG
John T. Orchard, USCG
Larry N. Osborn, USA
John Parham, USAF
Garry Parks, USMC
Fred Peck, USMC
Thomas M. Pesses, USN
Chet Pino, USMC
Stephen P. Plusch, USCG
Thomas Powers, USN
Pratt
Daniel E. Price, USN
Michael Prothero
Nile Radcliff, USA
James Ransom, USAF
Bill Rasco
Robert Reining, USCG
Garace A. Reynard, USCG

Stevan Richards, USAG
Richard J. Robbins, USN
Peter Roberts, USN
Ronald Roberts, USAF
Willie Rodgers, USAF
Bruce F. Rogers, USA
Robert Roush, USA
Charles Ryan, USAF
Ron Sable, USAF
Ray Sasaki, USAF
Thomas Scanlon, USAF
Ed Schlichter, USN
Roderick A. Schultz, USCG
Bruce Schwanda, USMC
David A. Schwiering, USN
Terry Scott, USA
Douglas Sims, USA
James Sims, USMC
Richard J. Singer, USN
John Smith, USAF
William Smith, USAF
Clinton Smoke, USCG
James J. Steward, USMC
Thomas Surles, USA
Ronald Susi, USAF
Victor J. Tambone, USA
Gary Taylor, USN
Joseph A. Telep, USCG
Elliot Tepper
Dick Theokas, USAF
Charles Thomas, USAF
John Thompson
Paul Thompson, USN
Col. Torres, USN
Paul Tuohig, USA
Ted Tzavellas
Dennis Van Buskirk, USNV
Amilicar Vazquez, USMC
Robert L. Vence, USCG
Robert Vlasics, USA
James Voss, USA
John Wallace, USCG
Skip Watkins, USN
Thomas A. Watts-Fitzgerald
Christopher Weaver, USN
William Westfall, USMC
Larry Wheatley, USCG
Stewart N. White, USCG
Raymond Wilkstrom, USN
Lt. Col. Will, USAF
James Williams, USMC
Grayson Winterling, USA
Merlyn Witt, USAF
Talmadge Womble, USN
George Worthington, USN
Florian Yoste, USAF
John Zebelean, USAF
John Zimmerman, USAF

THE INAUGURAL COMMITTEE IS DEEPLY INDEBTED TO THE MEN AND WOMEN OF THE ARMED FORCES. THEIR GENEROUS ASSISTANCE AND SUPPORT WAS GREATLY APPRECIATED.

T.V. PRODUCTION STAFF
Executive Producer/Director:
Marty Pasetta
Producer:
Michael Seligman
Terry Adams
James Balden
Andy Bamberger
Juan Barrera
Peter Barth
Andy Bass
Barbara Benjamin
Harvey Berger
Lee Bernhardi
Doug Berry
Best Audio
David Brand
James Brennan
Carrie Bryant

Joan Buday
Meredith Burch
Bruce Burns
Hank Cattanco
Wendy Charles
Kathy Chase
Barton Chiate
Vincenzo Cilurzo
Louise Coleman
Bill Conroy
Brenda Cooley
Ed Cowling
Michael Cressey
Ed Crosby
Tony Csiki
Leard Davis
Michael DeBlases
Sue Devlin
Anthony DiGirolano
Willie Dickerson
Joe Disco
Al Dotoli
Tom Durell
Laurence Estrin
Robert Estrin
Marty Farrell
Mike Farrell
Jim Feeney
John Feher
Barry Fialk
John Field
Sue Friedman
Bill Friel
Michael Garguilo
David Gass
Jim Gates
Timothy A. Gibbons
John Gorski
Ed Greene
Nate Halpern
John Hamlin
Bob Hankal
Eugene G. Hanna
David Hilmer
Linda Hobkirk
Marshall Jamison
Russ Kabeisemann
June Kendall
Susan Kerber
Mike Kerner
Bob Keyes
Steve Kibbons
Deedle King
Gordon Klimuck
Richard Kline
William Knight
Mitch Kolata
Terry Kulcher
Cheryl Kurk
Bob Lanning
Dave Levisohn
Bill Lorenz
Marilyn Lowey
John Luff
Jean MacClean
Thomas Mahony
Paul Malatich
Pat Maloney
Tony Marshall
Vincent Marvaso
Ted McConnell
Mick McCullough
Shawn Murphy
Nikki Nash
Ed Nebler
Mikel Neiers
Henry Neimark
James Nomikos
Frank O'Connell
Mike Onofiro
Wayne Orr
Ken Palius
Debbie Pasetta
Lynn Peggs
Jim Petlow
Bill Philbin
Carol Pratt
Frank Quintoni
Susan Reynolds
Tom Rickard

James Roberts
Merritt Roesser
Debbie Ross
Ray Rowe
Milton A. Rudin, Esq.
Norman Schwartz
Larry Sedwick
Sara Shafer
Ron Sheldon
Alan Shevlo
Sheldon Shimmer
Judy Simon
Harlan Singer
Dick Smith
Bruce Solberg
Ken Stein
Don Stern
Ron Stutzman
Jack Sumroy
Glen Swanson
Robert Tourkow
Bill Upwood
Paul Van Haute
James P. Washington
Richard Weiss
Garry Westcott
Andy Wilk
Keith Winikoff
Nicole d'Amecourt

ENTERTAINERS

OPENING CEREMONIES
The Mormon Tabernacle Choir
The United States Army Band
Efrem Zimbalist, Jr.
Osmond Productions

CONCERTS
Mikhail Baryshnikov
Grace Bumbry
Jerry Hadley
Karen Hunt
Dana Krueger
John Mauceri
Roberta Peters
Richard Stilwell
Warren Ellsworth
Alan Barker
Natalia Makarova
Patrick Bissell
Suzanne Farrell
Peter Martins
Patricia McBride
Jacques D'Amboise
Robert Irving
Scott Nickrenz
Leslie Parnas
Paula Robison
Marcus Thompson
Mstislav Rostropovich
Robert Noerr
Norman Scribner
Robert Shafer
Eugene Istomin
Rudolf Serkin

GALA
Debby Boone
Grace Bumbry
Johnny Carson
General Omar Bradley
Charlton Heston
Bob Hope
Rich Little
Ethel Merman
Donny Osmond and Marie Osmond
Charley Pride
Frank Sinatra
James Stewart
Mel Tillis
United States Army Herald Trumpets
United States Naval

Academy Glee Club
USNA Drum & Bugle Corps
Ben Vereen

SMITHSONIAN
The Double Decker String Band
The Federal City Four
The Airmen of Note
The Army Blues
The U.S. Navy Commodores
The Country Current
The Singing Sergeants
The Coast Guard Singing Idlers
The Icebreakers
The Chamber Orchestra of the United States Marine Corps Band
John Robilette
David Perry
The Smithsonian Chamber Players
The Romantic Chamber Ensemble
The Twentieth Century Consort
Buddy Charlton
The Seldom Scene
The Country Gentlemen
Foggy Bottom
The New Sunshine Jazz Band
Hot Mustard
John Eaton
Buck Hill
Bill Harris
Keter Betts
Rick Henderson
John Malachi
Marc Cohen and Toni Wilson
Bill Kirchner
Mariachi de las Americas
The Toho Koto Society
The Irish Breakdown
Magpie
Dewey Balfa
The Piney Ridge Boys and Patsy
Ralph Case Square Dancers
Norvus Miller & Company
The Howard Gospel Choir

BALLS
Fats Ammon's Band
Count Basie Orchestra
Tony Bennett
Pat Boone
Glen Campbell
Ray Charles
Mike Connors
Robert Conrad
Johnny "Scat" Davis
Tommy Dorsey Orchestra
Peter Duchin Orchestra
Chad Everett
Johnny Grant
Lionel Hampton Orchestra
Woody Herman Orchestra
Houston Pops Orchestra
Harry James Orchestra
Sammy Kaye Orchestra
Frankie Laine
Patti LuPone
Carol Lawrence
Ed McMahon
Glenn Miller Orchestra
The Mills Brothers
Jerry Naylor
Wayne Newton
Anthony Newley
Hugh O'Brian
The Osmonds (Alan, Wayne, Merrill, Jay, Donny, Marie & Jimmy)
Patti Page
The Pointer Sisters (Anita, June & Ruth)
Lou Rawls

Doc Severinsen
Robert Stack
Tanya Tucker
Elizabeth Taylor Warner
Washington Jazz Battalion
Efrem Zimbalist, Jr.

YOUTH CONCERT
The Beach Boys
(Alan Jardine, Bruce Johnston, Michael Love, Brian, Carl & Dennis Wilson)

SWEARING IN CEREMONIES
Juanita Booker

The 1981 Presidential Inaugural Committee is bipartisan and non-political.

DONORS
A. H. Baker & Company
AMC Motor Corporation
ASAE
AT&T
AT&T (Bell System)
AT&T Long Lines
Advancement of Science
Aebi Nursery, Inc.
Air Florida Airlines
Albin Hagstrom & Son, Inc.
Allegro Studios
Almaden Vineyards
Ambassador Travel Service, Inc.
Amer. Audio Video Resources, Inc.
American Can Company
American Cafe
American Center
American College of Cardiology
American Legion
American Motors General Corporation
American Security Bank and Trust Company
American Sightseeing Company
Americar Rental System
Amix Employment Company
Amvets
Andrews Baarlett & Assoc., Inc.
Anthony's Pier 4
Anton's Restaurant
Arata Expositions Inc.
Ruth Arden
Arlington County Manager's Office
Arlington Printers & Stationers
Armellini Express Lines, Inc.
Arthur Anderson & Co.
Associated Builders, Inc.
Atlantic Parking
Avon Products, Inc.
B&B Caterers
Ballantine
Baltimore/Washington Int'l Airport
Bank of Virginia
Charles R. Barker, Jr.
T. D. Barre
Beaulieu Vineyard
Beringer Vineyards
Bill Suyeyasu Wholesale

Florist, Inc
Blinded Veterans Association
Bob Peck Chevrolet
Booz, Allen & Hamilton
Bovello Plumbing and Heating
Braniff Airlines
Bridge Litho Company, Inc.
Brown Williamson Tobacco Corp.
Marion B. Brown
Bullfeathers
Burlington Industries
Burnsed Ferney Florist
C & P Telephone Co.
CIBA-Geigy Corp.
Calzada del Sol
Camera Graphics
Campbell Chain Company
Angelo Campitelli
Capitol Centre
Capitol Hilton
Capitol Magazine
Cardinal Management Associates
Carter Hawley Hale Stores
Casa Grisanti
Central Tours
Champion Home Builders Company
Champion/Titan Motor Homes
Charlie's Crab
Chateau St. Michelle Vintners
Chesapeake & Potomac Telephone Co.
Chevron U.S.A., Inc.
Chevy Chase Chevrolet
Chrysler Corporation
City of Fairfax Chamber of Commerce
Coca Cola, Inc.
Coca Cola, USA
Colorado Greenhouse Growers Assn.
Columbus and Stevens St. Paula Commers
Composition Systems, Inc.
Computer Infor. Technology Corp.
Constatine's
Cook, Purcell, Hansen and Henderson
Coopers & Lybrand
Csikos Hungarian Restaurant
Maurice J. Cullinane
Curtis Chevrolet
Davis and Vinson
Dean Witter-Reynolds, Inc.
Delta Air Lines
DiCesare and Associates, Inc.
Diplomat National Bank
Direccion General De Policia y
Disabled American Veterans
District News
Division of Visitors Services
Doggett Enterprises, Inc.
Doggett Parking Co.
Domestic Flag Air Carriers
Joseph L. Donnelly
Dulles International Airport
Walter Dunne
Dupont Plaza
E. F. Hutton Co., Inc.
Eastern Airlines
Edison Electric Institute
Embassy Row Engineering Reproduction, Inc.

Enomoto, Inc.
Ernie's Restaurant
Ernst & Whinney
Exhibition Decorators, Inc.
Exxon Oil Company
F. Korbel Brothers, Inc.
Fairfax Co. Chamber of Commerce
Fairfield Maxwell, Ltd.
Financial Management, Inc.
Firestone Tire and Rubber Company
Firestone Vineyards
First American Bank, NA
First Federal Savings & Loan
Flight Attendents of Eastern Air Lines
Floral Greens International
Ford Motor Company
Ford Motor Corporation
Forman Brothers
Fort Lesley J. McNair
Fox & Company
Frank Gumpert Printing
GSA, Room 1007
Gacques, Inc.
Genasys Corporation
General Motors Corporation
General Services Administration
General Telephone Directory Co.
George's Appliances
Georgetown University
Gilliam & Colbert
Giovanni's
Giumarra Vineyards
Gold Seal Vineyards, Inc.
Goodyear Tire & Rubber Co.
Michael Govan
Government Services, Inc.
Grove, Jaskiewicz, Gilliam & Colbert
Gulf Oil Company
Gus Duda & Associates
Department of the Army
Harshe-Rotman & Druck, Inc.
Hay Adams
Hechinger Company
Herman Goelitz Candy Co., Inc.
Herman Miller Co.
Heublein, Inc.
Bill Hoffman
Hoffman-La Roche, Inc.
Holiday Inn—Capitol Hill
Home Federal Savings and Loan
Houlihan's Old Place
Housing Assoc. of Washington, D.C.
Howard Johnson's Motor Lodge
Hueblein, Inc.
Hyatt Hotels Corp.
Hyatt Regency
Hyatt Regency Atlanta
IGM Communications Northeast
I.G.S. Design
Ikebana International
Ill. State Soc. of Washington, D.C.
Imperial Palace Restaurant
Inglenook Vineyards
International Distributing Co.
International Harvester Company
International Inn
Ivor B. Clark Co.
J. Lee Donnelly & Son
J. Walter Thompson Ad. Agency
Jartan Truck Rental
Jefferson Hotel
James Jennings

187

Jewel Foliage
John F. Kennedy Center for the Performing Arts
John William Costello Assoc.
Johnny on the Spot
Johnsen's Nursery
Johnson & Wales College
Jones Plymouth, Inc.
K. Nakashima Nursery Co.
KDEA
KSLO
KTXR FM
Kato Cut Flowers
Kettler Bros., Inc.
Kingsley Inn
Kitayama Brothers
Betsy Koons
Kwick Kopy Printing
L'Enfant Plaza
L. T. Delyannis & Assocs.
La Famiglia
La Scala Restaurant
La Vieille Maison
Lane E. Burnsed Fernery
Lanier
Le Bon Greens
Le Mont
LeBon Greens
Leather Etc.
Legal Sea Food
Legion of Valor
Nick Lewnes
Victor Litz
Loral Corp.
Lord and Taylor
Louis M. Martini
Kathy Lowe
Loyola School
Lustine Chevrolet
MEDDAC DAH
Macke Vending Company
Madison Hotel
Magyar Hungarian Restaurant
Maisonette Restaurant
Management Concepts, Inc.
Management Systems Applications, Inc.
Marat School
Marine Corps League
Market Growth, Inc.
Marketing Coordinators Int., Inc.
Marriott Corporation
Marriott Hotels
Marriott Key Bridge
Marriott Twin Bridges
Marriott Tysons Corner
Martin Enterprises
Martin Lithographers
Maryland Cup Company
Masionette Restaurant
Matsui Nursery, Inc.
Maxim's de Paris
McGraw-Edison
McLachlen National Bank
Meade Corporation
Mechanical Contractors of America
Melwood Horticulture Trng. Ctr. Inc.
Metro Washington Board of Trade
Metropolitan Restaurants Assoc. of Washington, Inc.
Michelle Vintners
Microwave Specialties, Inc.
Mid-America Expositions, Inc.
Midway Airlines
Mike's Donut & Deli
Military District of Washington
Military Order of the Purple Heart
Milton S. Kronheim & Co.
Minn. State Soc. of Washington, D.C.
Mirassou Vineyards
Mobil Oil Corporation

Monsanto Co.
Montgomery Co. Chamber of Commerce
Mottahedeh & Co.
Mount Eden Nursery
Mr. Smith's of Georgetown
N. Bernstein Mgt., Inc.
NALEO
NCO Assn. of the U.S.A.
Nakashima Nursery Co.
National Association of Home Builders
National Bank of Washington
National Corporation for Housing Partnership
National Direct Mail
National Geographic
National Housing Center
National Park Service
National Restaurant Association
National Rifle Association
Netherlands Flowerbulb Institute
New York Air
Nieman Marcus
Ninomiya Nursery Co.
Non-Commissioned Officers Assn.
Norbert Beauty Salon
North Carolina State Society
North Dakota State Society
Numbers Restaurant & Club
O'Connor & Hannan
OLD CARS WEEKLY
Occidental Petroleum Corp.
Ocean Front Floral Co.
Oklahoma State Society
Oku Brothers
Old Dominion Travel
Old Original Bookbinders
On-Line Systems, Inc.
One Biscayne Tower, Suite 3660
One Wayland Drive
Florenz Ourisman
P.M.I.
PBS, GSA
PEPCO
PMI Parking
PS Printing
Pajaro Valley Greenhouses, Inc.
Pan Am
Paralyzed Veterans Association
Park Schenley
Landon Parvin
Patton, Boggs, & Blow
Paul Masson Vineyards
Paul's Wholesale Florist Co., Inc.
Peat, Marwick, Mitchell Pennsylvania Ave. Development Corp.
Pepsi-Cola Bottlers
Pepsi-Cola Company
Pepsico International
Pepsico, Inc.
Perpetual Federal Savings & Loan
Philip Morris Tobacco Company
Pier 7

Pitney Bowes
Polar Water Co.
Polaroid Corporation
Postal Service Headquarters
Potomac Distributing Co.
Premium Distributors
Price Waterhouse & Co.
Prince George's County Cham. of Com.
Quality Inn—Pentagon
R. Robert Linowes
Radio Communications, Inc.
Rand McNally Maps
Raytheon
Reasoner, Davis & Vinson
Reserve Officers Association
Restaurant Associates
Richmond Hotels, Inc.
Ridgewells Caterer
Riggs National Bank
Ristorante da Gaetano
Robert A. Beer
Robert H. Carter III & Assoc., Inc.
Robert Mondavi Winery
Robert N. Pyle & Associates
Rockmont Chevrolet
Rockwell International
Rosenthal Chevrolet
Rough Creek Oil Internat'l, Inc.
Ruan Transfer Corp.
Ruder-Finn Public Relations, Inc.
SW&V Association
Sacramento Chamber of Commerce
Safeway Stores, Inc.
Jeanne Sanders
Sardine Factory
Savin
Scandia Restaurant
The Schneiders
Sebastiani Vineyards
Security Concepts
Shell Oil Company
Sheraton Carlton
Sheraton Washington Shoreham
Sierra Research Corporation
Smith, Hinchman & Grylls
Smithers Oasis
Smithsonian Institution
Society of American Florists
Sonoma Vineyards
Southern Railway
Spanish International Network
Sport Chevrolet
Sterling Institute
Sterling Vineyards
Stouffers National Center Hotel
Suburban Printing Service, Inc.
Peter Summerville
Sun Oil Company
Suyeyase Wholesale Florist, Inc.
T.P.C.
THIS WEEK Magazine
TIME, Inc.
TOSCO Corporation
TRAVEL HOST Magazine
TRW
Tandem Productions, Inc.
Terry Taylor Enterprises
Texas International Airlines
The Aluminum Assn.
The American Cafe

The American Gas Association
The Dolphin Group, Inc.
The Fairmont Hotel
The Flower Shoppe
The Forge Restaurant
The Goodyear Tire & Rubber Co.
The Greater Washington Bd. of Trade
The Hecht Company
The JN Company
The Macke Company
The Mayflower Hotel
The Society of Virginia, Inc.
The Taylor Wine Co., Inc.
The Tobacco Institute
The View
The Waterford 311
Thomasville Furniture Industries
Thompson Rose Co., Inc.
Time & Life Building
Time, Inc.
Tony Roma's
Total Patient Care, Inc.
Trude Ball's Empress Restaurant
Turnberry Isle Yacht & Racquet Club
Tuxedo Rental & Sales
Typographic Images, Inc.
U.S. Brewers Association, Inc.
U. S. Postal Station
U. S. Tobacco
U.S. Department of the Interior
U.S. Park Police
U.S. Postal Services Headquarters
U.S. Army Military Dist. of Wash.
Union First National Bank of Washington
United Airlines
United Brands Co.
United Fresh Fruit & Vegetables
United States Park Police
Universal Restaurants
Urban Electrical Supply & Equipment Corp.
Vanni Nursery, Inc.
Veterans of Foreign Wars
Victor A. Powell Fernery
Victor Business Products
Visual Aids Electronics Corp.
W. Bell and Company
WADB
WAKK
WAVC
WBBR
WBIG
WBRL
WBRO
WBZY
WCSP AM
WDAR
WEBO/WWWT
WECP/WWYN
WFEA
WFLO
WGPA
WHERE MAGAZINE
WHIP
WHSY-FM
WHZZ
WICO Radio
WICY
WISU
WJW
WNEG Radio
WONN
WOOW
WPCM/WBBB
WPTM

WKAL
WKHJ
WKNE Radio
WKNG
WLCM/WPAJ
WLIT Radio
WLMD Radio
WMIM
WMTM-AM
WQLM-FM
WRAM
WSBH
WSCP
WSHE/WSRF
WSLC
WSST
WTCY/WTOO
WVIN FM/AM
WWEE/WLVS
WWGA
WWKE/WMFQ
WWSC
WYNA
WYPR
Walter C. Davis & Son, Inc.
Washington Dining Guide
Washington Fish Exchange, Inc.
Washington Hilton
Washington Hotel
Washington National Airport
Watsonville Roses, Inc.
Weaver Brothers, Inc.
Wells Fargo Guard Services
Wente Brothers
Western Airlines
Westminister Motor Company
Wheaton Plaza Shopping Center
William P. Gelberg, Inc.
William J. Walsh
Wisc. State Soc. of Wash. D.C.
Woodstream Corporation
Woodward Bldg., Suite 930
Woodward and Lothrop
Xerox Corporation
Zuckert, Scoutt & Rasenberger

SPECIAL ACKNOWLEDGEMENTS
Dr. and Mrs. Lawrence Adams
Mr. and Mrs. David Margolis
Mr. and Mrs. David Murdock
Mrs. Lorena Nidorf
Donald L. Bren
Dr. and Mrs. Simon Ramo
Mr. and Mrs. George Roberts
Mr. and Mrs. Gwynn Robinson
Robert Six
Mr. and Mrs. Charles Thornton
Evelle Younger
William Boeing
Jack Courtemanche
Mr. and Mrs. Robert Tuttle
Bernadette Casey
1977 Inaugural Co-Chairmen, Bardyl Tirana & Vicki Rogers

EXECUTIVE CLUB*
Air Florida
Allbritton Communications
J.D. Allen Industries
Allison/Walker, Inc.
Amax
American Asian Bank

American Bankers Association
American Express Co.
American International Group, Inc.
American Laundry Machinery, Inc.
American Textile Manufacturers Institute
Archer-Daniels-Midland Company
Armco
Ashland Oil, Inc.
Atlantic Richfield Company
Bank of America
William A. Barnstead
Mr. and Mrs. Stephen D. Bechtel
Beneficial Corporation
Mr. and Mrs. Frank Briscoe
Bristol-Myers Company
Brown & Williamson Tobacco Corporation
Brownfield, Bowen, Bally, & Sturtz
The Budd Company
Burlington Industries, Inc.
William T. Burton Industries
John R. Butler, Jr.
California Savings and Loan League
Centronics Inc.
The Chase Manhattan Bank, N.A.
Citrus Central, Inc.
City Investing Company Corporation
Chevron, U.S.A.
Club Corporation of America
Compressor Engineering Corp.
Computer Sciences Corporation
The Coca Cola Company
Mr. and Mrs. Joseph Coors
Mr. and Mrs. Mark T. Cox, III
Conoco
The Continental Group
Mr. A. Samuel Cook
D.C. Bankers Association
Dannenbaum Engineering Corporation
deKieffer Berg and Creskoff
Deere and Company
Dow Chemical Company
The El Paso Company
ENSERCH Corporation
Evans Construction Co.
Exxon Corporation
Financial General Bankshares, Inc.
Florida Savings and Loan League
Fluor Corporation
Folger, Nolan, Fleming, Douglas, Inc.
Food Marketing Institute
Four Winds Enterprises, Inc.
Genasys Corporation
General Mills, Inc.
General Motors Corp.
Mr. and Mrs. Kenneth R. Giddens
Grumman Corporation
Gulf Oil Corporation
Gulf Resources and Chemical Corporation
Hamady Brothers Food Markets, Inc.
Mr. Leon Hess
Hines Industries
Mr. and Mrs. Charles G. Hooks
Houston Atlas, Inc.
Hughes Aircraft Company
Illinois Savings and Loan League

International Bank
International Business Machines Corporation
International Paper Company
ITT Corporation
Kroger Foods, Inc.
R. L. Lipton Distributing Company
Litton Industries
Lockwood, Andrews & Newnum, Inc.
Mr. and Mrs. Jose Pepe Lucero
Marriott Corporation
Mr. C. J. Marshall
Martin Marietta Corporation
Masco Corporation
Merill Lynch & Co., Inc.
Metropolitan Life Insurance Company
3 M
Mobil Oil Corporation
Phillip Morris Incorporated
Morrison-Knudsen Company, Inc.
National Photographic Laboratories, Inc.
Occidental Petroleum Corporation
Ohio League of Savings Associations
Mr. Thomas A. Pappas
J. C. Penney Company
Pennzoil
Pension Administration, Inc.
PepsiCo. Inc.
Republic National Bank
Republic Steel Corporation
R. J. Reynolds Industries, Inc.
Sanders Associates, Inc.
Seabrook Shipyard
Security Pacific Corporation
A. A. Seeligson, Jr., Co.
Sharon Steel Corporation
Shell Oil Company
Morgan Stanley, Inc.
Sun Company, Inc.
Mr. and Mrs. Carl W. Swan
Tenneco, Inc.
Texasgulf, Inc.
Thornton Oil Corporation
Time Incorporated
Times Mirror, Inc.
UMC Industries
Union Oil Company of California
United States Steel Corporation
U.S. Tobacco
United Technologies Corporation
United Telecommunications, Inc.
Underwriters Inc.
Mr. and Mrs. Michael A. Valerio
Vannerson Insurance Company
Vicksburg Refining, Inc.
The Watergate Companies, Inc.
The Western Company of North America
Wheelabrator-Frye, Inc.
Sir Yue-Kong
Mr. and Mrs. Henry Zenzie

PATRONS*
Abbott Laboratories
Aetna Life & Casualty
Allegheny Ludlum Industries
Alice Manufacturing Company
Allis-Chalmers
Allstate Insurance Co.
Aluminum Company of America
American Automobile Association
American Brands, Inc.
American Cyanamid Company
American Standard, Inc.
The American Thread Company
Anheuser-Busch Companies
Arkansas Savings & Loan Association
Arkansas S & L League
Avco Corporation
Avondale Mills
American Textile Manufacturers Institute
Armco Inc.
Becton Dickinson & Company
Bethlehem Steel Corporation
B. F. Saul Company
The Black and Decker Manufacturing Company
The Boeing Company
C & P Telephone Co.
Central Soya Company
Cherokee Spindale Mills
Chevy Chase Savings and Loan
Chicago Bridge & Iron Company
Chicago & Northwestern Transportation Co.
Cities Service Company
Clark Oil & Refining Corp.
Collins & Aikman Corporation
CMI Corporation
Coachmen Industries, Inc.
Coca-Cola Bottling Co. of N.Y., Inc.
Cone Mills Corporation
Control Data Corporation
Coopers & Lybrand
Corning Glass Works
Dart & Kraft Inc.
D.D.I., Inc.
Dillon, Read & Co., Inc.
Dixie Yarns, Inc.
Mr. and Mrs. John Dixon
Mr. C. A. Doolittle, Jr.
Dow Corning Corporation
Mr. and Mrs. John Henry Dudley
Eastern Air Lines Incorporated
Eastman Kodak Company
Jack Eckerd Corporation
Edison Electric Institute
E.I. duPont de Nemours & Co.
E., G. & G., Inc.
Electronic Memories & Magnetics
Ethyl Corporation
Fairchild Industries
Fieldcrest Mills, Inc.
The Firestone Rubber and Tire Company
FMC Corporation
G. K. Technologies
General Electric
General Motors
Corporation
The General Tire & Rubber Company
Georgia League of Savings
Getty Oil Company
The Gillette Company
Herman Goelitz Candy Co.
Goodyear Tire & Rubber Co.
Gould, Inc.
Hawaii League of Savings Associations
Roy M. Huffington, Inc.
INA Corporation
Internorth
Iowa Beef Processors Inc.
Savings and Loan League of Indiana
Mr. E. O. Jefferson
Johnson & Johnson
Kaiser Aluminum & Chemical Corporation
Kansas Savings and Loan League
Kerr Glass Manufacturing Corporation
Lear Siegler, Inc.
Lockheed Corporation
Louisiana Pacific Corporation
The LTV Corporation
Magic Chef, Inc.
Mapco, Inc.
Marathon Oil Company
Maryland Savings & Loan League, Inc.
McGraw-Edison
McGraw-Hill, Inc.
The Mead Corporation
Merck & Company, Inc.
Metropolitan Washington Savings and Loan League
Michigan Savings & Loan League
Milliken & Company
Savings & Loan League of Minnesota
Mississippi Savings and Loan League
Missouri Savings and Loan League
Mitsui & Co.
Morgan Guaranty Trust
Murphy Oil Corporation
Nabisco, Inc.
Nalco Chemical Company
National Association of Broadcasters
National Distillers and Chemical Corporation
National Restaurant Association
NCNB Corporation
New Jersey Savings League
North Carolina Savings and Loan League
Northrop Corporation
Mr. Richard L. O'Shields
Pacific Gas and Electric Company
Paine Webber Inc.
Panhandle Eastern
Pfizer, Inc.
The Pillsbury Company
Phillips Industries, Inc.
Phillips Petroleum Company
Potomac Electric Power Company
Procter and Gamble Company
The Proprietary Association
Raytheon Company
RCA Corporation
Rexnord, Inc.
Riegel Textile Corporation
Rockwell International
Sanders Associates, Inc.
Savings Association League of New York State
SCM Corporation
Mr. Benno C. Schmidt
Seafirst Corporation
Seattle First National Bank
Smith Kline Corporation
The Southern Company
Southern Pacific Company
The Sperry & Hutchinson Company
Spring Mills, Inc.
The Standard Company of Indiana
Sterling Drug, Inc.
St. Joe Minerals Corporation
Sunstrand Corporation
Texas Savings & Loan League
Texas Utilities Company
The Tobacco Institute
TRW, Inc.
Mr. Fred E. Tucker
Union Carbide Corporation
United Gas Pipe Line Company
United Pacific Corporation
US Air
Virginia Savings and Loan League
Julia M. Walsh & Sons, Inc.
Washington National Corporation
The Washington Post
West Point Peppercll, Inc.
The Williams Companies
Savings League of Wisconsin
Wynn's International, Inc.
Xerox Corporation

SPONSORS*
ACF Industries, Inc.
A. E. Staley Manufacturing Company
Air Transport Association
Akzona Incorporated
The Amalgamated Sugar Co.
American Airlines
American Apparel Manufacturers Association, Inc.
American Broadcasting Companies, Inc.
American Can Company
American & Efird Mills, Inc.
American Insurance Association
American Iron and Steel Institute
American Meat Institute
American Mining Congress
Amsted Industries, Inc.
ARA Services
Arkansas Best Corporation
Arkwright Mills
Armtex, Incorporated
Associated Credit Bureaus, Inc.
Association of American Railroads
Baker International Corporation
Mr. Malcolm Baldridge
Ball Corporation
Bank of America N.T. & S.A.
Bankers Trust Company
Mrs. Walter H. Beech
Belmont Heritage Corporation
Blair Mills, Inc.
Bliss & Laughlin Industries
Mr. Asa W. Bonner
Borg-Warner Corporation
Braniff International
Burlington Northern
The Burroughs Corporation
Butler International, Inc.
The Cabot Corp.
Cafritz
Campbell Soup Co.
Capital Cities Communications, Inc.
Carpenter Technology Corporation
CBS
CF Industries
Champion Spark Plug Company
Chatham Manufacturing Co.
Chicago Prumatic Tool Company
Citibank N.A.
Cities Service Company
Clinton Mills
Cluett, Peabody & Co., Inc.
Coats & Clark Inc.
Elliot H. Cole
Coldwell Banker
Colt Industries Inc.
Commonwealth Electric Company
ConAgra, Inc.
Connecticut Mutual Life Insurance Co.
Conner & Moore
Cosmetic Toiletry and Fragrance Association
Crompton Company, Inc.
Cubic Corporation
Delta Air Lines, Inc.
Deluxe Check Printers Inc.
Dennison Manufacturing Company, Inc.
Detroit Bank Corporation
Dixie Yarns
Dorchester Gas Corporation
Dover Mill Company
Dundee Mills, Inc.
Eaton Corporation
Economics Laboratory, Inc.
Elcor Corporation
Eli Lilly and Company
The Elk Cotton Mills
Esmark, Inc.
Family Lines Rail System
First Boston Corporation
First National Bank of Boston
First National Bank of Maryland
Fleetwood Enterprises, Inc.
Flintkote Stone Products Co.
GEICO
General Cinema Corporation
General Telephone & Electronics
Georgia-Pacific Corporation
Gerber Products Company
Gerli & Company, Inc.
Giant Food Inc.
B. F. Goodrich Company
J. Peter Grace
Graniteville Company
Mr. William R. Grant
Greenwood Mills, Inc.
Greyhound Corporation
Hadley Peoples
Manufacturing Company
Hammermill Paper Company
Hamrick Mills
John Hancock Mutual Life Insurance Company
Heublein Inc.
C. Howard Hardesty, Jr.
Harmony Grove Mills, Inc.
Mr. Frank E. Hedrick
Hercules Inc.
Hesston Corporation
Homestake Mining Company
George A. Hormel & Company
Hughes Tool Company
Human Services Group, Inc.
E. F. Hutton & Company Inc.
Ingersoll-Rand Company
IC Industries, Inc.
Ideal Basics Industries Inc.
Illinois Tool Works, Inc.
Inman Mills
International Multifoods
International Snowmobile Industry Association
Iowa Bankers Association
Kaiser Cement Corporation
Kerr-McGee Corporation
Kimberly-Clark Corp.
Knight-Ridder Newspapers, Inc.
Robert H. Krieble
The Jefferson Mills, Inc.
Jostens, Inc.
Lance, Inc.
Leggett & Platt, Incorporated
Libbey-Owens-Ford Company
Liberty National Life Insurance Company
Liggett Group Inc.
Litton Industries
Locktite Corporation
The Louisiana Land and Exploration Co.
M. Lowenstein Corporation
Ludlow Corp.
Macfield Texturing, Inc.
Man Made Fiber Producers Association
Mark Controls Corporation
Masonite Corporation
Mayfair Mills
MCA, Inc.
Media General, Inc.
Meridian Roofing & Construction Company, Inc.
Mid-Continent Oil & Gas Association
Miles Laboratories, Inc.
Monsanto Company
Mr. Charles H. Morin
Motorola, Inc.
National Association of Life Underwriters
National Association of Realtors
National Association of Wholesale Distributors
National Bank of Detroit
National Machine Tool Bldrs. Assoc.
National Soft Drink Association
Norfolk Shipbuilding & Drydock Corp.
NLT Corporation
Northwest Energy Company
Oak Industries Inc.
Mr. and Mrs. Bernard J. O'Keefe

189

Olin Corporation
Omark Industries
Opp and Micolas Mills, Inc.
Oregon Savings League
Owens-Illinois
Pabst Brewing Company
Pacific Resources, Inc.
Pan American World Airways, Inc.
Parkdale Mills, Inc.
Mr. Daniel Parker
Pogo Producing Company
PPG Industries, Inc.
Price Waterhouse & Company
The Prudential Foundation
Reeves Brothers, Inc.
Republic Corporation
Reynolds Metals Company
Dan River, Inc.
Roadway Express, Inc.
A. H. Robins Company
Russell Corporation
Santa Fe Industries, Inc.
Schering Plough Corporation
Scientific Atlanta Inc.
Sears, Roebuck and Company
Southern California Gas Company
Southern Railway Company
Spartan Mills
Sperry Corporation
Stauffer Chemical Company
Sunbeam Corporation
Sunbury Textile Mills, Inc.
Talley Industries
Texas Eastern Transmission Corporation
Textron Inc.
Ti-Caro, Inc.
Todd Shipyards Corporation
Tracor, Inc.
The Travelers Corporation
Twentieth Century-Fox Film Corporation
United Airlines
United Refining Company
United States Fidelity and Guaranty Company
Universal Leaf Tobacco Company, Inc.
Valley National Bank of Arizona
The Wachovia Corporation
Walgreens
Walton Mill, Inc.
Washington National Corporation
Mr. W. L. Wearly
Webster & Chamberlain
Western Airlines, Inc.
Whirlpool Corporation
Mr. Luke G. Williams
Wometco Enterprises, Inc.

PRESIDENTIAL INAUGURAL TRUST*
Trustees
William H. G. FitzGerald
Robert K. Gray
J. William Middendorf, II
Charles Z. Wick
Founding Members
Financial General Bankshares
Litton Industries
John Garabedian
Occidental Petroleum Corp.
Pepsico Foundation, Inc.
United Telecommunications
Henry Salvatori
C. A. Doolittle
E. F. Hutton & Co.
Hamady Food Stores, Inc.
Hamady Brothers Food Markets, Inc.
Joseph E. Uihlein, Jr.
Hardill Enterprises
Folger Nolan
Fleming Douglas
Hughes Aircraft
Tom Pappas
T. Peter Pappas
Nicholas Salgo
Dwayne O. Andreas
Glen A. Holden
Arthur K. Salomon
U.S. Tobacco
Masco
Stephen Jernigan
Richard De Vos
Jan Van Andel
Charles W. Steadman
General Dynamics
Joe Rodgers
Anna Chennault
Wayne G. Horst
Set C. Momjian
American Financial Corporation
Food Marketing Institute
The City Investing Corporation Foundation
Richard Taylor
Belmont Towbin Underwriters, Inc.
Jack A. Krautler
Rockwell International
Mae Sue Talley
Richard Heffner
Financial General Bankshares
Leon Hess
L.F. Rothschild and Company
Denk International Ltd.
Carl Lindner
United Technologies
International Telephone & Telegraph
The Kroger Company
Contributing Members
Mobil Oil Corporation
John Garabedian
Park Tower Realty
Gates Lear Jet
Ohio Drive
Ohio Conference of Teamsters
Beech Aircraft Corporation
Moya Olsen Lear
Magic Chef
Electronis Memories & Magnetics Corporation
D. K. Roberts
Douglas A. McCrary
William E. Timmons
Jim Kaufman
Steiffel Raymond Advertising
Mrs. Thayer Gilpatric
William J. Diamond
Donald R. Philbin
Hing Lin Chang
Joe Rodgers
Accountants
Ernst & Whinney

Photo credits

Photo credits listed clockwise when there are more than one per page.

Cover: Roloc/Uniphoto, 1: Bill Weems/Woodfin Camp, 3: Michael Pettypool/Uniphoto, 4–5: George Galicz/Photo Researchers, 6: Michael Pettypool/Uniphoto, 8: Fred Ward,

10: Roger Sandler, 11: Roger Sandler, Michael Pettypool/Uniphoto, 12: Milt Graham, Milt Graham, Roger Sandler, 13: Roger Sandler, 14: Milt Graham, Mark Higbie, Mark Higbie, Roger Sandler, Roger Sandler, 15: Roger Sandler, 16: Roger Sandler, Milt Graham, Roger Sandler, Roger Sandler, 17: Roger Sandler, Milt Graham,

18: Karl Schumacher/The White House, 19: Associated Press, 20–21: U.S. News and World Report, 22: Library of Congress, Wide World Photos, 23: Library of Congress, New York City Library, 24–25: Fogg Art Museum,

26: Harry Langdon, 28: Roger Sandler, 29: Roger Sandler, 30: Dirck Halstead/Gamma Liason, 31: Roger Sandler, Dirck Halstead/Gamma Liason, 32: Micheal Evans/Sygma, 33: Micheal Evans/Gamma Liason,

34: Dirck Halstead, 35: M. Abramson/Gamma Liason, 36: Cynthia Johnson/Gamma Liason, 37: Cynthia Johnson/Gamma Liason, Roger Sandler, Dirck Halstead, 38: Dirck Halstead/Gamma Liason, 39: Dirck Halstead,

40: Harry Langdon, 42: Roger Sandler, Michael Pettypool, Roger Sandler, 43: Roger Sandler, Michael Evans/Sygma, Roger Sandler,

44: Roger Sandler, Michael Evans/Sygma, 45: Michael Pettypool/Uniphoto, Roger Sandler, 46: Roger Sandler, 47: Roger Sandler, Bud Gray, Michael Pettypool/Uniphoto, Diana Walker/Gamma Liason,

48: Dirck Halstead, 49: Dirck Halstead/Gamma Liason, 52: Bud Gray, Dirck Halstead/Gamma Liason, 53: Dirck Halstead/Gamma Liason, 54: Dirck Halstead/Gamma Liason, Cynthia Johnson/Gamma Liason, 55: Cynthia Johnson/Gamma Liason, Dirck Halstead, 57: Raymond Crowell, 58: Roger Sandler, 59: Roger Sandler, Muffy Stout, U.S. Dept. of Agriculture, Yoichi R. Okamoto.

60: Ralph Becker Collection/Smithsonian, 62: National Gallery of Art/Smithsonian, National Portrait Gallery/Smithsonian, Ralph Becker Collection/Smithsonian, 63: Ralph Becker Collection/Smithsonian, New York Historical Society, 64: Smithsonian, White House Collection, 65: Ralph Becker Collection/Smithsonian, 67: Architect of the Capitol, 68: Ralph Becker Collection/Smithsonian, 69: Ralph Becker Collection/Smithsonian, 70: Library of Congress, Smithsonian, 71: Smithsonian,

72: Harry Burnett/Architect of the Capitol, 74: Roger Sandler, Michael Pettypool/Uniphoto, 75: Raymond Crowell, 76: Raymond Crowell, 77: Raymond Crowell, 78: Raymond Crowell, 79: Raymond Crowell,

81: Raymond Crowell, 82: Raymond Crowell, Jeff Tinsley/Smithsonian, Raymond Crowell, 83: Roger Sandler, Marty LaVor, Michael Pettypool/Uniphoto, Robert Sherbow/Uniphoto, 84: Robert Sherbow/Uniphoto, Roger Sandler, Robert Skillman, 85: Raymond Crowell, Raymond Crowell, Robert Skillman, 86: Roger Sandler, Robert Sherbow/Uniphoto, Robert Sherbow/Uniphoto, Roger Sandler, 87: Robert Sherbow/Uniphoto, Roger Sandler, Roger Sandler,

88: Michael Pettypool/Uniphoto, 89: Raymond Crowell, 90: Raymond Crowell, Marty LaVor, 91: Raymond Crowell, Robert Sherbow/Uniphoto, Roger Sandler, 92: Raymond Crowell, 93: Roger Sandler, Marty LaVor, Raymond Crowell, 94: Marty LaVor, Robert Sherbow/Uniphoto, 95: Jeff Tinsley/Smithsonian, 96: Roger Sandler, Roger Sandler, Robert Skillman, 97: Robert Sherbow/Uniphoto, Roger Sandler, Robert Skillman, Robert Skillman, 98: Raymond Crowell, Leslie Cashen, Leslie Cashen, 99: Leslie Cashen, Muffy Stout, Muffy Stout, 100: Muffy Stout, 101: Robert Sherbow/Uniphoto, Raymond Crowell, 102: Raymond Crowell, Robert Skillman, Raymond Crowell, 103: Robert Sherbow/Uniphoto, Raymond Crowell, Smithsonian, 104: Raymond Crowell, Michael Pettypool/Uniphoto, Robert Sherbow/Uniphoto, 105: Michael Pettypool/Uniphoto, 106: Michael Pettypool/Uniphoto, 107: Michael Pettypool/Uniphoto, Roger Sandler, 108: Robert Skillman, 109: Robert Skillman, 110: Robert Skillman, Robert Skillman, Roger Sandler, Raymond Crowell, 111: Robert Sherbow/Uniphoto, Robert Sherbow/Uniphoto, Marty LaVor, 112: Marty LaVor, 113: Roger Sandler, Marty LaVor, 114: Roger Sandler, Marty LaVor, Roger Sandler,

115: Roger Sandler, Robert Sherbow, 116: Roger Sandler, 117: Muffy Stout, Roger Sandler, Muffy Stout, 118: Muffy Stout, Roger Sandler, Roger Sandler, 119: Muffy Stout, Muffy Stout, Roger Sandler, Raymond Crowell, Roger Sandler, 120: Robert Skillman, Roger Sandler, 121: Roger Sandler, Muffy Stout, Leslie Cashen, 122: Raymond Crowell, Roger Sandler, Roger Sandler, 123: Raymond Crowell, Roger Sandler, 124: Roger Sandler, 125: Roger Sandler, Marty LaVor, U.S. Army Photograph, 126–127: Milt Graham, 128: Roger Sandler, Roger Sandler, U.S. Army Photograph, Milt Graham, 129: Milt Graham, Milt Graham, Roger Sandler, 130: Milt Graham, Roger Sandler, 131: Robert Sherbow/Uniphoto, Roger Sandler, Robert Sherbow/Uniphoto, Marty LaVor,

132: U.S. Army Photograph, 133: Michael Pettypool/Uniphoto, 134: Milt Graham, Milt Graham, 135: U.S. Army, Ankers Capital Photographers, Milt Graham, 136: Barbara Cebuhar, Michael Pettypool/Uniphoto, 137: Ken King, Roger Sandler, 138: U.S. Army Photograph, Michael Pettypool/Uniphoto, Roger Sandler, 139: Milt Graham, Raymond Crowell, Michael Pettypool/Uniphoto, Michael Evans/White House, 140: Michael Evans/White House, Muffy Stout, Muffy Stout, 141: Michael Evans/White House, Muffy Stout, Michael Evans/White House, 142: Milt Graham, Roger Sandler, Billy Shaddix/White House, 143: Roger Sandler, 146: Karl Schumacher/White House, Milt Graham, 147: Roger Sandler, Marty LaVor, Robert Skillman, 148: Mary Ann Fackelman/White House, Raymond Crowell, Roger Sandler, 149: Pomponio, Roger Sandler, Raymond Crowell, Pomponio, 150: Raymond Crowell, Robert Skillman, Michael Evans/White House, 151: Howard Wickham, Kim Nielson/Smithsonian, Robert Skillman, Roger Sandler, Robert Skillman, 152: Robert Skillman, Raymond Crowell, Robert Sherbow/Uniphoto, 153: Michael Evans/White House, Bill Fitz-Patrick/White House, 156: Roger Sandler, Leslie Cashen, Muffy Stout, 157: Leslie Cashen, Milt Graham, Roger Sandler, 158: Marty LaVor, Nachtwey/Black Star, Roger Sandler, Leslie Cashen, 159: Roger Sandler, 160: Michael Pettypool/Uniphoto, Roger Sandler, Robert Skillman, 161: Michael Evans/White House, Roger Sandler, Frank Alexander, 162: Robert Sherbow/Uniphoto, Roger Sandler, Roger Sandler, 163: Milt Graham, 164: Robert Sherbow/Uniphoto, Dendmark, Roger Sandler, Milt Graham, Milt Graham.

166: Roger Sandler; 167: Roger Sandler; 168: Michael Evans/, White House, Roger Sandler, 169: Roger Sandler, Michael Pettypool/Uniphoto, Michael Evans/White House, Michael Evans/White House 170: Roger Sandler, Roger Sandler, Carl Schumacher/White House; 171: Roger Sandler, Roger Sandler, Michael Evans/White House, Roger Sandler, Bill Fitz-patrick/White House 172: Roger Sandler 173:

A Great New Beginning—The 1981 Inaugural Story
was created and produced by the Presidential Inaugural Book Committee

The 1981 Inaugural Book Committee Staff. From left to right, Raymond Crowell, Jane Johnson, Dorothy Johnson, Doug Vega, Peter Pierce, Anne Voss, Dennise Balzano, G. Raymond Martin, Barbara Cebuhar, D. Diane Hill, Maureen Martin, Art Lahr, (In Front), Carl Sfferrazza, Howard Leaman and Karen King. Editor: F.C. Duke Zeller (Not pictured are Roxanne Christ, Donna Hazzard, Ron Leymeister, Sharon Peterson, Joseph Reynolds, Martha Rispoli and Nancy Rodgers)

Editor: F.C. Duke Zeller
Associate Editor: Barbara Ann Cebuhar
Research: Ronald Leymeister and Jane Johnson
Design Director: Art Lahr, Wickham & Assoc., Inc.
Book Design: D. Diane Hill

Inaugural Book Committee
Honorary Chairman: Mrs. Ursula Meese
Vice-Chairman: F.C. Duke Zeller
Director: Barbara Ann Cebuhar
Deputy Directors: Ronald Leymeister and Jane Johnson
Staff assistant: Karen King

Honorary Advisors
Mrs. George Aiken
Mrs. Howard Baker
Mrs. Jake Garn
Mrs. Mark Hatfield
Mrs. John Heinz
Mrs. Paul Laxalt
Mrs. James McClure
Mrs. Robert Michel
Mrs. Robert Packwood
Mrs. John Rhodes
Mrs. Ted Stevens
Mrs. Strom Thurmond
Mrs. John Tower
Mrs. John Warner

1981 Book Committee
Admiral Herb Anderson
Carolyn Bacon
Joseph A. Bruno
Lawrence J. Brady
Anna Chennault
Thomas E. Crowell
Herbert R. Collins
Lynne Davis
Thomas Davis, III
Ann E. Delahanty
Mrs. J. Edwin Dietel
Mrs. Anita M. Essalih
Carol Fitzsimmons
Peg Garland
John Howerton
Mary Ann Keeffe
James T. Kolbe
Karen Koon
Ron Lasch
Merle Lefkoff
Joseph E. McMahon
Charles K. McWhorter
Dr. Robert Miller
Thomas C. Moncure
Betty Southard Murphy
Donn Murphy
Marie Osmond
Mrs. Doray Saddler
Audrey Meadows Six
Dr. Barbara Smith
William Stover
Donald Webster

Contributing Writers: Robert Keith Gray, Vic Gold, James J. Kilpatrick, Victor Lasky, Abagail McCarthy, Ursula (Mrs. Edwin) Meese, Hugh Sidey, Mary Jane and Charles Wick and George F. Will.
Staff Writers: Barbara Cebuhar, Roxanne Christ, Byron Kennard, Maureen Martin, G. Raymond Martin, Landon Parvin, Peter Pierce and Carl Sfferrazza.
Official Inaugural Photographer: Raymond Crowell
Inaugural Photographers: Frank Alexander, Leslie Cashen, Milton Graham, Marty LaVor, Michael Pettypool, Roger Sandler, Robert Sherbow, Robert Skillman and Muffy Stout.

Layout Assistants: Bill Bickel, Sandy Webbere-Hall, Tom Heffner and Gayle Monkkonen

Acknowledgments: The Editors would like to thank the following people who offered invaluable assistance in preparing this book for publication: Ken Bastian, Vice-President Bush's office; Lee Bataglia, Ed Broughton and the staff of the ICA photo division; Ralph E. Becker, Historical Consultant; Clem Conger, Curator of the White House; Jennifer Crowley, Gamma-Liason Agency; Dixie Dodd; Helen Dorn; Michael Evans; Robin Gray, White House Press Office; Dirck Halstead; Shirley Jackson; Julie Jaroshenko; Cynthia Johnson; Caren Keshishian; Jim Moore, and the Minority House Photographers; Lawrence C. Merthan; Ray Nelson, Joint Congressional Inaugural Committee; Jean Pierre, Sygma Photo Agency; Sheila Patten, Press Secretary to the First Lady; Sharon Peterson; Michael Pettypool and the Uniphoto agency; Jean Tolson of Dossier Magazine; Ron Thompson of Nikon Professional Services; Jerrold Scoutt; Ann Radice, Curator of the Capitol and the Art and Reference Staff; Billy Shaddix, Chief of the White House Photo Office and his staff members Diane Powers and Donna Hawker; the Still Photograph Division of the Library of Congress; the Smithsonian Institution; the Photo Office of U.S. News and World Report; Peter Teeley, Press Secretary to Vice-President Bush; Fred Ward; Jerry Werbel of Booz-Allen and Dena Zeller.

Color separations by Lanman Corporation, Composition by Monotype Composition Co., Inc., Printed by Merkle Press, Glenn Dale, Maryland, Bound by Holladay-Tyler.
Design by Wickham and Associates, Inc.

Special thanks to Howard Leaman, Merkle Press